SKAIFEY

Mark Skaife and **Andrew Clarke**

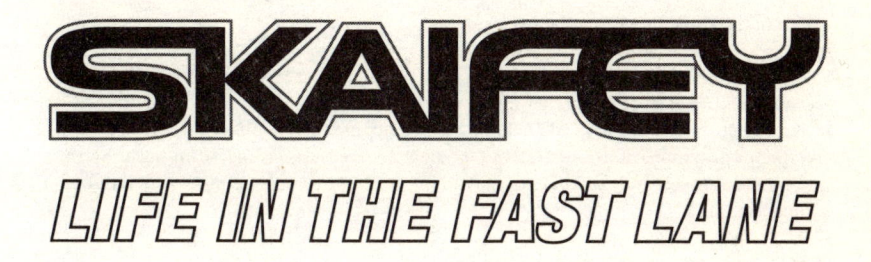

SKAIFEY
LIFE IN THE FAST LANE

EBURY PRESS

An Ebury Press book
Published by Random House Australia Pty Ltd
Level 3, 100 Pacific Highway, North Sydney NSW 2060
www.randomhouse.com.au

First published by Ebury Press in 2010

Copyright © Skaife Enterprises 2010

The moral right of the author has been asserted.

All rights reserved. No part of this book may be reproduced or transmitted by any person or entity, including internet search engines or retailers, in any form or by any means, electronic or mechanical, including photocopying (except under the statutory exceptions provisions of the Australian *Copyright Act 1968*), recording, scanning or by any information storage and retrieval system without the prior written permission of Random House Australia.

Addresses for companies within the Random House Group can be found at
www.randomhouse.com.au/offices.

National Library of Australia
Cataloguing-in-Publication entry

Skaife, Mark, 1967–

Skaifey / Mark Skaife.

ISBN: 9781741668995 (pbk.).

Skaife, Mark, 1967–
Automobile racing drivers – Australia – Biography

796.72092

Cover design by Luke Causby/Blue Cork
Front cover photo (Skaife): courtesy of HRT
Front cover photo (car): Robert Cianflone/Getty Images
Back cover photo: Robert Cianflone/Getty Images
Typeset in 12.5/17 pt Minion by Post Pre-press, Brisbane, Queensland
Printed and bound by Griffin Press, South Australia, an accredited ISO AS/NZS 14001:2004 Environmental Management System printer.

10 9 8 7 6 5 4 3 2 1

The paper this book is printed on is certified by the © 1996 Forest Stewardship Council A.C. (FSC). Griffin Press holds FSC chain of custody SGS-COC-005088. FSC promotes environmentally responsible, socially beneficial and economically viable management of the world's forests.

FSC
Mixed Sources
Product group from well-managed forests and other controlled sources
Cert no. SGS-COC-005088
www.fsc.org
© 1996 Forest Stewardship Council

CONTENTS

Intoduction by Andrew Clarke   1

1	This is what we do	7
2	New scenery	57
3	Who do you think I am?	111
4	Getting into the fast lane	129
5	Climbing the peak	151
6	The best of times and the worst of times	157
7	The good and the bad	167
8	Winning is everything	187
9	Life on the edge	219
10	The things that matter	249
11	Spheres of influence	267
12	It can be a cruel sport	283
13	Other perspectives	301

Mark Skaife Chronology   335

INTRODUCTION BY ANDREW CLARKE

Oran Park was a track that had provided so many key moments of Mark Skaife's life. His first karting win in the rain here back in the 1980s; his first pair of Australian Touring Car Championships sealed at this sinuous piece of bitumen in Sydney's south. It was a track rated for its complexity, for the rewards that were available for that last little bit of commitment. This was classic Skaife territory.

In December 2008, Oran Park was hosting its final round of the V8 Supercar Championship Series and Skaife was doing the same. It was a big weekend on any score. Immersed in his own personal space, Skaife felt a flood of emotion as he left the grid for what was most likely his final ever warm-up lap as a full-time V8 Supercar driver. The last faces he saw on the grid were those of his wife Toni and 12-year-old son Mitch.

Toni was a mess. Minutes before when she went in for a final hug, the tears were streaming down her face just as they had been weeks earlier when her husband announced his retirement from the main game. The more reserved Mitch, in many ways the introvert is father is not, held back his tears – but it took a bit of effort and it showed on his face.

As he had for more than two decades, Skaife had the shroud of his helmet to hide all but the most significant of emotions. On this day, you could see it in his eyes, there was a watery glaze as the crowd dissipated from around his car and he needed to deal with it before embarking on a race to end his time as a regular driver in Australia's top motor racing series.

Toni and Mitch stayed on the grid as long as they could. The pain wasn't in the knowledge that this may have been the last time they saw him race in anger – for there was a certain inevitability that he would at least compete in the endurance races – but it was very much about the closing of a career. A sea change for a father and husband succumbing to the inevitable in sport and ceasing to do what he loved doing and at which he had excelled for so many years.

After dealing with all that, Skaife released what he called 'the real Mark Skaife' one more time. If he wasn't going out at the top of his game, this final drive proved there were reasons other than just Mark Skaife, race driver, for that dip in performance. Two DNFs in the previous races had him starting 26th for his final race, and by the end he was sitting in 12th.

He made holes where there weren't any. He grabbed every

opportunity; he intimidated, bullied and bustled people out of the way. In the end, only one locked tyre sat between him and a top 10 finish in this race. But this was Skaife as we'd known him for so long, a driver with enough confidence to try just about anything – a driver with arrogance and flair.

Skaife is both a perfectionist and a control freak. There is always one way to do things, and that is generally his way, unless you have his full trust. The engineers he has worked with over the years talk of an articulate driver who was hell bent on winning. He would spend hours with them at times poring over data, and if he wasn't the fastest guy on the track or the one with the best race car, he wanted to know why.

The external manifestation of this was often misread by the media and pundits. One year at Bathurst when Jason Bright was faster than him in the same team, the media centre was buzzing with some pretty wild talk. Skaife appeared moody and distracted – the media thought he was having a tantrum because Bright was faster and that he'd walk back to the pits and get Bright slowed down. His theory was that if Jason Bright could do that time in an HRT Commodore, then so could he. And in the end he did, not by getting Bright held back but by improving his own game.

My personal relationship with Skaife has had its ups and downs. Once I was told to never darken his door again, but after I let him cool down we had a chat and resumed situation normal. He is a driver one must respect, not just because of his imposing record but because of his attitude and approach to the sport, which coupled with a certain skill level allowed him to get the best out of himself and those around him.

The past few seasons weren't a lot of fun for Skaife. The

ownership of Holden Racing Team, which Skaife took over on 1 June 2003, was taken on for all the right reasons and struck trouble for all the wrong reasons, and it challenged his driving. I had one interview with him in a board room at HSV in Clayton when he was preparing for a legal battle of some sort, and the entire board table was buried in piles of paper. It was three weeks before the start of a season, but it was clear where his mind was placed at that time, and it wasn't about getting ready for a season in the cockpit.

During those past few seasons we saw a driver on the edge, we saw flashes of brilliance in an amazing run of outs where he couldn't win a round to save himself. He had the speed, he had race wins, but the flow of round wins had dried. And so it was that at Phillip Island in 2008, with Garth Tander, he recorded his 39th and possibly final round win after more than 20 years in the sport.

But there is more to Skaife than just a race driver. Dressed in a suit and tie, he looks the part in Collins Street. Always immaculate and equally articulate, he is a more than capable performer around the boardroom table, although recent history may indicate otherwise to the naïve. His troubles of the past few years were not as reported, the reasons for the dramas were driven by ulterior motives and hidden agendas of others.

One journalist in particular seemed to delight at the latest Skaife rumour, and the stories flowed freely and without the proper checks and balances. Others were also caught in the whirlwind and the buzz of the great scoop. It made Skaife angry, it affected him and his family. At one stage, Toni felt like skipping work to avoid answering questions and correcting the errors of a story in Melbourne's *Herald-Sun*.

INTRODUCTION BY ANDREW CLARKE

But we'll get into all that later, my only word of caution until you get to that part of the book is that not all is as it seems.

There is another Skaife too and that is the very personal one who I really only started to know in the past year. He is a man motivated by and for people, and I believe that story comes out quite strongly. But there are bits you generally wouldn't read about as well. My daughter spent some time in hospital during February 2009, and during her stay she watched a video about living with asthma, and Mark Skaife featured in that video. In all my time of knowing him, I had no idea that both he and Mitch suffered from asthma.

What I saw from Mark was genuine compassion with a desire to find any way he could to help, and without going into detail, he did help and I will be forever grateful for that. As too perhaps are the people who have earned a living off Mark Skaife, or had their jobs saved when he risked everything to take on HRT.

What I know now is that the reason teams rallied behind Mark Skaife was that he won their trust, he rewarded their efforts and was honest with those around him. And in motorsport, there are not many who can say that.

In essence, Skaife is as accomplished in a race suit as he is in a business suit, and this story is about both of those, as well as Skaife the person. As a perfectionist, he is strangely and eloquently capable of picking holes in his own veneer.

In Skaife-land, there is but one story. And this is it . . . well most of it, anyway.

Andrew Clarke

1

THIS IS WHAT WE DO

MOTORSPORT IS AN odd sport. It's an individual pursuit on so many levels, but the reality is that the driver is also part of a team with as many critical roles as there are members. There are also mechanical issues and clowns who can end your run in a manner that just isn't a factor in other sports.

I've been very fortunate that for a long part of my career I've been in a team and in an environment where I knew that if I did a good enough job, I could win races. In my full-time driving career, I've only driven for two teams and you could argue they've been the two best teams of the past two decades or more.

Back in 1991 I started to gain the self-belief that I could win races on a regular basis, and that feeling was cemented in 1992 when I won my first Australian Touring Car Championship. The greatest part of that feeling comes from your own self-knowledge. You're so reliant on yourself for much of the race – it's a very personal feeling and somewhat selfish. It's about finding the zone that works, getting into the winning frame of mind without the sort of arrogance that lets things slip. For me, that feeling and that zone started when the car was wheeled out of the truck for the first time on a weekend.

For most of my career, as I said, I had enough faith to know that 90 per cent of the time the boys would give me a car that could win, and the rest was up to me. On the days I didn't win, the media and fans didn't say, 'Oh geez, the bloke on the left-hand front wheel didn't do a very good job,' or 'Do you think the shock absorber wasn't the right rate?' or 'It would have been good if it had more power.' It was me people pointed the finger at when it went wrong, and conversely treated me the opposite when it worked. But it was always very much a team and, in many respects as the driver, I was the captain, albeit one with the ability to ruin a weekend for everyone.

None of the big picture motorsport things matter one ounce when you're lined up on the grid sitting there by yourself. No one's going to help you then, and that's why I say it is a very individual sport. Perhaps the only other sport I can think of where it's the same is boxing – all the trainers and all the strappers count for nothing when you've got to trade punches with someone.

When you put the helmet on it is a defining time. But that is not enough on its own, it really all starts from a willingness to be there. I remember reading Alan Jones' book *Driving Ambition* and one of the really pertinent things he wrote was that when you put your helmet on and you're sitting in the car and you're ready for a race or for qualifying, you actually have to be happy that you're there to do that; that you're happy to go and drive the car to the edge of disaster. That you're happy to commit to whatever that task is and you don't feel like you want to be anywhere else. Without that you can't possibly do your best. When you put your hat on and you've climbed aboard, you absolutely have to be 100 per cent happy and committed to what you are about to do.

I remember lots of times driving out of pit lane, saying to myself as a trigger, 'This is what we do,' because you actually have to understand it and live it. If it's qualifying, man, you commit yourself to things people would never believe. You put your foot on the brake pedal at a point on the road that you think, 'Fuck, I'm not going to make this corner.'

Like at Bathurst when you fire it into Reid Park with a wall right next to the car, in qualifying you've gone in there so fast that you don't know if you're going to make it around – if that's not wild then I don't know what wild is. You've lobbed it at the corner and you pull out at the end and you've subconsciously held your breath. If you've climbed onboard, you've put your helmet on and you've decided that's what you're going to do, the level of commitment and the courage to do that is out of this world.

I always felt like I would rather go off the road and ruin a lap like that by over-committing to it than to soft-cock it and put my foot on the brake too early. Nothing in my world would be as disappointing as to put my foot onto the brake on the back straight at Pukekohe half a car length early and make the corner easily. I would be so feral with myself and that would be much more disappointing than if I put my foot on the brake two and a half metres too late and ran wide.

You've got to be honest with yourself at the end of the day if you want to get the best out of yourself; no-one else would know what you went through. You might look at the data and they'll say you were slightly early on the brake, but you'd know the real story.

Just put it into perspective. You might have just run a qualifying session and made the top 10 shootout. You might have had two goes on warm tyres to get yourself to a point of being fast enough to be in the shootout. So you're organised, you're pretty much up to speed. You then sit around for 15 minutes or half an hour or sometimes even the next day, and now you're sitting in the car and you've got cold tyres. You're going to drive out and both you and the team expect you to put your foot on the brake as deep you've ever gone, and I can tell you right now, anyone that does that is very good. Your brain's not acclimatised to the speed, it's not acclimatised to the level of grip or the tyre condition or whatever else has changed since you were in the car with everything maximised. You go out and fly down to a corner not knowing whether the car's going to make this or not and you actually purposely put your foot on the brake so late, so deep and so hard that you think to yourself, 'Why did I do that – there's no way it's going to stop.'

You get to the point where you actually scare yourself, and sometimes you get it spot on, other times you could have gone a metre deeper or you needed to be a metre shorter, even if you haven't gone off. There is absolutely only one person who will know what went on, no data will show what you felt.

Qualifying in the rain at New Zealand's Pukekohe track in 2004 was one of those times we got away with it. We had a shithouse engine and it rained, so our eyes lit up – we thought we were back in it because in motorsport if it rains it can often take some of the engine power dramas away and this was one of those days. I was fastest in qualifying and Marcos Ambrose was out before me in the shootout and he did a ripper lap. I went out on my run and it was pissing down. I arrived at turn one – which is fifth gear in the dry and maybe 240km/h – and there were massive puddles of standing water. I turned in and it just bolted on me. It's a big fast right-hand corner, hard on the throttle with full opposite lock and I speedwayed my way around it because there was no way I was going to give up that easily on the first corner of a qualifying lap.

We made it through there and the chicane to get onto the back straight, and the whole way down the back straight, while aquaplaning, you're trying to work out where you're going to brake. You've got no possible idea because you don't know how much tyre grip there is or how wet it is down there because you haven't fired at that corner in anger for more than an hour.

So I went blazing down there pulling gears up to 260 kays and I remember when I put my foot on the brake the wheels locked – and when the wheels lock in the rain the engine turns off; it goes silent because the tyres just slide over the wet road. The whole way in I was modulating the brake trying to make the corner, and by the time I got to the point where I needed to turn the car it was bordering on gone, but I let go of the clutch and the brake and it turned and made the apex and fired straight out of the corner. I couldn't believe it. I could have had a hundred goes and wouldn't have got it that good.

When you're driving really well, all that just happens in slow motion. The wheels are locked and the car's sliding, you're gathering up and gathering up, you know the corner's coming so you try to predict the retardation to a point where you say, I've got it slow enough now I can turn the corner. The amount of decision-making in a short space of time is just incredible. So you've done that corner – *phew*, unbelievable. But then you've got to get it out of the corner, you've got to put your foot on the throttle and you don't know how much wheel spin you're going to get, you don't how much grip you've got. Then it's nice and gentle gear changes and get out of the corner, and then the two fastest corners to finish the lap off. I remember the tyres at the apex on the first of those quick corners and thinking if I turned it in and slid it, by the time I got there I'd miss the tyre bundle, and it worked perfectly. Honestly, another coat of paint would have been enough to have hit the tyres. We got pole by a hundredth of a second, I think, and I remember that lap was absolutely the best I could have possibly driven that car on that day.

It's a very odd sport and that's what makes it great. When I'm being wheeled around the nursing home, that lap and that feeling will live with me forever. When you scare yourself, when it's so wild that you're wondering how you got away with it, that is an amazing feeling.

THIS IS WHAT WE DO

I didn't know it back in 1989 when things were ramping up with Fred Gibson's Nissan team, but that feeling would become my addiction. I'd been in Melbourne for a couple of years at that time and I'd won the two litre touring championship in 1987, but 1988 was a very tumultuous year. The new Nissan Skyline HR31 was a difficult car and Glenn Seton leaving the team at the end of 1988 which made the following year tough. We had Jim Richards join us and George Fury and I remained, with me still the third driver. I was learning a heap from Fred about every aspect of motorsport, but having someone like Jim join the team accelerated the rest of my learning.

In 1989, the Australian Touring Car Championship was eight rounds, with four extra events, including Bathurst. Nissan Motorsport Australia (Gibson Motor Sport) ran two Skyline HR31s for Jim Richards and George Fury for the entire season and another car for Skaife from round 5 onwards. Only two cars were entered for Sandown and Bathurst and Skaife shared a car with Richards. Dick Johnson won the ATCC in a Ford Sierra, his team winning the opening six rounds before Fury won at Winton, where Skaife also scored his first ATCC podium. Peter Brock won the final round in his Sierra. Johnson and John Bowe also won Bathurst, while Richards and Skaife won the Sandown 500, which was Skaife's first outright win in a touring car.

I was more frustrated by the car not being good enough than I was about how many race laps I was getting. It was very heavy at the front, the turbocharger was too small and it didn't make good enough power, and it was unreliable. Probably the only thing that was a real kick for me was that we had Jim Richards – who I rated as the world's best touring car driver – join the team. I knew I could learn a lot from him and I was hungry for it.

In the off-season of '89 we did a huge amount of testing, primarily at Winton and at Amaroo Park, and we knew, at least from a car perspective, that we were in better shape than the year before. Fred brought Jim into the team because he knew we'd get 100 per cent out of him, and we did. He came along and he drove the wheels off the car – which was just fantastic. At that point he wasn't any faster than me on our best lap for the day – I remember we both did a 52.3 on old tyres at Amaroo Park and there was nothing in it at Winton either – but he was able to do more of those times than me and he could string them together.

Jim was driving the car harder and he demanded more of the car than I did at the time. So although the development of the car wasn't necessarily based around Richo, it was being developed at the highest level because he was very hard on the car, which is what he was told to do. Fred's theory was: drive it until it breaks and then we'll fix it and make it stronger. Everyone used to say, 'Isn't Richo lovely on the car?' Well, they couldn't have been more wrong. He was an animal; he drove the car so hard it was unbelievable. He brought it in and brakes were melting off it, and everything was destroyed. 'Gentleman Jim' was an absolute fallacy.

But it gave us a real mandate to fix the car, and he dragged a result out of it all year. For me it was my first proper year of having someone like that around; it was good to have someone from left field. By the end of the year, we did a big test at

Phillip Island during which we simulated Bathurst and it was probably the best I'd ever driven at that stage. There wasn't the same sort of data available back then, but when you averaged all the laps I was only fractionally slower than Jim and faster than George.

So when we went to Bathurst I was still pretty inexperienced in terms of my Bathurst miles. I was, at worst, two seconds slower than Jim at the start of the weekend and at best a second slower than him from a race perspective. Because we didn't have data and you were in the same car so you couldn't follow him, I really had no idea at that stage where I was slower than him. It was a real eye-opener at such a difficult circuit.

We got away with it, though, and we ran third with Jimmy doing most of the driving. But my first Bathurst podium didn't really feel like mine – it was a good solid result but not good enough based on my desire to be at the level of Jim Richards.

We'd worked very hard for that result. We had nowhere near the power of the Ford Sierras at the time, and they blew us away in a straight line, but all that work we did on how the HR31 put its power down and how it handled and what development we did with Yokohama to get better tyre life, traction and grip was really starting to work for us. We won Sandown a few weeks earlier and I was almost as fast as Richo there, and for me just having Richo being happy to have me as his co-driver was almost an endorsement.

He wasn't really a fatherly figure even though there was a big age difference, but he certainly spent time with me, helping me along and giving me guidance, which was important given I was doing a lot of testing and not as much racing.

In 1990, the Australian Touring Car Championship was still an eight-race championship followed by a three-race endurance championship with a support race program for the Australian Grand Prix after Bathurst. Nissan Motorsport Australia (Gibson Motor Sport) started the season with two HR31 Skylines for Jim Richards and Mark Skaife, with Skaife debuting the Skyline GT-R at Mallala in the sixth round of the series. Both Richards and Skaife qualified the GT-R for the next round in Perth, although Richards raced the more reliable HR31, with which he had already won two rounds. The final round of the series was at Oran Park, and Richards qualified and raced the new car while Skaife switched back to the HR31. Richards won the title from Peter Brock (one win) and Dick Johnson (two wins), who were both driving Ford Sierras. Colin Bond also won two rounds in his Sierra. Win Percy was the best placed Holden with eighth in the championship. It was also Skaife's first year in the Australian Drivers' Championship and he finished third to Simon Kane and Mark Poole. Skaife won the final round of the series.

We worked bloody hard on that car in 1989 and then in 1990 it effectively won the Australian Touring Car Championship – which was just outstanding. Jim and I were really competing hard against each other that year, although I still missed a couple of rounds. We knew the GT-R was coming and we knew what its potential was, but we still had to compete with the old HR31. Jim won the opening round at Amaroo Park and then again at Winton, which was the halfway point in the championship and I hadn't even finished a race. But we had the car working well and we were pretty proud of that while excited by what lay in front of us.

I got points at Lakeside which was the round that Jim moved into the championship lead with Dick Johnson in his Ford Sierra dropping to second. In hindsight, it was a no brainer to give me the new car at Mallala – we needed to get race miles into it and you couldn't risk Jim's championship with what was potentially fragile and untested. As it turns out we were fast at both Mallala and Wanneroo but failed to finish at both, and then Jim was given the car for the final round at Oran Park where he won the race and sealed the title.

We'd made the old car very driveable, but all the work we'd done on shock absorber stuff and suspension geometry meant nothing on the new car – there wasn't one single part that was the same. When we first got into the GT-R it was pretty much in Japanese spec as it arrived and we had a lot of work to do. Fred purposely put me in it to be a bit of a guinea pig and that's what the boys called me after that. If there was anything that was a bit risky, Jim used to say, 'Give it to guinea pig – if he makes five laps then that'll be all right.'

You didn't need to be a lawyer to work out that the specs on the GT-R stacked up well, that for power to weight, and for all the good things that it brought along, it was going to be a pretty special car. But no one really understood the level of technology nor did they understand the engineering requirement to make it reliable. It was a nightmare, it was just an unbelievably technical and fragile piece of equipment.

It had four wheel steering, and that was the first thing we disconnected but even that wasn't easy. It had another steering rack on the back and we had to make that into a solid rear toe adjustment; it wasn't just about cutting a wire or not turning the thing on. We had Ross Holder, Steve Curtis and a couple of other technical guys helping us on all the electronic parts of it because there was plenty of electronic engineering, as well as the mechanical. We had to work on the four-wheel-drive system so we had adjustments that we could make from wet to dry, full four-wheel-drive versus 20 to 30 per cent at the front. It wasn't necessarily just a linear thing either, we could change it at certain speeds, change it with lateral and longitudinal g-sensing – it was incredibly complex.

That's really where I evolved this assessment of the five segments of the corner when most people were still talking about three. The nature of this car was such that you couldn't simply talk about entry, apex and exit, you needed to break the entry and exit into two more blocks each. The last segment of the corner – basically the exit drive – was all about how straight you could make the car. You could treat this differently in the GT-R to any other car I'd driven; you could alter the four-wheel-drive as it was accelerating based on road speed and on the g-forces. So sometimes you had to determine why it was getting sideways. Was it actually lateral grip or was it because it was spinning wheels? A lot of that discipline really served me well in later life in terms of how you set the cars up and being able to determine what the real issue was with the car.

Largely it was seat of the pants stuff, but data was just coming on properly and we were able to quantify what we were feeling. I laugh about this because it sounds ridiculous, but good engineering people want to help you. If you've made a comment about a car they want to go and find the data that shows it, then they can understand and rationalise and work out what to do to fix the car. Guys like Ross Holder, Richard Hollway and Dave Swenson would go looking for entry understeer in turn two if that's what I said I felt, then they'd work out why and try to fix that specific complaint.

But the reality is that there are a lot of engineers who firstly don't believe the driver, and then actually want to prove the driver wrong. Because if they can say that the car is good and that it's the driver's fault, they've done their job. With that sort of mentality you have this constant problem between driver and engineer and it just doesn't work.

As I mentioned, we'd seen the GT-R in Japan, but when we saw it as a race car I was turned on by it. It was a tough looking, muscley car with great road presence – all the things that make a great looking race car. When I first got in it I couldn't believe it, you put pressure on the throttle coming out of the corners and it was unbelievable how hard you could accelerate. It had great power but it also had such great traction; however we had to work bloody hard to get it to work consistently on the sort of bumpier and tighter tracks we had in Australia.

It wasn't Fuji or Le Mans or Spa – these were mongrel circuits like Lakeside, Winton and Amaroo Park. Getting it to behave was just one part of it, we had to get it to survive those kind of tracks too – they have such different loads and put such different stresses on a car. We had to keep on developing all the way through the life of the car, especially when CAMS (Confederation of Australian Motor Sport), as 'rule makers', started to handicap its performance.

When we debuted the car at Mallala it was really on a wing and a prayer, we had no idea how it was going to stack up reliability-wise. So when it was clear Jim was the contender in the 1990 championship and I wasn't, I started doing most of the work on the GT-R. On debut it was quick but fragile. I used it for two rounds and when we thought it was OK we put Jim in for the final round to tie up the series.

That's where Fred was outstanding – his understanding of racing and his strategy was absolutely the number one in the country. He also had good engineers around him and he made educated decisions which clearly stood the test of time. He could have put Jim in that race at Mallala – it would have been easy to put him into the faster car just as the media and many at Nissan wanted us to do at the time, and it would have stopped because it broke a left front hub and he wouldn't have won the championship.

So when we wheeled the GT-R out at Mallala for its first race meeting, we had a major drama with it in practice and we got out to do one flying lap for qualifying, because we had a brake issue with the car and scored some damage when it dropped on its nose at speed. I remember blazing out and doing one lap in the second part of qualifying and sitting third behind Peter Brock and Tony Longhurst. But off the start, it was just unbelievable. You could basically give it full revs and dump the clutch and the thing would rocket away being four-wheel drive. So in no time in the race, I passed them for the lead and bolted. We were a mile in front when I got down to turn three and my brake pedal went straight to the floor after it broke another of the little lightweight hubs. But it was an incredible debut.

We could probably have backed off when we got the lead – we could have sprinted into the distance and we had plenty in reserve. I was driving it hard and I was driving it to win the race, so I wasn't going to make a mistake, but we needed to test it out – that was the whole point of what we were doing. Obviously the GT-R got better each time we went out with it, and come the final round Jim used it to really good effect.

We then went to Bathurst and pretty much led all day, but there was always a doubt about its reliability. We had no way of Australianising it by that stage and it didn't make it even though we ran conservatively. HRT won that race with Win Percy and Allan Grice, and Fred just kept telling me to let Grice go when all I wanted to do was race him. I remember Fred yelling at me over the radio, 'Let him go, let him go' – I think I was pissing him off. It was one of those races where we had to drive the car conservatively because we just weren't in a position to race, which was strange for us. As I've mentioned, Fred had always told us to 'drive as hard as you can and we'll fix it', which is a great philosophy because it's what eventually made the cars we built so good, but this was Bathurst and we had to try and be smart. The car didn't finish, but we did learn more about it.

After Bathurst, we started working away at it, gradually fixing what we saw as the cars' weaknesses. Back then, the Australian Grand Prix was held in Adelaide and in November, so for us the support race for that meeting was another chance to test. We were going to go as hard as we could to see what broke, and in the process I had the biggest crash of my life to that point. Richo and I were battling for pole position and it was my first lap in qualifying. We now had Formula 1 spec Pi System data loggers in the cars and we could get measurements around what was happening – and importantly we could find out exactly what the car was doing in any given part of the lap. I knew I was getting big gains on Jimmy coming on to the back straight, which was onto Dequetteville Terrace, a really fast right-hander where Mika Häkkinen had his big crash a few years later.

It was a great corner, a really fast fourth-gear corner that is a little bit like turn eight now but slower. There was a big kerb on the inside and a massive kerb on the outside, I remember driving up over the kerb in practice and knew I could get away with it in qualifying, no problem. So I blazed in there, turned in and slid towards the outside kerb. But it had a bit more force in it than other laps because we were on new tyres and it was pretty wild ride. When it hit the kerb the impact broke the bottom out of the wheel; it turned straight over on its roof and was still going fast. I remember turning down to try and stop the car from turning over, but it didn't really work. No matter how hard I pressed the brake pedal, the car just wouldn't slow down – usually the brakes don't have much effect when the car's on its roof.

Jesus, it hit hard.

As it was running towards the fence on its lid, the road ground its way through the top of the A pillar and the roof and into my helmet. So it's got grazes all over it and it flattened a big section of my helmet as it was heading to the fence. When it hit, the force was incredible. The car bounced right back into the middle of the track and it was rotating on its roof and when it stopped they couldn't get me out because the door was so damaged. A heap of guys pulled up, like Joe Sommariva who was driving a BMW 635, Colin Bond and I think Peter Brock too. But when I was stuck in there the marshals started yelling out, 'Fire! Fire!' God, it wasn't getting any better now. I was stuck in there and she was going to light up. It was just unbelievably frightening.

No-one knows this, but I actually damaged my right eye in the crash. I was so sore I lay in a Nissan Patrol the whole of the next day. I went to the medical centre, I was chewing Panadeine Fortes like Smarties and I've never been so sore in my life. It was really hot over in Adelaide that time of year and I just lay there in the Patrol with the air conditioner on, I couldn't move. I kept blinking all the time and there was a black spot, like a fuzzy spot, in my eye.

I couldn't get my brain around what it was – it was very strange. So I went back to Melbourne and Fred's wife, Christine, took me to the hospital to have my neck and everything checked. We did all the MRI stuff and then the doctor said I should have all these others scans to see why my eye was funny. Most people just said it would get better, but it hasn't, although my brain has rewired itself to make it a non-issue – but if I take the time to find it I still can. If you've ever been knocked out you'd remember all those little fuzzy spots which go into your vision – it was like they were all compacted together in one little spot, a small spot right in the middle of my eye.

Earlier in the year, I had a rock come in the window of the car and hit me in the eye at Lakeside and Dr Kevin English, an ophthalmologist in Brisbane, looked after me then, so I got on a plane and flew up to see him. He went through a whole host of checks and said I had scarred the retina with the impact. Everything in your head moves in a crash like that, and some of the movement scarred my eye.

We never told anyone, though – we kept it quiet the whole time. Kevin said my eyes would find a way to work around it, and they have, but it is still there.

That crash was a real drama. I almost missed the next race meeting which was the Nissan 500 at Eastern Creek and Neil Crompton was drafted into driving with Jimmy just in case, but I arrived pretty late and got in the car and drove. It was obviously good to get back on the horse and get back in the car and drive, but it was also very frightening because I didn't know how much the vision thing was going to hurt me. Fortunately, when I drove the car I was on the pace. But it was quite a nervous time.

There was also some damage to the L4/L5 discs in my lower spine which had been dislodged and it was basically crushed. The roof had been pushed down and the seat wasn't moving, so something had to give, and it was those discs in my back.

We worked incredibly hard in the offseason after 1990 to make the GTRs more accepting of Australian circuits from an endurance standpoint. We knew we needed to have reliability if we were going to win in 1991 and I put a huge amount of pressure on myself with that. Richo came up to the Central Coast to have Christmas and New Year with us and he brought the whole family. Freddie was there too. I remember having a beer with Dad and I said to him, 'If I can't beat Richo, I'm stuffed.' The energy that I used to try to beat Jim Richards was as much as I can remember with anything. I knew he was the one I had to beat first and foremost, but we also had to get the cars to survive.

One extra round was added to the ATCC in 1991 which made for 11 race meetings for Skaife in the Nissan GT-R (which was by now dubbed Godzilla). He also ran seven rounds of the Australian Drivers' Championship, winning six of them and the title. Both Richards and Skaife were in the GT-R for the 1991 season and Mark Gibbs joined them in a third factory prepared being nominally run by Bob Forbes. Richards won four of the first five rounds of the series to set himself up for back-to-back titles, winning the championship 137 points to 132, but only after Skaife had to drop his worst score – 10 points from Winton. In all, one of Richards or Skaife was on the podium at every round, and each missed the podium only once. Tony Longhurst, now in a BMW, was the only other round winner for the season as the Sierras proved fragile trying to chase the GT-Rs, and the Commodore simply didn't have enough speed. Skaife and Richards won Bathurst together for the first time.

We went into 1991 in pretty good shape. It had all our own front uprights, front spindles, hubs, wheels, all new top-hats and brake arrangement. We now had our engine staff doing the turbochargers and we also had new suspension geometry and shock absorbers. We'd virtually changed everything. We even did all our own four-wheel drive maps and had our own six speed gearbox.

If you lined it up against any GT-R in the world, it would have been the best. So 1991 was arguably one of the better years for Nissan Motor Company in motorsport – we just smashed them. It came down to Jim and I in the last round of 1991 and Jim won the title.

I won my first round of the touring car championship in

Perth that year, and yes it was significant and I remember really valuing it. I think on that day Jimmy and I were in a class of our own, and to me I'd already gone past where I thought the threshold was where I should have already won a round. It was overdue in my eyes, and I drove well but I didn't drive fantastically. I didn't drive it out of its skin, and when I won, I thought, 'Oh yeah, that's great.'

There were lots of times when I drove better for less reward. At Mallala a few rounds later, I bolted on everybody, even Richo. I drove it better at Mallala to win than I did at Perth. So there are times when you really know. It's such an individual pursuit like that, you really know when you've done a great job.

The year-long battle between Jim and myself was fantastic, although it was a drama for Fred. We were driving the cars so hard to beat each other that we'd gap the field by too much, so there was this constant talk of handicapping hanging over the team and Fred trying to slow us down to not encourage the handicappers. But he didn't want to play favourites or whatever and that meant that Jimmy and I needed to beat each other. It was a bit like Senna and Prost where you can have great rivalry within the team which makes for great race cars and great team development, but it makes it difficult sometimes.

It was a funny year though, and I ended the season with more points than Jim but I didn't win the title because we had to drop our worst round – which for me was the Winton round where I used the old pit lane exit road during the start and got penalised – and that moved Jim in front. Then we went to Bathurst together and won, which was my first

Bathurst win. So 1991 was an exceptional year for the team and for me personally. At that stage I felt like I was driving well enough not only to compete with Richo, but also that on some days I could beat him.

We won the Australian Drivers' Championship in that year too, and that was a good effort, especially mixing the two different cars and championships. I was doing so much driving I was never out of a car and was often driving two cars on the same day at some places. I finished second in the Australian Touring Car Championship, won Bathurst and won the Drivers' Championship. My career was pretty much heading down the right road and there was only one way to get better, and that was to win the ATCC as well, which we set about doing in 1992.

Winning Bathurst meant a lot, but I was also young and naive. First Bathurst, that's pretty cool, no drama, I was 24. But I also didn't finish in the car and I reckon there's a lot about that race which is all about being in the car at the end, because it's got much more emotional appeal and a much greater sense of reality about it when you cross the finish line.

But this stage in my life was definitely a glassy-eyed Mark Skaife. This was Hollywood. This was as good as it gets. I was in the best race team with the best overall sponsorship against the best driver in the same equipment, and week-in, week-out I was speeding around a racetrack somewhere. It was just fantastic.

I did have another big crash in that year; well, a lucky escape really. Jim and I had this thing where if we damaged a car – even something like knocking a headlight out running into someone – we had to pay the boys a slab of beer.

So the whole funny thing was that after that crash at Adelaide, Jimmy reported back to Fred over the radio saying, 'He's rolled it over.' Fred said, 'What? He couldn't have rolled it over, it's only the first lap in qualifying,' and Jim said, 'No, he's rolled it over.' Fred asked, 'What's the car like?' and Jimmy replied, 'I think he owes the boys a small bottle shop!' That's how much damage was done. So that was our gag and that just ran for years.

In 1991, Symmons Plains was one of those race meetings where they had cars and bikes in a 4 × 2 race meeting, and we went down to watch the guys through the fast kink in the back straight in the rain which, honestly, was as good an experience as I've ever had. There were these mad pricks on motorbikes arrowing through there in the rain – it was out of control. I said to Richo at the end of that session, 'Do you reckon you could get through there flat-out?'

He said, 'I don't reckon. Why don't you have a go at it and see if you can get away with it, and if you can I'll give it a run. I haven't seen a good accident for a while.' He's such a funny bastard and that's where we get our great relationship, just the rapport of that stuff. It was very funny but it was also like a red rag to a bull. So I went out in qualifying and I came down the main straight on the first flying lap and it was actually going to be quite easy to get through the kink flat, so I turned the corner, and when I turned, the left hand (the loaded side of the car) front brake rotor exploded and sliced the wheel in two. The disc was hot from the big stop at the hairpin which was the previous corner and with all the water splashing onto it from the rain it just started to crack and it let go. I'd just pulled sixth gear and it had exploded and I was a passenger. It was doing maybe 250 km/h when it let go and the car was spinning down the track and onto the grass and it felt like it was getting faster. There was the massive tyre wall off to the left, and of all the times I've been scared in a car, this was just terrifying – the brake pedal was on the floor, I had no steering and it was going fast. I couldn't do anything about it.

It was heading for the tyre wall on the left, and in those days there was a flag marshal's box right down the end of the main straight on the inside. I remember clearly as the car was going backwards, I looked at the tyre wall and pulled myself forward as hard as I could in the seat, and the car just kept on rotating and I had no idea how it was going to hit. But it ended up going between the tyre wall, which is really just a dirt bank with some tyres on front of it, and the marshal's box – either would have killed me, but it went between them. Dead set.

Allan Moffat was standing at the corner and he reckons I was doing 120 miles an hour (200 km/h) when I went between them. It went across the circuit, down through all the mulga that was down the end of the run-off road, through the pit, through the barbed wire fence, and out into the Yules' property and onto the potato farm. That's how far it went. It would have been 200 metres from the track, if not more!

Moffat ran down to me not knowing what he was going to find, and he was white. He said, 'Fuck, man! That was going fast!' He knew if I'd hit anything it would have been 'goodnight, nurse'. Absolutely the luckiest thing ever in my career – if I'd hit either of those it was just over-red-rover, you're dead.

The off-road adventure tore everything from under it, so even though the panels were straight it was a big job to fix it. Everything that hung down under the car was just pulled off. They had to clean it first because there was mud and shit everywhere. And the funny thing was, again on the radio, Richo goes to Fred, 'That idiot's trying to get through the kink flat – I told him you couldn't get through the kink flat.' He'd come round the corner down the straight and seen my car right down there rooted and he was already counting in his head how many slabs this was going to cost me. So there was a bit of humour in a really bad situation.

1991 was my second year doing both the Australian Touring Car Championship and the Australian Drivers' Championship in my SPA Formula Brabham. It was pretty easy to get my head around the different cars, even on the same day. Yes, some cars like certain things and have their own little idiosyncrasies, but essentially all you can do is just go and drive the car to its absolute limit, and in some ways it really is as basic as that. I've always said that if anyone was as fast as us, all they'd done was driven that car to its limit.

The racing driver's job is very basic – drive whatever car you're given to its absolute limit. When you do that, when you get the best from it, you'll get the rewards on the time sheet. You see differences in Formula One teams – one bloke's got the absolute best from it and the other guy hasn't. But you'll see at racetracks like Monza where the track is relatively easy that you get them in pairs on the grid – two Ferraris, two Brawns, two McLarens and so on. Driving the car to the limit there is easy. But you don't see that at somewhere like

Spa where it is all a lot harder, the pairs get broken up as one driver decides he's happy to take a bit more of a risk there, or conversely less. At tracks that demand more from the driver you rarely see the grid formation in teams on each row.

We did get handicapped at the end of 1991 and that meant we had another big off-season to get our heads around all the new issues. How would we deal with the extra weight? How could we get more power and driveability out of the engine with turbocharger 'boost' restrictions? There were a lot of issues that made one giant headache for us. And then you add in that we'd signed Winfield with the biggest single motorsport sponsorship ever in Australia at that stage, so there was a lot of work turning everything that was blue into red. It was a very busy time.

> *The ATCC was again held over nine rounds in 1992, and Skaife and Richards were now driving Winfield sponsored GT-Rs. They recorded back-to-back Bathurst wins that didn't prove too popular with a lot of the crowd since the car had crashed out of the race only for it to be red flagged and awarded to them. In the main championship, Skaife recorded four wins on his way to the first of his five touring car titles. Richards didn't manage a win in the now handicapped GT-R, but did finish second in the series. Tony Longhurst and his BMW were again the best of the rest and with one win he finished third overall. John Bowe had a DNF (did not finish) that blunted the three round wins and Glenn Seton won a round too. Peter Brock had switched back to Holden after spells with both BMW and Ford. Skaife also won his second Australian Drivers' Championship, this time with three round wins from five starts.*

Rothmans spent money over and above their Winfield motorsport sponsorship – they leveraged it properly in terms of the extras such as press advertising, PR, merchandise and the like, so their spend overall was in really big numbers. Believe me though, we needed all that money. It was a time when some of the top guys from Rothmans were just mad motor racing people . . . guys like John Devine, Gary Krell, Des Hancock, Robert Paige, Ian Kleeman and Peter Turner were happy to live and breathe motorsport with us. But they also knew what there were doing, they'd been involved in the Peter Stuyvesant time with Allan Moffat and it just blew me away how well they used us, but it also added a little to the pressure we were feeling.

We rolled out not just the GT-Rs but the Formula Brabham car and the whole thing was Winfield-ised. We changed everything from blue to red and it was an exciting time. From a branding standpoint, even though it was cigarettes, it wasn't as controversial then – Benson & Hedges, Peter Jackson and now Winfield were all involved, and there was a lot of brand competition between them. They were the three market segment leaders and were heavily into sports and arts sponsorship with around $100 million invested per annum.

So we started 1992 with a car that was up to 1500 kg from its original 1260 kg, and that doesn't just slow you down, it stresses every component on the car that little bit more. We had turbo boost restrictions to limit the engine power output, the same tyres and no real downforce to speak of – if you did a modern aero test on those cars I reckon they'd have lift rather than downforce, and that meant with all the other bits running against us it was a very hard car to drive.

Yes, it was still quick but we were miles away from driving around with an arm on the door. I had some real stoushes off the track through the year with people like Larry Perkins, who used to say we were just cruising. I made him the offer one day at Lakeside in 1992, that as well as giving him a backhander, if he wanted to come and drive the car he was welcome to have a crack at it.

Skaife was angered by suggestions that he and Richards were foxing to keep the rule makers away from his car. Most of the time he was able to keep his emotions in check, but in the post-qualifying press conference at Lakeside, Skaife suggested Larry Perkins was a candidate for a punch in the mouth, and then offered him a steer in the car. 'You come and drive the car in the morning, Superstar, and see for yourself.' Perkins never drove the car.

We still had the advantage of four-wheel-drive, but that wasn't too much use everywhere. At Symmons Plains, for instance, the only place it was of any use was coming out of the hairpin; for the rest of the track you'd rather just have the rear wheels driving. The Sierras were much faster in a straight line than us, so we had to make it up under brakes, which wasn't easy with 1500 kg to pull up. Jimmy and I just weren't happy, we were complaining a lot about the cars, and Fred had to cop a lot from us, not that he could do much. I wouldn't have liked to be Gibbo at the time.

We got some results at places we probably shouldn't have; I won at Amaroo Park which was amazing with that weight. Coming into the final round I'd won three of the eight rounds up to that point, and Jimmy had none, but I had a bad round at Wanneroo and Jim finished on the podium which kept him in the hunt. All the other wins had been shared around – although John Bowe had won a few, he also had a DNF earlier in the year which hurt him. So going into the final round at Oran Park, only Jim could beat me for the touring car title, and in the Formula Brabham on the same day I had to fight Mark Larkham for the drivers' championship.

In the Nissan I got a great start and was able to win the race which meant I won my first Australian Touring Car Championship, and that was probably the best day of absolutely driving at the highest level I had to that point. I won both titles, and given that no-one else at that point had even won both titles before, it was amazing to do it on the same day.

There was a lot of pressure to perform. Pete Geoghegan came out and drove my car as a publicity stunt because he was the youngest touring car champion to that point and if I won I was going to beat that record. I drove the old Cortina that he won the touring car championship in 20 years or so earlier, which was good fun but it was just another distraction. For me, while my whole weekend was about winning the ATCC, there was always this thing in the background of winning the drivers' championship on the same day. Neither race was easy and they both went right to the chequered flag, but I won both races and both titles.

I don't think I've ever felt pressure as high as that. I remember lying in bed that morning hoping the cars would hang together and that I could do the job. I think as a race driver you've always got a certain level of confidence in yourself, but you know there is always the spectre of mechanical failure. The simplest things can cost you; unlike other sports, it's very cruel in that way. In an AFL grand final, for instance, one little mistake generally won't end the game. In motorsport, that's all it takes.

The mechanical part of it is always a lingering issue out there in the big wide world of 'are the cars going to finish the races?'. If the cars are going to finish the races, can I be fast enough to win, can I cope with all those demands? Can I drive it at such a high level that no one's going to beat me today? You've got to qualify well and be on the front of the grid in both. You've then got to make good starts. You've got to not make mistakes in the early laps. You've got to be able to gap the blokes when you need to. I've always said that when you're operating really well, everything happens slowly and you've got the car on a piece of string – on that day in both cars that's how it was.

It was a great feeling to go to Bathurst two months later with number one on the door for me rather than Richo, but what a day and what a Bathurst to win. It was our second in a row, but it almost didn't happen. It was so wet at the end I'm glad I wasn't in the car. I still think it's the heaviest rain I've ever seen there.

Poor Jimmy was caught out; Crompo came in just before him to put wets on and that kept Jim out for a lap. And as Jim came out of The Cutting and came up over the rise at the right-hand change of direction, there were rivers of water running off the hill and it just pushed the car straight into the fence. We were all standing there horrified – we knew the race was over for us. A minute or two later, the car was just washed off the road at Forrests Elbow for a big crash, it was just extraordinary. There were six cars parked there and it looked like a wrecking yard.

The look on Jim's face, and the level of disappointment around the garage, was like you could not believe. But all the technical guys in the team were saying, 'This race is going to be stopped and we were leading before it got red-flagged – we're going to win this.' When Jim arrived back, though, and I ran over to him, my first reaction wasn't that we'd won, my first reaction was to console him. I actually got the message that we'd won as I ran out and it came over the PA at the same time. I remember looking over at Richo and his face was just white; the crash had obviously frightened him and his level of disappointment was extreme. When I told him we'd won, this morbid white face turned to absolute elation in seconds.

There had been a lot of gags over the years but that wasn't one, and he knew I wouldn't joke about that; it was an unbelievable moment for the two of us.

It was truly an unforgettable day. Denny Hulme (the 1967 world F1 champion) died during the race and he was a great mate of Jim's, so he was pretty raw. Never in my life has it been that dangerous – 285 km/h down the straight and you couldn't see two car lengths in front of you.

That's what made the crowd reaction so gutting. We, like many other drivers, had put it all on the line and people should have been able to say, 'Well done today, boys.' We didn't make the rules, we just drove for our lives. Everyone went feral, though – we were getting booed and they were getting stuck into us – so Jimmy gave them a burst. He was the senior member of the team so I was letting him do the chat – it would have been a much uglier experience if I had the chance to speak freely because I was getting pretty fired up just standing there and copping that shit.

Winning Bathurst was a great way for us to close off the GT-R chapter; with the work we'd put in as a team to get that final result, I thought it was a just reward. As an automotive engineering exercise it was phenomenal and that was probably what made what was happening to us in terms of the rule changes for the next season even more astounding.

At that stage, we still had to look after our existing sponsors – including Nissan – and get the best results possible. Other teams were able to start working on their 1993 cars because they were already with Ford or Holden, we didn't have that luxury. Some teams even ran cars at Bathurst, and for those already running Holdens there was a big carryover of technology so we were already on the back foot for 1993 if the rules changes went ahead. We clearly wanted to win as many races as possible in the closing stages of the year and that meant we had to keep going ahead full steam with the GT-R.

But the switch to the new rules which effectively banned our car (and the BMWs) wasn't all as clear cut as it appeared and there was a lot of controversy and drama. Fred actually took CAMS to court about the legality of the rule changes and there was a lot of action being taken in the background, but basically television got together with CAMS to go and seek Ford and Holden as a two-horse race. We'd invested so much energy and money into developing those cars, the redundancy of equipment was devastating. All we had left out of it was the best sponsorship package in the country. Whatever we did we knew we could change to the new class and do well, but all the technical work that we'd done to make this car so great was effectively thrown away.

It wasn't just the cars for us – there was all the equipment and the intellectual property. We'd spent so much money to resource ourselves up to that level we were making a heap of race parts inside our facility, we were making all our own turbo components, and all that work was basically being dumped. So when we went to Holden we probably had four to five million dollars worth of stuff in plant and equipment – a lot of money in those days – that was essentially worthless. We sold a couple of cars overseas and bits and pieces, but Fred would have lost a lot of money on it all. And because we had contractual obligations, a championship to win and Bathurst, we couldn't change over to the new rules as early as many of the other competitors like Seton and Johnson. We were on the back foot for 1993 before it had even started.

I'd gone to Europe straight after Bathurst to do the final couple of races of the F3000 season (the open wheeler category that had taken over from Formula 2 as the class one rung below F1, competing against future F1 drivers David Coulthard, Rubens Barrichello and Olivier Panis) and by the time I came back the decision had been handed down – the GT-R was officially gone from the local racing scene and we now had to work out whether to race Fords or Holdens. We had a bit of blueing about which car we'd use and we could've gone either way – it could have been Ford or Holden. In fact, Rothmans wanted us to go with Ford because they had a massive company car fleet with them. Fred, possibly because of his previous Ford ties (he had won Bathurst with them), thought Ford was the right way to go too. We had some real heart-to-hearts: everyone wanted to go Ford ... except me.

We met with the Holden heavies Rob McEniry, Ross McKenzie and John Lindell to seek support in late 1992. They were immediately onside with our plans and could pick up the level of energy Fred and I had to make the new venture work for all of us. We were pretty motivated to make this work, as a team we were sick of people saying the only reason we were winning was because of the car. We knew we were a pretty good operation and I certainly wanted to prove a point personally.

I thought Holden was the best alternative and part of my reasoning was that I believed Tom Walkinshaw Racing (TWR) – which was running the homologation program for Holden – would do the best job on the aero-kit. And how wrong I was. Within the first year we had to have a parity adjustment because the Ford had a clear advantage. The 150 mm perimeter skirt that we had in the front spoiler was technically deficient compared to the Fords' complete undertray. We went with Holden and we struggled in terms of front grip, but when the parity adjustment was made we were immediately competitive.

With the Nissan banned for 1993, Gibson Motor Sport changed to the Holden Commodore for the nine round championship. Skaife and Richards were on the pace but were not consistent. Richards won the final two rounds of the series while Skaife had to make do with a pair of podiums – in the end, they were the first two Holdens in the championship hunt with fourth and sixth. Glenn Seton won the title comfortably from his teammate, 1980 Formula One World Champion Alan Jones. The two Dick Johnson Racing Falcons also finished the season well, Bowe winning a round. At Bathurst Skaife qualified second, but a late race run-in with a back marker forced Richards up an escape road and Larry Perkins cruised to the flag. Skaife won his third Australian Drivers' Championship in a row with four wins from six rounds, knocking off Mark Larkham for the second time.

We had Bob Forbes' GIO Commodore in our workshop because we were preparing his GT-R, so we used that in the off-season to start our Holden program. It had a lot of Perkins bits in it and we basically blazed out and started doing work with Yokohama to see what we needed to do with the tyres. At that point in time Yokohama was very proactive and its tyre technology was very good coming out of Japan, and there was a very experienced European gentleman called Burt Baldwin (ex-Goodyear F1) who was handling the development and the whole program in Australia with Keith McCormack. At the advent of the new series, there really wasn't much between Bridgestone, Dunlop and Yokohama, but it was still a massive change for both Yokohama and us to adjust to the new cars – we were back to rear-wheel-drive for instance and changed our needs from the tyre massively. Now we only needed the front tyres for steering and the rear tyres were for traction.

We started buying new bits for the car to deal with the issues we were uncovering. We would rather have engineered our own solutions, but we didn't have time if we were going to roll it out at Amaroo Park. So we started with what was just a kit car. There was a lot of fudging going on too. Because we were the new boys on the Commodore block, we'd buy stuff from blokes and it wouldn't fit – it was just unbelievable. We got our first engine from HRT and we couldn't even close the bonnet. It was about three inches too high.

Their car must have been lower in the cross member and the engine mounts to get that thing in. I can remember standing with Andrew Bartley and Jeff Grech trying to close the bonnet after we got the engine in place. We all thought we were at the cutting edge of technology back then, but by today's standard we were all lagging.

So under these new rules with new cars and new regulations, the engine should have been in the same spot in a Ford and in a Holden, but we couldn't even get it lined up from one Holden to the next. There was actually a lot of drama about how to get it right between Ford and Holden at the time too. Without being too technical, the Chevrolet engine had Siamese ports on the inlet manifold which basically dragged the air from each other but the way the Ford cylinder head was configured was much better because the ports were separated and it wasn't taking air from itself. This meant the inlet trumpets were different, and then the Chev engine sat forward more than the Ford so that even closing the bonnet was hard in a Holden. That said, we felt we should have been able to do that, even on a kit car.

We resolved it all as well as a few other things and got it all together for Amaroo, finishing on the podium. I don't remember a more satisfying day than our first race meeting in the Holden in 1993 at Amaroo Park. That was the roughest, toughest race I've ever been in – it was like a fight when you're inside the fence and you can't get out and you can do whatever you want because the umpire isn't intervening. In those situations, you can do whatever you have to do to get a result and we were certainly taking liberties.

I miss tracks like Amaroo. Brock always used to say, 'Great racetracks have consequences,' and Amaroo had consequences. In a Formula Holden car we were doing 38 second laps around there – you could get the car across the top of the hill flat and that was amazing because it was totally blind. It was an unbelievable racetrack, perhaps not suited so much to a big touring car, but you had to take a risk to do anything there. It's why that race was so much fun. Lakeside was similar too. If you compare them to the modern places that we go to now, it's just a joke. Compare Amaroo Park to Queensland Raceway – it's not even in the same league.

You had to be really aggressive to pass because it was so hard. I remember serving Tomas Mezera straight off the road at Honda, totally on purpose because I couldn't get past. He was blocking me everywhere and no-one said 'Get the bad sportsmanship flag out' to penalise him for him blocking. It was like, Who cared? When I pushed him wide there were no repercussions, unlike today's racing. I remember getting right through the field and the car had half the front spoiler missing, and that was when we first picked up that the front spoiler would have been more efficient with an undertray.

I served up so many blokes and I ended up on the podium as the first Holden. It was an incredible race, especially considering the first and second place getters – Glenn Seton and John Bowe – had been running the Falcon at the end of the previous year's races.

That was our first race for Holden and our first foray into what everyone was saying was a level playing field. I don't remember ever being more motivated and we were absolutely into it. By the time we got to mid-season we were far and away the strongest Holden. We should have won Bathurst that year: we had a great battle with Larry Perkins, but Jimmy had to go up the escape road at Hell Corner late in the race which cost us any chance of winning, and we ended up second.

The first engine had 511 horsepower and it was a customer shit-box, it was very average. We made it as good as we could in the early part of the season. We had to wait while our own engine program switched from Nissan to Holden and got up and running because that doesn't just happen overnight. You can't turn one tap off and another on.

What people don't really understand about touring car racing – or V8 Supercar Racing as we now know it – is that the front of the field has always been exceptional. The fields may not have been massive, but the front has always been great. So on the day we ran our first Holden, there were the likes of Peter Brock, Tomas Mezera, Wayne Gardner, Larry Perkins and Neil Crompton in Holdens, and Dick Johnson, John Bowe, Glenn Seton and Alan Jones in Fords, and obviously Richo and I in our Winfield Commodores. The names at the top of the field were a who's who of Australian motorsport; it was just outstanding.

To achieve what we did then, in the face of that competition, with a car that was clearly handicapped to some of the field, and having pieced together a customer car from whatever sources we could use, was amazing. We were very proud of what we did then, and we knew that once the parity issue was dealt with we'd have a reasonable shot.

Personally, after what had gone on with the GT-R I wasn't as motivated as I would have liked and I was thinking about overseas. My F3000 run hadn't been a lot of fun and I wouldn't have wanted to race that car in 1993. There were a couple of different configurations of front suspension geometry at that time – some had a single mounted mono-shock and others had twin-shock, which is what we had, and it was a shocking car to drive.

At the faster circuits it was OK. When I tested at Magny-Cours in the south of France I was about third or fourth fastest, but on slow tracks like Nogaro it was just a dog; it had the worst understeer of any car I've ever driven. So I didn't come out of that feeling really good about F3000 because we didn't have a car that was good enough to do the job. I was initially really motivated about doing F3000 and what was happening to us in Australia was boosting that, but my motivation didn't stay high because the car we had was ordinary. It was a bit of a restless time for me, and maybe if I'd enjoyed those races more I may have bailed out of touring cars and had a real crack overseas.

Amaroo Park probably killed any hankering for Europe – I don't remember ever feeling better at a press conference than I did that first round. To be on the podium on that day, to be the best of the Holden teams, was awesome. I knew after that race meeting that the Ford was a lot better than the Holden too, so it was a very good result. What was good for us was that I knew we had a lot more to come; ours was just a customer kit car with bits from HRT, Perkins and Harrop Engineering.

I remember saying in the press conference, 'This is an unbelievable effort, this is a car that privateers in Sydney could have bought,' and I meant it. By our standards there was nothing special about that car, and anybody with money could have pieced it together as many blokes were doing in what was referred to as a privateer operation. We had to do the opposite to the GT-R program: everything on the Nissan was light and fragile and we had to make it suit Australian conditions. But these things were engineered in Australia and it felt as if truck engineering had been applied; it was never going to break because it was over-engineered. So we made our own front uprights and our own diff housings and started to go better. We were the first team with an offset diff housing in back, and we did that because the chassis rails were stopping us from running the rear ride height that we wanted. So we built a diff housing which had the axle running offset within the tube and the whole diff housing was offset compared to where the centreline was for the ride height we wanted.

Everyone was asking how we could get the ride height so low – they were sure we were cheating. But it was within the rules and it was clever; we were good at thinking outside the square. By the time 1994 came along we had our own engine program, inlet manifolds, front and rear upright and it was on for young and old. We just smashed them in 1994.

Not that 1993 was a bad year; I mean, we were competitive at most places while we played catch up and we could easily have won Bathurst. We were very unlucky. Perkins and I basically raced each other all day and right near the end, Jimmy was in the car and got caught up with the lapped car.

He had to brake down the wet line at Hell Corner and went down the escape road. It cost us the race but it was the closest finish in Bathurst history at that stage.

We were having a beer with the crew in the garage later and Richo gave me the biggest compliment I think I'd ever had. He said on that day that was the best drive he'd ever seen at Bathurst and it was better than any of Brock's drives. For me that was a fantastic accolade from a guy like Jim.

We'd been pretty determined during 1993 to prove to the world that our dominance hadn't just been because of the GT-R, and while a Bathurst win would have confirmed that, I think we still showed we were a good team, GT-R or not. It was equal footing and we were right in the game.

> *Now sitting at 10 rounds, the 1994 ATCC was dominated by Skaife in the Gibson Motor Sport Winfield Commodore, the first Holden title win since Peter Brock back in 1980. Skaife won four rounds and comfortably had the series tied up at its penultimate round in Perth before recording a DNF at Oran Park. Jim Richards in the other team Commodore finished the series in sixth. Glenn Seton and Alan Jones each won rounds in their Falcons, while Peter Brock and Larry Perkins recorded victories in their Commodores. Bathurst was won by John Bowe and Dick Johnson in a Falcon, Skaife and Richards retiring after 39 laps when Skaife crashed in the rain.*

The off-season was reasonably calm for the first time in a long while. We were building new cars and we had a very comprehensive development list, but it wasn't out of control. It was still very early days for our engine program, but we were seeing real gains in outright power (now we had around 580 hp or 430 kW) and the refinements that made it easier to use. We were very, very busy but working to a plan that was ours and not influenced by rule changes. We won at the first three race meetings in 1994 and got a jump on everybody and from there they had to catch us, and I wasn't going to let that happen.

There was a lot of drama starting up about what was going to happen with tobacco sponsorship. I think at the time cigarette companies were spending about $100 million a year on sport, so a lot of sports were going to take a hit, and clearly we as a team stood to lose a lot.

I'd cut back my open wheeler stuff by now too. We'd won three titles in a row and sold the car. We had a 1993 model Lola F3000 car, an ex-Heinz-Harald Frentzen car from Nova Engineering in Japan, and we ran that a bit, but we were scaling it all back so I could focus all my attention on the touring car. By that I don't just mean the driving, I mean everything – all the little developments, the running of the team, sponsorship . . . the whole lot. We also needed all our money for the touring car operation, so we just phased the Formula Brabham out and eventually sold the car to a New Zealander.

I was running the workshop in those days and was also running the business in 1993/94. I think we had about 35 guys in those days, which was certainly keeping me busy. Fred was involved day-to-day, but he was really consumed with trying to replace Rothmans as a sponsor.

We came out in 1994 with fantastic car speed, and that felt great. When you think back on it now, we had worked so hard to win a championship and win a Bathurst, and we had all that machinery taken away from us, all that effort basically meant nothing in terms of the future. But we rolled our Gibson team knowledge into a new program and within a year we were able to win it all again.

We got to the point where our cars were the best in the field. We were winning titles and should have won Bathurst, but we had two issues at the time: Yokohama was starting to go a bit soft on development and Bridgestone was improving; and the massive issue for us was clearly from a commercial standpoint in replacing Winfield. What people didn't understand about the Winfield connection was that normally with sponsorships, the best way to get a new sponsor is to promote a current one from a junior investment level and evolve their spending because they determine that it's good value. So if you've got a sponsor for a couple of hundred thousand dollars, to be able to ramp them up along the way is the best way of moving forward.

With Winfield, no other sponsor wanted to be on the cars, other than Holden and Yokohama, because it was not socially acceptable, so we didn't have the ability to grow a smaller sponsor into a replacement for the cigarette money. Looking back we probably didn't handle it the right way. I remember trying to do a lot of it myself but I was only 28 and still learning. We moved to a new factory and we did a huge amount of things to show potential sponsors that we had all the infrastructure and that we were the best team. But the cost base was so high we had to use our capital to go racing the next year.

But it was a tough year on other levels. Ayrton Senna died in May 1994 and I remember thinking to myself a couple of times that if the best driver in the world could die doing this, it's not too flash. Because his crash was through mechanical failure, it was a reminder that if you have a failure at the wrong spot you can be in real trouble. I'd had a couple of lucky escapes so far, but Senna's death really resonated some of my innermost fears.

On the track, though, it was great. We could have wrapped up the series in Mallala with two more rounds left to run, but Fred wanted Jimmy to improve his position in the championship and I had to let him win the first race for the weekend. Fred said over the radio, 'Let Jimmy through.' I think there were two laps to go, so I let him through at the second hairpin and he won the race and I ran second. That meant I had to go to Perth to win the championship, which really wound me up and led to some tense words back in the garage. I would love to have gone to Perth without any of that pressure so I could have just enjoyed it more; in the end we had a rough weekend in Perth but still sealed the title because both Glenn Seton and Peter Brock went worse. So off to Oran Park with nothing at stake and Longhurst fired me out through the paddock off the start, so I had a terrible weekend but we still had the championship.

We had a jammed throttle at Sandown after battling with John Bowe all day, and that cost us any chance there, and then at Bathurst I had a crash in the rain. It was raining so hard, I couldn't see where the left-hand kink was entering The Cutting, but I soon found it. It hit pretty hard and that was the end of that. We didn't finish the year off very well and that just compounded the pressure to come back in 1995 and do better.

Craig Lowndes was an emerging talent in 1995, scoring pole at Bathurst in one of his few races for HRT that year. Bathurst was won by Larry Perkins and Russell Ingall while Skaife and Richards again failed to finish. In the championship, Skaife and Richards struggled a bit as the belt tightened at Gibson Motor Sport after the cigarette money was legislated off the cars. Skaife scored only one win for the season and languished sixth in the end of season score. John Bowe won his first ATCC title which made him only the second driver behind Skaife to win both the ATCC and the ADC. In addition to Bowe and Skaife, Seton and Perkins were the only other round winners.

But the year started badly with a massive crash at Eastern Creek. We were doing wet weather tyre testing and I had the shits because the decision was made to put the same bad tyres on the car instead of going to a new spec tyre – it was the most ordinary tyre I've ever driven on. I kept on saying, 'I don't even know why you're base lining it, just get it off the car and it'll never go back on again.' Anyway, I went barrelling down the straight thinking, 'What a bunch of dickheads.' Driving this thing in these conditions with that tyre just wasn't fun and it was useless in terms of development.

At the end of the main straight where the drag strip joins our track, there was drag racing compound on the road and that stuff is just like glass when it's wet. I turned the corner and the car just didn't look like making it and that's about the last thing I remember. It went off the road and hit the wall. I blacked out and woke up when they were dragging me out to the ambulance. The seat ended up in the back seat of the car and everything was broken; I was very lucky not to have been killed.

My ex-wife Belinda was pregnant with Mitch when that happened. She was at the movies with Jayne Seton and she came to Westmead hospital where I was for a week or so. She still reminds me that I tried to cheat on the memory card tests, with her help, to prove I was OK to go home. You'd have to be an idiot not to question what you did for a living at that stage. At the end of the day, it's what you do and the reality is that you make a decision to take those risks or not. We know that the sport's inherently risky and the mechanical failure thing is always the one that's scariest – when the brake pedal goes to the floor, or the throttle jams open, steering or brake failure or a tyre blowing. Those ones are all pretty wild because you have so little control, but the rest of the time you take an educated risk as to how much you want to put on the line. As committed as you might be – and you might be right on the edge – you don't ever turn into a corner thinking, 'I'm not going to make it,' because you'd be a goose and you'd crash. But you have to set your own boundaries as to how hard you want to push, how many risks you want to take. Lying in that hospital bed, with a child on the way, made me confront my own mortality – I knew I was lucky to be alive and that feeling was reinforced when I saw the photos of the crash.

I had two broken vertebrae and dislocated ribs. They call it a bucket-handle one where it pops out at the back and at the front. I also had whiplash, and all sorts of other stuff. I was pretty sore, and all the smart arses of the industry would come into the hospital and try and make me laugh because they knew it was going to hurt.

At the start of 1995 we built a new car and we were

organised, but then when I had that crash in pre-season testing it put us behind schedule. I might have been eager to beat everyone, but I missed the first round at Sandown.

So when I went out to Calder to drive the car after the crash during the lead-up to the next round and I remember I was bloody nervous. I did four or five laps and it hurt like you couldn't believe, although I had rib protectors on and all that stuff. I did four or five laps and did the same lap time as Jimmy and all the wiring seemed OK in my brain, but there was no way I could race. I qualified on the front row alongside Bowe in Tasmania for the next round, though, and that was a ripper thing – I knew then it was all OK.

There were certain race meetings in 1995 where tyres were really becoming a factor. By that stage Bridgestone was doing the best job with tyres and Dunlop was also doing a better job than us, because the level of commitment from Yokohama was starting to wane. The Yokohama guy in Japan who was one of our mates and was a very high-level race tyre engineer and designer had been replaced by a guy from the forklift department. Seriously, the bloke from the forklift department was brought in to run our motorsport program. I don't know how forklifts and race cars ever got hooked together in Yokohama-land, but he had no idea. We weren't getting the same response from Yokohama and the testing was average. He wanted to do silly stuff and I wasn't getting on with him very well. We then started to lose some of the competitive edge that Yokohama had in certain places.

The Yokohama was a great stop-and-go tyre and it had really good braking and good traction, which meant it was good at places like Winton. The Dunlop tyre had really good compound suitability for some places and not others, but when it worked it worked really well. At places like Lakeside it was far and away the best tyre and Russell Ingall and John Bowe just belted us there. Bridgestone was starting to get a characteristic of mid-corner grip which it was developing off the back of its Formula One program. The lateral grip from the belt angle that they used in the construction of the tyre meant their lateral grip was just so superior to ours. At places like Eastern Creek and Phillip Island they were unbeatable. Fortunately Bathurst has never been a tyre-sensitive circuit, so when we went to Bathurst we were the fastest car by a mile.

It was the end of the cigarette era and it was effectively our last race in Winfield colours. There was a lot of conjecture about me joining HRT, and yes, John Crennan (who looked after both HRT and Holden Special Vehicles at the time) and I had various meetings although nothing had been agreed. Peter McKay from the *Sydney Morning Herald* wrote an article during Bathurst week that I was going to HRT and that was a little off-putting for the team. But we went to Bathurst and we were just going to beat them all; in my mind it was that simple. Larry Perkins had an incident on the first lap with Craig Lowndes and we were leading by almost a full lap. Larry was just in front of me, though, when I came on to Conrod Straight and broke a tail shaft. When it broke it almost took my left leg clean off, but we had almost put a lap on the car that eventually won the race, that's how far in front we were. No-one could work out why Jimmy started the race, but people didn't know that we were only going to do three stops, everyone else was going to do four. We had them all hammered, but that is what happens in motor racing.

As I said earlier, there is always mechanical uncertainty waiting to bite you.

However, that weekend gave me enough confidence to stick with them. I wanted to stay with the guys because I was loyal to the team and knew how much work we'd done to build the fastest Commodore on the grid. I knew that if we rolled out a good car in 1996 we'd be right. I basically did a deal for half the budget for the following year with Tooheys and we were looking pretty good until that deal fell over.

> *With Skaife opting out of an HRT drive, Craig Lowndes took the seat and dominated the year, winning both the ATCC and Bathurst (with Greg Murphy). He won six of the 10 rounds while the best Skaife could muster was a lone podium at Sandown early in the year. Richards was now sidelined as Gibson Motor Sport could only afford one car. John Bowe, Peter Brock, Larry Perkins and Russell Ingall won a round each. Skaife with John Clelland finished seventh at Bathurst after Skaife qualified the car in fourth but landed ninth in the Shootout.*

I guess a lot of people questioned my decision not to join HRT at that stage, especially when we started 1996 with a plain white car. Even though the car looked fantastic with black wheels, it wasn't sustainable because we didn't have the funding to do it properly. Holden remained incredibly loyal, John Stevenson (Motor Sport Manager) continued his funding based on only one car and allowed us free white space to sell the signage. That meant we had to pull back to running one car. We couldn't afford to run a car for Richo. We went from having 35 people to eight or something. If you've ever heard of multi-tasking, that was the time. It was frustrating for me because we were competitive. Lowndes had taken the seat at HRT that I turned down, and he and Brock were going well there. Seton was obviously hard to beat too, but we could run with them for a while providing we had no disasters.

At Eastern Creek for the opening round it got hot in qualifying and we didn't qualify very well, Eastern Creek is a weird track like that, a couple of degrees difference in ambient temperature can totally change the track. You've got to stay on top of it, and we didn't. We raced OK though and made it into third spot. Glenn and I were having a bit of a battle, and Brock decided to drive around the outside of us at turn two. He got wide and went off the road then fired into the side of my car, smashing us both into the fence on the left-hand side of turn three. It was just not like Brock – I don't know what he was thinking because there was no way he could drive around the outside of both of us at that corner.

He was sort of half trying and he didn't get away with it, but the reality was that as a consequence I was caught up in his crash. The crash destroyed the car and that hurt us quite badly. In the end we also had to miss some rounds where the Yokohama tyres were so bad there was no point wasting our money. There were little snapshots where the car was good too, but it wasn't good enough. Holden continued to be really good with me during that phase and they pretty much sponsored the car for the whole year without any signage.

It was a pretty average time for the sport all round, though. The television coverage was ordinary and they were replaying events late at night. The series went to Western Australia and only had 10 or 11 cars competing; the sport was really struggling.

Tony Cochrane, who now heads up V8 Supercars, had come out to our workshop and I drove him down to Phillip Island. We spent a lot of time talking about where the sport was and what we needed to do. We've been really good mates ever since then. He came in and he ranted and he raved and he promised, but he also delivered. You look at it now on every measurable score – crowds, TV ratings, profitability, teams revenue, and you think, 'He's done a bloody good job.'

2

NEW SCENERY

WE GOT TO the end of 1996 and finished seventh at Bathurst with John Cleland. Our car was nowhere near as good as it needed to be, so I had some discussions in the off-season with John Crennan and Kevin Wale (Holden's Head of Sales and Marketing) about joining HRT throughout the course of 1997. I'd missed a few rounds because we didn't have the money to do them all and I was actually doing some commentary for David White at Channel Ten. I don't know what month it was, but John Crennan spoke to me very seriously and said, 'Are you going to do this or not? We've got an opportunity, Brock's going to retire and we'd like you to come and drive for us at Bathurst and who knows what happens after that?' Leaving Gibsons was a very difficult thing to do. I remember talking to the boys that were left in the workshop before heading to the Crown Casino for the media announcement of me partnering Brock for his final Bathurst, it was really very important for me to speak to all the guys face-to-face and shake hands.

They were all very much aware of my predicament. As it was I didn't have any other real options. It was HRT for me or continue battling to make it onto the grid, but making the change was not that easy. John had thrown Fred a bit of a lifeline too by getting him to run the Young Lions program with a young driver named Steve Ellery, who later went on to run his own team. If Fred hadn't been doing that as a fully funded deal, he would probably have had to shut the door totally. He was running the team very lean and mean at that stage but there was enough to keep him cracking.

Skaife was really only a part-time driver in 1997 competing in only half the rounds of the championship. Lowndes had left HRT to try his hand at F3000 in Europe and Brock announced during the season that this would be his last, and Skaife moved from Gibson Motor Sport to Holden Racing Team for the endurance races. He scored pole at both Sandown and Bathurst but had troubled races at each, including an engine failure at Bathurst that put him and Skaife out of the running. Larry Perkins and Russell Ingall won their second Bathurst together and Glenn Seton won his second ATCC, with Bowe, Ingall, Murphy, Brock and Wayne Gardner winning rounds. The category was now officially branded V8 Supercars.

I went to the workshop at HRT and I knew there'd be an issue with some of the guys who used to work for me after we'd had to let some of them go, but Jeff Grech was really good with me about it and he said that the gig with Brock was good for both of us. In 1997 they'd run Brock and Murphy while Lowndes was overseas, but with Lowndes coming back to Australia he was pretty much guaranteed a drive in 1998, and I think Jeff loved the idea of running the young outfit of Lowndes and Murphy. I wanted that drive to replace Brock, though, so I had some work to do in convincing him I was the man. So Brock and I went to Sandown and we were fastest in every session, qualified pole position, fastest in the race, but Brock had a throttle cable drama early in the race which put us out.

We did a few tests at the time too and I couldn't believe how good the Bridgestone tyre was – it was just unbelievable. It was like driving a different car, like they weren't even touring cars compared to what I was driving only a few weeks before. I was pretty upbeat at that stage.

At Sandown, I remember doing an 11.6 in practice, which was the fastest in the session, and I approached Ron Harrop and Richard Hollway (Krusty) – Ron was engineering and Richard was on data – and I said, 'I reckon this car will do an 11.3 or 4 if we just make a couple of changes.' So we buggered around for a little while, we changed the rear shock, and then did an 11.3. It was a good result – Ron and Krusty knew straight away then that I wasn't bullshitting and that I had a good handle on it all.

With data we can work out how much time is lost, but when you are at the top of your game as a driver you can work it out yourself pretty well. A bit of understeer here, a small locked brake there . . . that cost 2/10ths. You also get a good feel for the car and what small issues are costing you. You know if you can get it to turn better at one corner, you can get the power down earlier and you'll get a 1/10th gain, for instance.

It was a strange atmosphere at the time. Lowndes was clearly the golden boy and Greg was also pretty much the same, so to come along and put the 05 car on pole at both Sandown and Bathurst was just the sort of statement I needed to make.

Brock and I were fastest all weekend at Bathurst also, qualified on pole by miles, and did the first sub-2m 10s lap ever. In terms of qualifying, Brock actually went out and started the session. He did some laps and I think he was sitting fourth when he came in after he'd given the wall a little bump at The Cutting. We fixed it and I went out and only had one flying lap. Jason Bargwanna was actually fastest that afternoon in the Young Lions car and he was bowling around with a big grin on his face, but we knew we had more to come, so I was very quiet.

They ran a special warm-up then for the cars in the shoot-out and we did a 2m 9.89s lap on new tyres and were more than a second quicker than the next guy. In the shootout we didn't quite match that, but a 10.03 was good enough for pole by nearly 8/10ths. We went into the race in good shape – Brock was really upbeat and we were really well prepared. We were leading the race and Lowndes was racing with me when he fired into the fence at Reid Park on top of Mount Panorama. We were going to have our arm on the window for the rest of the day and then we had a flame out on the way up Mountain Straight and the race was over with a dead engine. Brock was actually pretty good about it all. He wanted to have the best job done for the team for the weekend and that's mostly what he really cared about – to him it wasn't about his last Bathurst at all.

At that stage I felt like I'd done everything asked of me, but I hadn't really spoken to John Crennan or Tom Walkinshaw (who was the owner of HRT through TWR) about it so I didn't know what the future held. There was a lot of conjecture about whether Murphy would stay or whether I'd come in to replace Brock and there was a bit of drama about it all. Murphy had driven for the team during 1997 and he had some loyal fans, but Brock was going and Lowndes was coming back from Europe to do the entire 1998 season and not just the endurance races.

Lowndes was guaranteed his spot, but they weren't sure whether to run with me or Murphy at that stage. It's hard to change both drivers and that was working against me. It took a couple of months to get an answer. Brock was making noises that I'd be the appropriate replacement, but he didn't have any real power in the decision-making process. Holden was lending support too, but it all came down to John Crennan.

He approached it in his typical fashion and came up with a document, which set out the strengths and weaknesses of Greg Murphy and myself. Crenno tried to put a bit of science into the decision – the document also had a score card for people like Jeff Grech and Ron Harrop to rate both of us in certain areas.

Fortunately, Crenno's decision went my way. Greg stayed close to the team and drove with us in the long-distance races. Eventually a sister-team, Kmart Racing was formed and Greg was drafted into that outfit.

> Skaife was really only a part-time driver in 1997 competing in only half the rounds of the championship. Lowndes had left HRT to try his hand at F3000 in Europe and Brock announced during the season that this would be his last, and Skaife moved from Gibson Motor Sport to Holden Racing Team for the endurance races. He scored pole at both Sandown and Bathurst but had troubled races at each, including an engine failure at Bathurst that put him and Skaife out of the running. Larry Perkins and Russell Ingall won their second Bathurst together and Glenn Seton won his second ATCC, with Bowe, Ingall, Murphy, Brock and Wayne Gardner winning rounds. The category was now official branded V8 Supercars.

After being so heavily involved in the running of Gibson Motorsport, it was very strange for me to just be a hired driver. I knew that wasn't going to be enough so I spoke to John Crennan about doing some more things and he was able to help out. I settled into the team really well, our speed was good straight away but I still had a bit to learn about getting the set-up right for races on the Bridgestone tyres.

I got five pole positions, which was half the series at that stage, but Lowndes was doing a better job in the races. He was very good at either getting the car right for the races or for driving around any issues that may have existed – his qualifying wasn't consistently good enough and that remains a factor today. Having said that, on occasions his qualifying is brilliant, it's just a bit spasmodic.

We qualified well for most of the season, but I also made some silly mistakes in the races. I remember at Sandown I was catching John Bowe in the race and I had a dive at the last corner and we both hit. I was on the inside, and normally in a hit like that Bowe would have been the one who'd spin, but not this time. He turned in in typical Bowe style, the blinkers were on and he was looking forwards only, and when we hit I had the spin.

I was really cranky with myself. That was a dumb thing to do because I could have gotten off to a much better start with the new team. Lowndes went on to win the round and had the momentum. I didn't win as many races as him, so I knew there was a lot of work for me to do with my engineers and we tried to wrap some science around tyre conservation and consistency.

That was at the start of what is known as comprehensive vehicle analysis where you could work out the mechanical balance of the car front to rear, for instance, and you actually had a number you could work with. If you went for a heavier front spring in the car, the number would change. It was those sorts of scientific things I was demanding of the team. It wasn't NASCAR, where you lick your finger and put it in the air, there was a bit of science to V8 Supercar racing – we had great engineers and a lot of brains in that team, and we were able to work out some numbers and I was happy with that.

I finished third in the series and then Lowndes and I joined up together for the long-distance races. We didn't get the results, but we could have just blown them all out of the water. At Bathurst, for instance, we were miles in front after we qualified on pole, did the first 2 minute 9 second qualifying lap after doing a 9 in practice the previous year . . . and then we blew a tyre in the Chase. We were 30 or 40 seconds in front of the Stone Brothers car that ended up winning the race, so that was the end of that.

It is true that Lowndes and I were different in the way we went about our business, but that was actually good. We gelled quite well and we brought different things to the table; along with great engineering staff, that's why HRT was able to become so dominant. We had all the bases covered.

My biggest drama in 1998 was Lowndes' start method and I could never work it out – even to this day, I haven't got a full handle on it. What he did was he left the engine hard on the rev limiter at 7500 rpm and just dumped the clutch. He then bounced it off the rev limiter and that kind of acted like a crude traction control. It just didn't make any engineering sense to me, but Craig and the team had perfected it.

I tried a couple of times and failed miserably, so I kept using my technique and that meant I wanted different things to him. I wanted better engine driveability low-down; I wanted more clutch modulation; I wanted a softer, longer clutch pedal so I had more room for error. I wanted to make it so that you used the clutch as a torque converter, like an automatic, rather than this incredibly harsh drop-the-clutch-stop-go method.

On a lot of the starts I just lost ground. At Symmons Plains where I qualified pole position, I was third or fourth to the first corner. Lowndes' starts were better than mine and he was getting the race results. He quickly got a bit of his swagger back and things were going well on his return to the class, but there was never any drama between us at all and our relationship was, and still is, very good. We were definitely testing each other in terms of who was fast and who wasn't and the amount of competition between us was certainly intense. But that was our game, it's what we do and ultimately we had respect for each other and particularly our differences in approach.

Richo and I at Gibsons kind of grew organically into a superteam, but this thing was put together that way. This was 'throw the best two blokes in arguably the best team and see how it goes' – which Walkinshaw has always been keen on.

As I've mentioned, we had a healthy respect for each other but there was also a fierce rivalry. We never had a bad word, though, and we never blued at all in any way. We had some bumping and jostling, especially in 1999 when I was more up to speed in terms of what the car wanted as a race car.

1999 was a dominant year for HRT with Lowndes and Skaife again finishing first and third in the main series. Skaife suffered badly in the title race with poor results at the Clipsal 500 and the Sandown 500, both of which were double points races. Lowndes won only two rounds (and had a monster crash at Calder Park which kept him out of one round) and Skaife recorded five wins, Garth Tander was starting to show some speed at Garry Rogers Motorsport and he recorded his first round win, while teammate Jason Bargwanna also won a round. Jason Bright, Russell Ingall and Larry Perkins also won rounds, while Greg Murphy and Steve Richards teamed up to win Bathurst (which was now part of the championship) for Gibson Motor Sport. Skaife was beaten to pole there by Mark Larkham and finished third in the race with Paul Morris.

At Phillip Island in the rain, for instance, you should have heard Jeff Grech on the radio! Man, was he into us. We were out in the lead and it was pissing down with rain and we were racing like you could not believe. We came through the Hay Shed (the fastest and most dangerous corner at the track) at the absolute limit and we arrived at Lukey Heights and both of us were gone, we were fully out of control. Lowndes was a bit wider than me and I was a little bit of the beneficiary of him seeing it first because he was leading, and as he ran wide I slid up the inside of him. We went over Lukey Heights together and all you could hear on the radio was, 'You fucking idiots! You fucking idiots!' Anyway, I passed him and came down the hill into MG, turned across and won the race. It was a ripper race – we were nose-to-tail and we had a massive gap over the next car. Those sorts of races were just fantastic, even if it did stress a few of the guys in the garage.

Queensland Raceway was another one. It was raining again and I came at Lowndes from way back because I thought he was being a bit of a skirt; I out-braked him but I had to hit him to get through. On the next lap he did the same to me and you could hear Jeff on the radio calling us fucking idiots again; it was kind of funny really – great reactions!

But what was good was that Lowndes was always up for a laugh and a joke on most things, so we'd get out of the car and laugh with each other over it all. That's the thing with Lowndesy – he has an uncanny ability to deflect the intensity with a good laugh. Not many drivers are like this. As intense as it was, it was a great time for us as motor racing drivers because we were in the best cars, we had the opportunity to win each weekend and we were trying bloody hard to beat each other. It was great fun.

Overall though, 1999 could have been a bit better for me. Craig had a big crash at Calder Park and I won more races but he won the series. They had double points rounds that year and I crashed at Clipsal and Queensland Raceway which were two of those races, which was disastrous for the championship and obviously hurt my points.

But really, a lot of the work I'd done with the team's engineers meant a lot of the technical stuff that I wanted was starting to come my way. We'd tried three or four different clutches, different clutch master cylinders and different pedal ratios and we got the starts right.

There were a few little bits and pieces already appearing in the media about Lowndes and that maybe he was looking at moving on after 2000, which was still a whole season away. And yes, I think he was starting to get a little bit dissatisfied, because a little bit of the supremacy that he once had in the team was starting to dissipate. But that's what happens when you start to talk about leaving. At the end of the day, though, we were still equals in the team.

Skaife was back on top of the table in 2000, winning the championship just as it was announced Lowndes was leaving HRT. There was speculation over him switching to Ford, but that wasn't confirmed until much later. Skaife won four of 13 rounds to win the title from Tander who won Bathurst with Bargwanna.

Lowndes, Paul Radisich and Steve Richards each won rounds of the series. Needing to finish 17th at Bathurst to win the championship, Skaife did it the hard way after a mid-race tangle with a back-marker. He ended up sixth on the day with Lowndes and won his third title and his first with HRT.

2000 was the big year for the increased hype and talk of Lowndes leaving the team and probably what made it catch fire a bit more was that his engineer, Rob Starr, was moved onto my car for the season. Maybe Craig read that as an indicator that the tide had turned a little bit more inside the team and that the emphasis was working towards my gig. There was a lot of contention about all that and 2000 was a great year for me – I had the last to first victory at Clipsal and I think I won four rounds of the series. I think if Craig was sitting here with me now, he'd admit he made too many mistakes during 2000. He went off the road in Darwin, for instance, and he just looked a bit desperate on occasions. The momentum of sport is a strange thing.

He had always believed that if he was in equal cars he'd probably beat you. But as time went by he knew that not only was I tuning the car probably better than him, he was now down my road on set-up more often than not. He knew how hard he had to try and that was starting to show in his driving at times – he was under pressure and there were cracks appearing. Those Lowndes battles were really intense, because at that stage it was really only he and I consistently.

In hindsight I can honestly say that I am grateful for his level of competitiveness. He pushed me. His happy-go-lucky demeanour should not be misinterpreted. He is one of the most competitive and hardest racers of all time.

There were others who came in and out of competitiveness, but they just weren't there at every round. Glenn Seton and Neil Crompton were the factory Ford team and at some places they were quite strong. I had a great battle with Glenn in that era at Phillip Island. I was leading and he was catching me, and out of turn one and up to turn two there was a guy in the middle of the road. I blazed up to him and I thought if I go round the outside, I'm off the road. I had to go across the dirt on the inside, all four wheels, and re-join. It was one of the most out-of-control bits of driving I ever got away with; it was a little bit like walking down the main street, the other bloke goes right, you go right, he goes left, you go left. I flicked left because I thought at least there's road over there and if I go the other way, I'm in the tyre wall. So I did that and went across the grass and it popped out the other side. When you're sideways off the track at Phillip Island you realise just how narrow the track is and I didn't think there was any way I could make it stick, but it came out at just the right angle and it stayed on the road – we cleared the mess and went on to win.

It was the same thing in 2000 in terms of it really being me and Lowndes across the course of the season, although Garth Tander was strong all year too. I had a good lead in the series going into the final round, which was Bathurst: if Tander won the race I had to finish 17th or better to win the series. Lowndes was teamed up with me and even though he was leaving the team he promised to put in 100 per cent to win the race and help me with the championship, and I think that tells you a lot about Craig as a person.

We led most of the day closely pursued by Garth (and Jason Bargwanna). Neil Crompton (with Glenn Seton) was in the battle also, and at around two-thirds race distance we got tangled up with British driver Matt Neal, who we were lapping. This was at Hell Corner, so I had a whole lap to run before I could get into the pits and I'd punctured a tyre. It was quite a tough race because it was wet-dry, wet-dry, wet-dry and we'd been pioneering for most of the day while we were leading. Because of the rain patches, everyone's strategy was all over the place and it meant we spent time during the day in the middle of packs we just didn't want to be in.

When I drove out of the pits I asked the boys where we were, and they said 17th. So then I asked where Tander was and they told me he was leading. 'Fuck, is anyone going to give me any good news?' It was as if we were following a script. I knew I had to get on with it to get back to a spot that gave me some comfort. We finished sixth that day so it was no problems winning the championship, but was that a tough and stressful day out!

Aside from not winning the race, perhaps the most disappointing thing was not being able to race with Seto and Crompton – they were really strong and could easily have raced us to the chequered flag. It was one of Glenn's best chances for a win, and it was an interesting scenario.

Because it was the last round of the series there was a lot of focus on winning Bathurst versus the championship. Like, would Tander or myself cough up a Bathurst win just to make sure of the title? Obviously for us, that didn't become a factor and I don't think I could honestly tell you what I would do.

NEW SCENERY

I know a lot of people were thinking that if it was Glenn and myself racing to the finish, and if he stuck his nose up the inside, that I'd back off and give him the corner to make sure of the championship.

What would I have done? I think logic and the broader view of the championship would disappear when you're racing for Australia's biggest motor race, but until you face that decision I just don't know. I was often in the position where people were talking about that scenario, but fortunately I was never called on to make the decision.

I do know you give it your all regardless. That Bathurst was one of those races where you were often on slick tyres on a damp track, and there are times just after a safety car, when the tyres aren't fully back to temperature, where the laps are just spooky. You have to fire into corners with no idea what grip you've got, but you've got to press on or you'll get caught, so you do. It is far from a safety-first approach to the race.

With sixth place in that Bathurst I won my first championship with HRT and with Lowndes moving on it was a massively important win, while from a personal point of view it was very satisfying. I had made the change to a new team for the first time in my career, I was battling one of the best drivers of all time in the same equipment and I was winning. The car was now how I wanted it and I felt like we were really on the verge of something special.

Motorsport's worst kept secret was confirmed early in 2001, with Craig Lowndes joining a three-car Ford team being run by Fred Gibson. Jason Bright joined HRT after a couple of seasons trying to forge an IndyCar career in the US. Marcos Ambrose joined the series after running openwheeled racing cars in Europe and he scored pole on debut at the Australian Grand Prix. Skaife was at the top of his game and dominated the series, winning comfortably from Russell Ingall. He had four round wins, including Bathurst with Tony Longhurst and the Clipsal 500. The TWR group was now running the two HRT cars for Skaife and Bright, an occasional HRT entry for Rick Kelly, and the Kmart Racing Team with Murphy and Todd Kelly.

In 2001, Jason Bright joined the team to replace Lowndes, who'd gone to Ford in a team being run by Fred Gibson and the racing licence owned by Bob Forbes, and we began the year really well. The season started at Phillip Island before moving on to Clipsal, and Phillip Island was one of the best weekends ever for the team because we were fastest in every session and it was a really dominant display. We were on the front row of the grid and finished first and second in the opening race with a few other drivers showing a bit of form too, so it looked like we were in for a cracker of a season.

Lowndes was immediately on the pace in his new Ford, which proved to me that the other Ford teams just weren't doing a good enough job, rather than them having a disadvantage, as they all claimed. Clipsal was a fantastic race with Lowndes, but when we had contact it put Lowndes out and left me with pretty significant damage. The race also turned out pretty weird. There was a safety car intervention at one stage which put Bright onto a strategy that left him on his own, and he ended up winning, which was great for the team. The real battle of the race, though, was between me and Lowndes and I thought we were going to battle for most of the season.

I'd also had a great fight with Paul Radisich and he turned me around at turn four at nearly 200 km/h and somehow I stayed off the wall. When cars spin like that, you need to half understand where the trajectory of the car is going to go and you have to know where the front wheels are pointed and try to guide yourself down a very narrow alley. You have a certain level of control, but you still need luck to spin around in such a narrow gap – on any other day you had a spin there, you'd knock every corner off it, so that was pretty lucky.

That was 15 laps into the first race and we dropped back to the middle of the pack before getting back to fourth. Lowndes actually won that first race which set up the Sunday fight. He was coming at me on fresher tyres and I was working pretty hard to hold him off, and this was where our intimate knowledge of each other's race craft could be a bad thing. I knew what gamesmanship he was going to use, and pretty much where it was going to happen. So when he went to do the criss-cross on me at turn six I knew what he was up to, so I purposely slowed up going into the corner. He gave me a thump which I was expecting, and that pushed me on a bit. But we kept the fight going down the little straight between turns six and seven and we got all tangled up. I think our front wheels interlocked and his car jumped in the air and there was a massive amount of damage to his Falcon.

I had a fair bit of damage too and the boys settled me down because I needed to finish and get points, but it didn't work out too well. Back then turn eight was a much slower corner than it is today and you dropped back to third gear, but I slotted it into first. As I was letting the clutch out I picked up that I was in the wrong gear and it just locked the rear wheels and turned me around. Because I'd worked out what was happening, I was able to keep it off the fence, but I finished well down the order. It was an average Clipsal but it was basically the start of a new phase of the competition with Lowndes. There were a fair few races throughout 2001 that were similar to that and it was again great rivalry.

There was a lot of conjecture at that time that Holden had an advantage over Ford, and I think Lowndes and Ambrose proved that was wrong. Ambrose came into the sport at that stage and was immediately on the pace, and I was clearly impressed by what Fred was doing with Lowndes and Ford. I knew a lot of the guys who were working on Lowndes' car and I was happy for them, but the fact that Lowndes was immediately competitive in a Falcon that had just been pieced together said the Falcon was actually a pretty good race package.

They were going to be a very good race team, they had significant Ford backing and were effectively the factory team and history will say that it was very much to Holden Racing Team's advantage that the relationship between Bob Forbes and Fred Gibson blew up. It killed the team when they were absolutely on track to being the strongest Falcon operation and they looked on the money. With Fred's ability to get the right guys together to build a car and do a good job, plus Lowndes' ability to drive the car, they were in a fantastic position. The president of Ford Australia, Geoff Polites, was really behind Fred and it looked like they could really challenge us long term. I had a lot of conversations internally, especially with John Crennan, about how surprised we were by their immediate speed. The car livery was designed in Ford's styling department by Nick Hogios and it looked great.

I was privately thinking to myself, here comes the competition. But as I said, history will say that the demise of the team probably saved us from a big duel with them, which I was genuinely torn about. I was happy that Fred was back at the front and I was also happy that Lowndes was in a car that kept him there too. I am on the record at press conferences saying, 'It's good to have him back in a competitive car,' and that was true sentiment as to how I was feeling; it wasn't just said because it sounded good.

I was getting a real buzz from how that competition was going to evolve and I loved the challenge. It was like me and Seto from the mid-'90s all over again. Red versus blue and Skaife versus Lowndes this time.

If you have a look at the race that we had at Eastern Creek in that same year, it was one of the best motor races I've ever been in. Lowndes and I were breaking the lap record lap after lap after lap after lap. I led the race early but he got the jump on me in the pitstop and I had to chase him.

I've still got the tape of the race and it was like we were continually running qualifying laps. It ended up that Lowndes made a little mistake at turn two and he trickled off the road and I won. It was just a classic race. They were only reasonably short races at that time, but we both got out absolutely buggered because of the level of intensity. When you do those sorts of laps, when you're almost off the road at every corner, that's the highlight of motorsport and it is incredibly rewarding if it all works out your way.

We had a few battles like that during the year – even at Bathurst it was on. When it rained, Murphy and I were battling for the lead and Lowndes was right there with us. I arrowed past Murphy between Reid Park and McPhillamy Park and went off the road, all four wheels into the sand and back out on to the track. On that same lap, Lowndes went into the fence at Forrests Elbow. We were all absolutely out of control because when it rains and you're on slicks you have very low grip and that's just how it is.

We went on to win Bathurst from Brad Jones (which was an amazing battle in the final stint), but it shows you how competitive Lowndes was in that first year with Ford. That was the win with Tony Longhurst and Bright was with Tomas Mezera in the other team car. Bright and I shared the car at Queensland Raceway, where you perhaps needed more flexibility than Bathurst and we felt we needed both of us in the lead car to have the best chance at winning, while at Bathurst it wasn't as critical and we were better served by having us in different cars. At Queensland, though, we had dramas – Brighty had someone blow an engine in front of him and there was a huge amount of oil on the windscreen, so he decided to flick the wiper on and it made it worse. We had to pit to fix that and we were still in the running later in the day when the rain stopped the race. That was the one where Radisich won the race in the sandtrap, much like we did at Bathurst all those years ago. Ironic really that it was a Dick Johnson car that lost out at Bathurst and then won in Queensland under the same ruling . . . I know which one I'd rather win!

Brighty and I then split up for Bathurst. His car was a

better qualifying car because it was stiffer and more suited to those conditions, but as a race car ours was just fantastic. I'll always remember Longhurst saying before the start, 'Just go and do what you do – just smash them in the first bit.' And we did. It was such a great race – there were so many cars with speed, but we were doing it easy early, we were just cruising and we were in control, even if some people thought we were running low on fuel near the end. So our speed as a race car was ultimately fantastic.

2001 was an excellent year and it was a really rewarding championship win, because there were some really good drivers in good cars. The Castrol cars were strong, with Perkins and Russell Ingall, Murphy and Todd Kelly were quick in the Kmart cars which were sister cars to ours, and Tander and Bargwanna still had speed. In Fords we had Radisich and Steve Johnson who were still winning races then, Seton was strong with Steve Richards, and Lowndes and Crompton in Fred's outfit were quick too. John Bowe was quick in places and Ambrose was sensational in his first year – he got pole at Bathurst at his first attempt and that was an amazing effort.

There was some really good, high-level competition, and we had some great battles with each of them during the year. We had to fight really hard, although it doesn't look that way when you see the championship table today. There was a real element of competition there with probably eight or 10 really red hot blokes in good cars who could win races, and in the end it was one of those race years where it worked out well for me. What helped us was that we were probably the only consistent front-runner on all the different styles of tracks.

Jason was an interesting teammate to throw into the mix. He'd come back to the V8s from an open-wheeler background and he was pretty hungry. Jason was fast and he was very precise about how he wanted the car, whereas Lowndes could drive almost anything. Jason wanted a much more stable car on a much stiffer platform – which in some ways was good, because some weekends if he had the speed it gave us a direction as to where we needed to be with set-up. Again, there was no real aggro with him, but there was plenty of competition.

By that stage we had such a good handle on the engineering that we were the pacesetters week in and week out. We had a level of consistency that no other team had, whether it was cold like Canberra or hot like Darwin (there were only two weeks between them), and we had good car speed. The Kmart cars were almost identical to ours at certain places, which was also important for getting that four-car thing running that John Crennan wanted. Time would say his plan was pretty good; even to this day, what he set up then is still working.

> *2002 was an amazing year for Skaife, with victory in the first five rounds setting up a relatively easy championship win over Greg Murphy and Marcos Ambrose. Skaife also won his fourth Bathurst, this time with old mate Jim Richards, to make it seven round wins from 13 for the season. Skaife and Bright shared the first eight rounds before David Besnard won his first and only round of the ATCC with Simon Wills in the Queensland 500. Jason Bargwanna and Greg Murphy also won a round, and Marcos Ambrose's final round win at Sandown was a pointer to 2003. 00 Motorsport was in trouble off the track and Lowndes left*

at the end of the season to join Ford Performance Racing which was set up under a similar model to HRT.

That consistency and speed is what set us up for 2002, and we brained them. 2002 was, for me, the standout year of my career in terms of just having an unbelievably good run and being able to win. We won the first five rounds of the series and six of the first seven, and I was annoyed we didn't get that win in Barbagallo and make it the first seven.

I should have won that round. As I was passing Greg Murphy, I did the criss-cross on him at the last corner and with his left foot he touched the brakes in the corner because he was going to run wide, and we bumped. From both our points of view it was a fair pass and, in fact, Greg came straight up and said afterwards, 'You were robbed.' As competitors I think you know what's acceptable and what's not, and if I thought there was a possibility I'd hit him too hard to get by or that it wasn't a fair bump, I would have let him go by and had another crack at him later – effectively redressing the situation as it's currently called.

I've had some really good races in Perth with guys like Mark Winterbottom, Tander and Steve Richards, and I had a ripper battle with Paul Radisich one year. I've had some of my best ever races there, but I've also had some shockers. Ingall fired me off one year when we would have probably won the weekend. In typical fashion we arrived at the first corner – when everyone thinks it's open slather – and he gave me a hit and turned me around at turn one. Another year with Marcos Ambrose, I was on pole position and we ended up hitting at the first corner and we should have won that weekend as well.

Barbagallo is actually a very, very good racetrack. It's very fast and it requires a lot of car control and is a very tyre sensitive circuit, so the better you have your set-up the longer they'll last during the race. Really good drivers go well there because you have to drive the car with a lot of sensitivity, a lot of real feeling.

When they resurfaced, it took a little bit of that harshness out, but it's basically got back there now because the sand wears the surface away. If you went to rank your favourite tracks it isn't going to rate with Bathurst and Phillip Island, but it is a really difficult track that has lots of great memories for me and it rates right up there with the best of the other tracks.

In 2002 we changed to the Dunlop control tyre, and we as a team got a handle on that better than anyone else. I know it's easy to look at things through rose coloured glasses, but I remember at the time being very critical of the team and what I saw as a lack of development for the year. I knew that with the Kmart team coming on, we had to be better at what we were doing, and I just couldn't see it. I was very critical that the extra team was diluting our efforts. I didn't want to worry about what I called the 'sausage factory'; I didn't want HRT to be worrying about spitting out cars – I just wanted my car to be right.

So on the outside everything was fantastic, but internally I was being very demanding about what we were doing with the cars and what we needed to do to move forward. The fact that we won the first five race meetings that year flew in the face of what I was saying, but I was really concerned about the lack of development. When we rolled the car out to win at Clipsal after already winning Phillip Island at the start of

2002, the only genuine technical change we'd made was that we had changed some of the paint from red to black on the back of the car!

I was off my head, I was ripping into everyone saying, 'How can you expect to win when you roll out next year and all you've done is made a paint change?' So everyone talks about what incredible levels of development we had at the time, but they were all kidding themselves. What we did better than anyone else was that we got a feel for the Dunlop tyre quicker than other teams.

Although I was critical of what was going on in terms of development, I still offered to pre-qualify for the Clipsal 500 so Rick Kelly had a guaranteed start. That was the year of pre-qualifying because there were so many teams and drivers trying to run in the main game, and that move worked well for us. Making that choice was very controversial but I knew that it was going to be in our best interests for us to have another effective test day on the Dunlop tyre at a place – Mallala – that was quite similar to a lot of places we were going to race at during the year. I'll always remember that day, right at the end on the very last lap – and that's when things are operating well for you – Lowndes was fastest and I knocked him off to top the times at the end of the session.

We went on to win both Clipsal races and on the Monday after the race I went up to the Barossa with the guys from Channel Ten, David White, Scott Young and Sam Heard. As we got in the limo the boys were saying, 'Bloody great job. Geez, that development work over summer was good.' I remember thinking as we were driving up, 'If you only knew that the only change was from red to black.'

So it looked from the outside like everything was fantastic, but it was only because the team was operating at a very high level and we were getting the best out of what we had. I felt we needed to be doing more, though, and we started to do some development work. We were pressing on and to win five race meetings in a row, missing out on the sixth, but winning the seventh, was an unbelievable year.

I certainly wasn't bored. I was having a lot of fun, and then to win Bathurst with Jimmy Richards again was something really special to me. That was just one of those weekends where everything worked out. We had pole position and no dramas through the weekend. It rained in the race and because Jim wasn't that familiar with the cars he was being conservative and very professional at that stage and we lost some ground, but it was no big thing given our car speed.

Ingall and Steve Richards were together and that was a very strong combination. As it turned out, after all the wet stuff, we went back out and caught them. Right near the end there was a safety car – Steve Richards was leading and he made a bad restart and I got up the inside at turn one and went on to win from there. Again, it might have looked reasonably easy from the outside but the radiator was covered by a plastic bag and it was overheating – Lowndes was already out of the race due to another plastic bag covering his radiator and causing engine dramas. Our car was OK cruising around behind a safety car, but I had to pass him quickly or I would have been in a bit of strife when it went green. I needed the clean air, so my move was pretty desperate but it had to be done. Steve just had a slide when he made the restart, I got a run on him, dived up the inside and then put two or three really good laps together before I had to start short shifting to look after the engine temperature. The alarm lights kept coming on, but I kept on cancelling them because there was no way we were going to stop. Even if they said to stop, I wouldn't have. I would rather have seen the thing smouldering as a shit-box on the side of the road than not win.

We were able to win the championship with a few rounds remaining on that day too, but that didn't even figure in my head. This was Bathurst and you do whatever you have to do to win. I was able to keep the revs down on the straights and that kept the temperature at manageable levels, but we'd never seen an engine survive at those sorts of temperatures before.

Poor Richo and his family – his wife Fay was in the garage and she was torn because it was between Steve, her son, winning the race and Jim, her husband. It was a fantastic battle too and she got both her husband and son on the podium, and in the right order for me.

After I finished with Gibsons I never thought at any stage that Jimmy and I would be back together for Bathurst. Jeff Grech and John Crennan had asked me who I wanted with me there, and while others were either pairing their regular drivers or going for younger blokes, Jim was at the top of my list – to me he was a no risk option. He's just a freak. Whatever you give him, if you allow him enough miles and you let him get his head around how to drive it, he is just extraordinary – probably the most gifted and versatile driver I've ever seen.

To win Bathurst ten years on from our last win together was very special and, for me, unforgettable.

We used him again in 2003, but with the engines the way they were we had trouble. I was driving with Todd Kelly and Richo was taking the second car, because at that stage most teams were starting to pair lead drivers and we felt we needed the same flexibility, and Jim out-qualified me at Bathurst. The engine that we had in his car was actually stronger than ours, but he drove it well and proved he could still do the job. I wouldn't normally accept that too well, but I thought what a ripper job he'd done, and at that stage I owned the team so it wasn't a massive issue, so long as both cars were strong.

2002 was a magnificent year, with the team winning the first eight rounds and then Bathurst – we were on top of the world. We knew some changes were coming in at the end of the year, some really big engineering changes under a program called Project Blueprint, which was designed to provide engineering equivalency for Ford and Holden race vehicles, but we were confident we'd be OK. Then it all started to come apart.

You could not believe the drama that was about to unfold. John Crennan was, and still is, one of my closest friends and we'd just done a deal for me to sign a new five-year contract with HRT. We were in the car coming back from a presentation to Hugo Boss for sponsorship of HRT and also an HSV customer rewards program, and he was on the phone to TWR's boss Craig Wilson, who was basically telling him how bleak things looked for TWR (as owners of HRT).

At the time, HRT had what I called the 'Collingwood scenario'. The club president Eddie McGuire was John Crennan, the coach Mick Malthouse was Jeff Grech, and we had Nathan Buckley as the captain – Mark Skaife. There was a great team of cohesive thinkers with a rare blend of older experienced guys, who'd been around enough, and younger blokes, who were so keen and so diligent and so eager – you couldn't have had a better team. What I was most concerned about, and I've got to be absolutely honest, was the number of people who were trying to purchase the team from outside. There were people who I knew were not going to fit the team culture or mould and certainly weren't going to operate in a way which was good for Holden, HSV, HRT and our race relations with HSV or our major sponsors or the people who supported the team.

The downstream effect of all this was staggering – it was a train smash. Holden viewed this structure as a critical triangle linking HSV and HRT with Holden, especially because a manufacturer was not allowed to own a team and Holden was only given a temporary reprieve on this rule. Ross McKenzie (head of sales and marketing for Holden at the time) was very strong on maintaining these critical links and wanted to keep John Crennan as the head of HSV, keep Jeff Grech by having him at Holden Motorsport, and they'd be able to keep HRT with me being there. Even though the new structure was more cumbersome, personally I wouldn't change the decision to buy HRT because I know I made it for the right reasons, especially for all the team members.

The biggest single thing for me was that so many of the guys felt like it was jeopardising something they'd worked so hard to create – the whole culture and environment that was there and a lot of them were worried about their jobs. Guys have mortgages, they've got families, they've got all the normal commitments without the security . . . it was a rough time for all of us.

In many respects, 2003 was the most significant year of all for both Mark Skaife and HRT. With the collapse of the TWR empire that owned HRT, Holden snapped up HRT to save it from the liquidators, but it had to off-load the team mid-season due to the rules of the series. Skaife stepped in and bought the team. On the track, it was a hard slog. Project Blueprint had forced a whole raft of changes on the Commodore and its competitiveness was hindered. Ambrose had shown at the end of 2002 that he and Stone Brothers Racing had a grasp on how to make the Falcon work, and they won the 2003 series with six wins from 13 rounds. Skaife won the Clipsal 500 and the Sandown 500 with Todd Kelly but just missed out on Bathurst after drama with an opening door. Greg Murphy and Rick Kelly won Bathurst after Murphy recorded the fastest ever lap at Bathurst, a record that still stands in 2010. Lowndes won in the rain at Phillip Island and Russell Ingall (now driving a Ford) scored a pair of wins. 2003 is perhaps more famous for the 'race rage' incident between Skaife and Ingall at Eastern Creek.

It was a pretty tough year on and off the track but we were still competitive. There was a huge cloud over the team and Project Blueprint had done so much to the car in terms of making significant engineering changes, but we went to the first round and won the Clipsal 500. You've heard me say before, but for us to go to Clipsal and win under that scenario was just amazing. It was the best win for Holden Racing Team in its history and for me personally as it was my wife Toni's 30th birthday. It was fantastic to celebrate afterwards.

I wasn't happy with my drive in the Saturday race – Ambrose won and I was right behind him. It was a good drive but it was an eight out of 10. I had the shits with myself because I detuned the car a bit too much when we changed from qualifying to racing. Geoff Polites, who was head of Ford at the time, came up to me at the press conference and congratulated me and said, 'Good drive'. I said, 'No, it was a shit drive, Geoff, it'll be a lot better tomorrow,' and he laughed.

I always got on really well with Geoff because he understood competitive sport and he understood the motor industry. When I said to him it'll be a lot better tomorrow, I was serious. I knew that the team would respond by having a better mousetrap for the next day, which they did. It was fantastic and I drove well. There are very few races at Adelaide where you can't think of making any mistakes, but that day in Adelaide I cannot remember one error. If you think about that, it is pretty amazing – it's not an easy track and it's a long and demanding race. At the hairpin you slow the car from 250km/h to 55km/h and to slide the car into that corner each time and to get it right 78 times was in itself monumental. It was a good race against Ambrose and Steve Richards was fast also. It was a cracker.

Ambrose was by now at the top of his game. I can't think of another guy coming from out of the V8 Supercar circus who was that impressive straight away – he could seriously drive. He was genuinely at it in 2003 and he was one of those blokes you rarely had contact with, and we raced pretty hard on the edge of disaster at a lot of places and never had an issue, which is more than I can say for some. He was really very committed, his laps were good, his qualifying was good, his whole act was good.

Ambrose always had the car very pointy, meaning that the car, from a balance perspective, was very reliant on front grip. In the first part of the corner he was very fast and he basically took the load from the car and made the tyre contact patch consistent which maximises mid-corner grip, as a consequence as he kept it flowing through the corner – which was a bit of an open-wheeler style that he brought with him. And really, he was bloody excellent using this technique. A lot of the time I didn't think he'd make the tyre live, but he did.

We fought him right to the end of the series at Eastern Creek where I had the run-in with Ingall who was his teammate at the time, which we'll talk about more later. That incident took a little bit of attention away from his championship win. However, it was a great fight, and although we didn't win, it was a bloody good battle.

Overall, 2003 was a bit inconsistent because of a series of things largely out of our control. Like at Bathurst, we had to use the new spec engines while Murphy was able to still use an older spec engine, which was at that stage a much better unit. I'm not taking anything away from Greg because that lap he did was fantastic, but his engine speed was just unbelievable.

Murphy qualified on pole but our race car was very good and the thing that stopped us from having any chance late in the race was damage to the left rear door, which came open. It was a race that really got away from us – even though we were on the back foot for most of the weekend, it just wasn't happening like it had the previous two years. I was pretty shitty about the mechanical black flag we were given, not because we didn't deserve it but because of when it was given to us. If they'd given it to us when it was first an issue we would have still had a chance, but they let it go for half a dozen laps. Then there was a safety car and they called us in after the green flag. It was just madness. I was feral because I thought I should have been called in earlier and that would have changed the way the race ran as we would have easily repaired the car and been able to finish strongly after the safety car intervention.

With the timing of the flag, we had to go to the back of the runners on the lead lap, and that was it for us. If the door's open, then it is open and you've got to fix it, so why didn't they call us in straight away? It was a very weird season and that just summed it up for us.

On 1 June the team was officially handed over to Skaife Sports, and from that moment on my racing life changed. With Holden's long term sponsorship commitment I was able to finance the $3.25 million to purchase the team from them, which was a lot more money than most people were saying at the time.

I still don't think splitting Holden Racing Team into the racing arm and the development arm being run independently by Holden was a good move, but that's what Holden wanted and that's what it got. Holden Motorsport was supplying us, as well as the new Kelly Racing Team which essentially took over Kmart Racing in a similar deal to mine, and Kees Weel's PWR team. There were more than 30 people trying to buy HRT, but Holden liked the concept of continuity that I provided and the Managing Director Peter Hanenberger was very supportive of my expanded role and the plan in general.

In January and February when this whole thing exploded,

there was only one option for me and that was to race with HRT. I had a contract and as long as the team was still in business I was in. I also had a sense of loyalty to the boys in the team and that's ultimately why I put my hand up to buy it, even though it was really only half a race team under the restructure.

Jason Bright had left the team and Todd Kelly was my new teammate, but given that he was only swapping over from the Kmart team he was already affected by the train wreck that was happening to us and TWR in general. In essence, he was already on the train; he just changed carriages.

Peter Brock rejoined HRT for Sandown and Bathurst in 2004, but it all turned upside down. Plato was collected by John Cleland at Bathurst and rolled 05. Skaife meanwhile was enduring his worst ever season with HRT and finished the year in 12th spot with no round wins. He had shown plenty of speed, but for one reason or another that didn't turn into round wins. Ambrose again won the series with five round wins, teammate Ingall scored one. Jason Bright in a third team being run by Holden Motorsport won rounds and finished third after running an older model Commodore for most of the season. Greg Murphy won Bathurst again with Rick Kelly while Ambrose won Sandown with Greg Ritter. Other round winners for the year were Todd Kelly and Cam McConville.

But we got through that year and believed we'd weathered the worst of the storm and held high hopes for 2004, but it was like I couldn't do anything to buy a round win. There was lots of drama about how the new engine we were forced to use breathed and what the air box was like because the inlet manifold layout was different and the installed engine power didn't match up with the dyno-rig testing. We were well down on power and our data from the dyno confirmed that. At some tracks we were down seven or eight kilometres an hour in a straight line – it was just unbelievable. It was a joke that Holden Motorsport had to use the lead factory team to be the pioneers for this new engine program and it hurt us through the back end of '03 and '04.

I was starting to get desperate about winning too. There were times I was driving races like it was qualifying; I was driving at 11/10ths just trying to get a round win. I should have won in the rain at Eastern Creek but went off the track – I passed Ambrose around the outside of turn four into turn five and a couple of laps later at Corporate Hill I passed a slower car on the outside but just couldn't get it back on line for braking at the next corner and spun off – not finishing the race.

You can only drive a car at a certain speed; it wouldn't matter if it was Michael Schumacher or Ayrton Senna, every car has a limit. If you don't drive it to that limit, you get beaten because you're not driving fast enough. If you drive over that limit then sometimes you get away with it, but if you consistently drive the car over the limit because you're looking for a better result then the propensity to make mistakes is higher. And that's clearly where we were. Our new engine program was delivering ordinary results and the overall level of development was way below what we needed to maintain a front running position.

By then all the compliance issues around HRT and its licensing had started and were snowballing. We had TEGA

(Touring Car Entrants Group of Australia) tribunals and spent a lot of time explaining structures and business models to people. Through that period I had some great drives but I wasn't consistent. One of the good ones was Oran Park. I'd won the first race against Ambrose and then the next race we were battling together, absolutely nose to tail. We were both going to come into the pits at the same time but I didn't know he was pitting and he was right in front of me. The pit entrance at Oran Park was very tight and it was a pretty hairy thing, and when he started to brake I was on full noise. I knew where I needed to lift off, but when he headed for pit lane all my markers shifted too.

I had to go sideways to miss him and then had to go back on the track rather than into the pits, or I would have crashed sideways into the pit entrance. Think about it like this: you're doing maybe 160 or 170km/h and you've got a plan for getting into your driveway as fast as possible, but then someone else goes into your driveway before you. Well, the fact is that you can't do it! So when he put his foot on the brake and I had all the wheels locked, I was going to hit him and park him in the driveway backwards. It would have ruined both our days, but I flicked left and missed him and did another lap. Effectively, to avoid him, I lost a hundred metres – which was the gap we had for the rest of the race – and I lost the whole weekend. We had the same points but he had a better finish in the final race and that meant he won instead of me.

People didn't come out of the weekend saying, 'What an unbelievable battle that was between Skaife and Ambrose, that was one of the best,' because all they could see was something that looked like a mistake. But Ambrose knew, and he came up to me afterwards, shook hands and acknowledged what a fantastic race it was. We were absolutely on the ragged edge of disaster lap after lap, miles ahead of the next car. But the press didn't say, 'What a ripper race that was on the weekend.' It was 'Skaife's mistake cost him the weekend'. Idiots!

I think what pissed me off the most was that we should have known he was coming in. We were scanning their radios and we were in the pits next door. That should never have happened and I went off my brain when I got back into the pits and we were debriefing afterwards.

We still went to every race at that time at least expecting to be competitive, and to be honest we still thought we could win anywhere and at any time. But it just wasn't happening. At Bathurst we suffered from a broken Watts Linkage (a bracket which keeps the rear suspension located in the car) in qualifying – it jammed up through the Dipper and we couldn't get it pulled apart and put a new one in during the session. That was the first time I hadn't qualified in the top 10 for 15 years – 18th was a long way back.

We were in the fastest three cars on race day. We certainly had the pace of Murphy and Rick Kelly but it just didn't fall our way and we don't even know what happened. Todd lost a lot of ground at one point because his back was hurting with some seat position dramas. It was a shit year and that race just summed it up.

Russell Ingall won his first ATCC in 2005, recording one round win on the way to the title. His teammate, Marcos Ambrose, announced at the start of the season that he was going to the States in 2006 to have a crack at NASCAR, and he finished third in the series with two round wins and seven podiums. Murphy, Tander and Steve Richards all won a round each, while Lowndes (now with Triple Eight) won four and Todd Kelly three. Skaife won his fifth Bathurst with Todd Kelly and finished fifth overall.

I think we'd started to get our heads around the engine problems a bit better in 2005, but we still didn't have the best engines in pit lane. I did a big presentation to all the board at Holden explaining a lot of the issues with the engine and how much better we'd made it in the off-season. Holden Motorsport was buying pistons that were so expensive I used to call them gold plated – they were the lightest pistons you could buy at the time and I wanted them in every engine of ours. I was putting a lot of demand on Holden Motorsport to get that right and as it turns out, our speed in lots of places was definitely better.

In China I was fastest straight away and qualified on pole. I had a clutch drama in the final race and Todd ended up winning the weekend which was good. That was HRT's 50th ATCC win too (which is a feat no other team has managed, even to this day), so that was a big thing. Todd also won the next round in Darwin, so we were definitely travelling much better than the previous two seasons. When we got to Bathurst we were strong.

Lowndes was now with Triple Eight and he was quick, but he tagged a wall early and was out of the running with a less broken Watts Linkage. We had a great battle with Murphy and Ambrose, but they crashed each other out. Our car got better as more rubber was laid on the track and it was a great race car at the end.

In the third segment of the race we were breaking the lap record lap after lap, and when Todd had his final pitstop and handed the car back to me I had to hunt down and pass Jason Richards to win the race, which I did with 20 laps left to run.

I didn't qualify the car well enough that weekend, but we had terrific pace in race trim. I remember at one stage during practice when I did a 2m 8.5 on a high level of fuel that I said to the guys in the garage that lap times like that on Sunday were enough to win the race. It was a heap quicker than anyone else at that stage in that trim, so instead of changing the car back for qualifying, we basically left that solid set-up and threw new tyres at it and it didn't really get any of the usual new tyre gain in the qualifying session or in the top 10. So I ended up fourth in the top 10 but I wasn't that worried.

By now, Tom Walkinshaw was heavily involved with Holden Motorsport to the point that he was going to buy it, which was pretty controversial given what had gone on with TWR and its previous bankruptcy in the UK. He asked me when I finished my first stint if we were fast enough to win. I told him that at that stage we weren't, but that we would be later. Tom was pretty keen across the board to make sure we had the right equipment to do the job, and he knew how we felt about it too – to ensure we had the latest and greatest of everything.

He went to a meeting that Ray Borrett, who was looking after Holden's involvement in the sport, had convened to listen to John Kelly, Kees Weel and myself talk about what Holden Motorsport needed to do for us. It was a pretty aggro meeting because we all thought we were getting shafted and I reckon Tom walked out and thought, 'Wow, this is an absolute minefield.' But he listened and he was starting to get a feel for what the car needed and I was very close with him in a technical sense. I spoke to him probably two or three times a week about what the car needed, what we needed to spend our money on, and what the emphasis or priorities were.

We had a great car at the end of the race. I think that stint was as good as I've ever driven there, and to win Bathurst on Todd's birthday was just unbelievable. Even though I'd passed Jason Richards he was still coming at me, so it wasn't really until the last lap when I got an amazing reaction going across the top of the mountain that it was starting to feel like a reality.

A lot of things go through your mind at the end of a race like that. One of the great things for me in that timeframe was that Robbie Starr and Richard Hollway and the rest of the team were there and they'd worked so hard to get us back to being competitive. One other thing that was fantastic for me was that one of my best mates, Craig Kelly, was in the pits too. Craig's a great sporting person – he'd played in an AFL Premiership with Collingwood – and he also understands the culture of business; he was acting CEO of HRT at the time and that made the result even more special.

But it had been a tumultuous day. There was the balaclava incident with Ambrose where he was penalised for not wearing one, which was against the rules, and that cost him any chance of racing with us at the end, and then he was involved in a crash with Murphy that nearly blocked the track, which would have meant an early end to it all. It was an extraordinary race.

Anyway, the first thing that came into my head when I crossed the finish line was that it was a great 26th birthday present for Todd, and I just said, 'Happy birthday, mate.' It wasn't planned or anything – it just came out.

Bathurst was the one highlight for me in a very tough year, and it looked like we were on the way back. Russell Ingall won the 2005 title in a consistency run with only one round win and Marcos Ambrose bailed out of the series to have a crack at NASCAR in the States, so I was a bit disappointed about both those things. I was very critical of the points system – drivers should have an incentive to pass people and you have to have a point score rewarding that. I think there were two points between each position; well, you have to be nuts to take a risk for that. But good luck to Russell and Rick Kelly the next year – they looked at the points and did what they had to do. I wouldn't want to win in that way, though. And I'd always enjoyed racing Ambrose so I was going to miss his competitiveness, but it also hurt Stone Brothers who suddenly understood just how important he was to them.

Rick Kelly took the consistency first shown by Russell Ingall and turned it into a fine art in 2006 – he won the title without winning a round, but with seven podiums for the year. Lowndes won the most rounds but was for the second year in a row the runner-up. Mark Winterbottom was starting to emerge and he won the Sandown 500 with Jason Bright, who also won in Bahrain. Jamie Whincup won a couple of rounds as Lowndes' teammate. Skaife won the round in New Zealand to equal Brock's record for the number of the ATCC rounds won, but finished the season in 16th with lots of mechanical dramas. Steve Richards and Todd Kelly were also round winners. 2006 will perhaps be best remembered as the year of Brock's death, the motor racing legend dying in a tarmac rally in the lead-up to Bathurst which was won by Lowndes and Whincup after Skaife dominated qualifying but lost a clutch on the grid. Tander was controversially switched from the Toll HSV Dealer Team to HRT for Bathurst and Sandown to partner Skaife.

With the championship rewarding consistency, a year like 2006 was also going to be horrible on the scoreboard. It could easily have been a great year for us with our speed, but we had a massive amount of mechanical failures. Walkinshaw had now taken over the Holden Motorsport totally and he was also negotiating with me to buy up to half of Holden Racing Team. I'd done the deal with Paul Little and Anthony Tratt from Toll Holdings to have Toll sponsorship and I handed it over to John Crennan to fund the other two cars as the Toll HSV Dealer Team. So we had two red cars and two orange cars for the year.

Tom and I have always been very similar in how we go about our racing. We never had an argument or a cross word about that, and our view of getting the best from the team and the car and the best from the weekend's efforts was always in line. He actually reminded me a lot of my dad in the stuff he did and the genuineness of his desire for me to go well, like when he came down to stand with me at the back of the grid at the Clipsal 500 in 2005 – he was there with my wife, Toni, and Craig Kelly prior to the race.

Tom laughed because I walked up and warned three or four of the blokes in front that I was going to be serious about coming through. We were all there having a water, he went and grabbed some ice, made sure that everything was right and it was seriously like my old man could have been there. Despite what you may have read elsewhere, Tom and I had a good relationship at that time.

We had four equal cars and we rolled out at the Clipsal 500, and I qualified on pole and beat Tander and Todd (who were 2nd and 3rd on the grid) by four tenths of a second. It was a great lap and it was as good a lap as you'd ever do at the Adelaide Parklands Circuit. I felt confident about the race – we had the speed and I felt like I was driving as well as I'd ever done based on the quality of qualifying and the shootout lap.

My race ended in the wall at turn eight. The car broke a hub on the left front and when I came up to brake at Wakefield Street the brake went immediately hard and it felt like a mechanical failure. I cleared the brake, ran down the escape road and I turned to head back to the pits. I warned the guys over the radio that there was an issue and I was just cruising back to the pits. I think I was doing something like 180 km/h instead of 240 on the approach to turn eight when it just sheared the wheel apart and fired me straight into the fence and, fuck, it hit hard. I remember thinking to myself when I hit that you couldn't humanly hit the fence any harder than that without killing yourself. I was so sore, and under normal circumstances I shouldn't have been driving the next day, but I did.

The boys did an unbelievable job on the car – they worked all night and got it ready. We went out the next morning and Tom was fantastic. I was either second or third fastest in the warm-up and Tom came up to me, shook hands and said, 'Well done.' There's not many guys who understood what that took, but he was a racer and he knew the level of commitment required to do that and how much it meant to the guys who worked all night.

We were making up ground in the race; basically it was a car a lap. We came up to turn eight and there were four cars all tangled together – Paul Dumbrell was involved and Murphy too. A couple of laps earlier I'd passed two cars there, so I was right onto it. I backed off a little bit and I fired through the corner to get the best run I possibly could, so I could pass them going into the hairpin at turn nine. When I got out on the other side of the corner – because you can't see – Murphy was already parked in the fence. So I saw him, put my foot on the brake and slid to try to miss him, and all it did was go straight into the back of his car.

Here I was, thinking I was going to go from seventh or eighth to, say, fifth on this move, and I'd parked it in the fence at the same corner as the day before, and they were both hard hits. Murphy was in the fence and I got out to see him and he was 'nigh-nighs' – the impact was so great, he was knocked out.

For me personally, this was devastating and a turning point. Two big hits in two days at the same corner. A lot was riding on my result and I knew that this would add to the pressures I was already feeling – despite the issues being mechanical. Turn eight at Clipsal is notorious – an off there is as daunting as it gets and this hit was reminiscent of my crash at Eastern Creek 12 years earlier.

Toni was at home with our first daughter, Mia, who was

only three weeks old, and I recall a feeling of real consequence and my relief to be alive. I was coming up to my 39th birthday and I remember thinking that I nearly didn't make 40! Moments like these can and do bruise you, and I don't mean physically. It's not that they soften you; it's just that they make you acutely aware of your life and how you want to live it.

I knew I wanted to race, but I started to think about a life off track. In hindsight, it was a pretty significant weekend for me.

We had lots of other silly failures during the year too. At Oran Park I was leading by miles when the gearbox broke. There were about four race meetings in a row where we didn't put the left-hand rear wheel on properly after the pitstops. We were going to win at Symmons Plains too, so it was very frustrating to have to stop again to fix a loose rear wheel.

There were just so many stuff-ups that were infiltrating our world and it was draining. However, that year I still won in New Zealand and equalled Brock's record of the most number of Australian Touring Car Championship round wins. The next race weekend we should have broken the record but I didn't get enough points in the reverse grid race despite winning both the other normal races. At Oran Park we came from last to first in the final reverse grid race, probably the best drive of my career – Lowndes and I battled the whole time through the race. So there were events where people were saying, 'Skaife isn't driving as well,' but there were drives in that year that were just as good as I'd ever driven – absolutely rock solid professional efforts.

Bathurst that year was very painful. If you think about

what had happened in the lead-up given we were dominating in terms of car speed in all sessions, I was able to get pole position and the car was an absolute jet. With all the Brock hype relating to his death a month earlier, there was such expectation from Holden fans and the like, and I felt a lot of pressure on us as the official Holden factory team. It couldn't have gone any better up to the start of the race we were super confident, and all the signs were there for Tander and I to win. And then disaster struck. It was exactly the same clutch that we'd used the previous year to win the race – there were no experimental clutches or anything else I was reading about. It was in the right gear (1st gear) and immediately after disengaging the clutch at the start it had massive slip which was so bad that we went back in the field to almost last. I limped up Mountain Straight with the clutch still slipping and as cars began to pass and I was hit from behind by Jack Perkins and slammed into the fence. Standing in the pits, watching a very similar thing happen to Tander when we drove together again two years later was just eerie.

It was devastating, easily one of the worst moments of my career, especially after being such red-hot favourites at perhaps one of the most important Bathursts ever. We wouldn't have made it to the top of the hill even if Jack hadn't hit me, we would have been parked on the road coming out of Griffin's Bend at the end of Mountain Straight. I felt sorry for Jack, he was almost the last car to catch me and he hit me when he pulled out from behind another car; not that it mattered to us because it was already over.

What made it even more unpalatable was the crap people were saying – 'Skaife left the car in third gear', 'he had the handbrake on,' or that we were running an experimental clutch. All the critics that wouldn't have had a clue. And as I mentioned it was exactly the same clutch that we used the previous year that won. It had been re-shimmed to make sure it was set up correctly. Bathurst is always a drama for clutches because of the start and the final drive ratio you have to use, and this was about as bad as it gets. Yes, we got off the line but the race was all over at that point.

There is a certain level of greyness in engineering land. This was one of those situations and one of the races where when we reviewed the clutch issue, the damage was so severe it was hard to determine which part had actually failed first. Based on speed Tander and I were going to win by a mile at Sandown and the bolts had come out of the steering arm. Bathurst was just another piece of crap like that with another mechanical failure.

2007 saw the debut of the VE Commodore. This car represented a completely new era for V8 Supercars because of the way it was built – it also looked the part with bulging guards and a clearly defined wedge. It did nothing to turn around Skaife's fortunes, though. Garth Tander won the series by two points from Jamie Whincup and they traded round wins for most of the season, with Lowndes also winning three to remain in contention. Rick Kelly won a round, as did Todd Kelly, Skaife, Winterbottom and Lee Holdsworth. For HRT, the year was punctuated by as many legal appearances as races as TEGA sought clarifications on the team's ownership before letting it race at all. Lowndes and Whincup won Bathurst again.

We then had to start getting VE Commodores ready for the start of 2007. That was a big job at the time and Walkinshaw was basically in full swing, in that he had total ownership and control over Holden Motorsport and they were doing all the VEs for the Toll HSV Racing Team and for us and the whole thing was blazing along.

If you take the mechanical failures of the previous year and you have a look at the finishing results of one team versus the other in terms of us against the orange team (HSV Toll), there were certainly some issues. If you wanted to, it was pretty easy to control that sort of thing by lifeing components – which is an aviation term for working out how long parts are safe to use – and taking risks on components failing must be carefully assessed.

There was a lot of effort going into the Toll HSV team at that point and Tom was very keen to acquire part or all of HRT. There were a lot of arguments over who had priority and why. Clearly, given Tom's ownership status of HSV and their sponsorship of the Toll team, that did ignite some concerns about competing interests of the teams – especially internally from the staff of each team.

In fact, there was so much stuff going on that looking back now I can't remember either the 2007 or 2008 seasons all that well. I have a more accurate recollection of 1997 than I do of those years, so that has to tell you something. I do remember at one stage I wanted to tell everyone to just get the hell out of my life and just let me go and drive the race car, but that wasn't going to happen. There were a lot of people close to the situation who believe these internal pressures were engineered to make me feel this way. But for me it's blurry; all I know is that there were a lot of wild and varied agendas going on.

The pressure through those couple of years was pretty intense. There was all the normal stuff from myself, but that was amplified as the owner of the factory Holden team, a team with such history and expectation. I've said over the years that there are times in your career when you can't lose a race and other times in your career when you should be winning and you can't win a race. You've got to take those situations for what they are, and when there is media scrutiny that tends to make the burden greater.

It means you sort of get negative about it: 'Oh, do I really want to be here, I'm really sick of this crap.' It's more that I wasn't enjoying the whole ambience of it. Going to the races was hard work. There were times I said to Toni that I just didn't want to get on the plane, I simply didn't want to go to the race meeting.

For most of the time it was OK when I was there, but if the car wasn't good and I wasn't enjoying it as much, my feedback to the engineers probably wasn't as good as it had been in previous years. If the car wasn't good I'd get too frustrated with it and I wouldn't head down the right set-up or technical path. There are issues on all levels when it gets like that. If you don't operate at the right level in every sphere – and that's what makes the complete race package – you'll struggle at times especially in terms of consistent performances.

There was obviously a lot of weirdness about my last season with the speculation around my future and the up and down results and I felt it was probably one of the most demanding, tedious years from that standpoint. But there were glimpses of really good stuff. I always say that the first race meeting is a great indicator of how the season might go, and when I wheeled out and did exactly the same time as Whincup and Winterbottom at Clipsal in the first session, I knew straight away that we could definitely go all right – we were the fastest three drivers and were only split by thousandths of a second.

There were times in that year when it was all working well. But there were other times when I knew it wasn't really Mark Skaife in there, I didn't value it enough and it was frustrating me. I didn't get a feeling that I was doing something special in the car.

When I won Eastern Creek in 2007 I'd said to the boys that if Tander was competitive I wanted everything the same as his car to the millimetre. Everything – cambers, ride heights, shock absorber settings, coil spring rates, suspension geometry, the lot – not one single change. We did exactly that and we dominated the weekend, qualified on pole, won two out of three races – absolutely hammered them. On that weekend those cars were identical. I knew as a driver I could still do it if I was given the equipment to do the job and I was in the right frame of mind, but I was being let down too often with technical problems and it was getting me down – I wasn't enjoying it.

I won't do you the disservice of trying to recollect those two years because, in all honesty, my memories of them are pretty foggy and I'd rather forget them. There were times when I would have rather been somewhere away from racing, and that was unusual for me given this was my life long passion.

That Eastern Creek win was the one where I broke Brock's all-time record and that was significant. The first bloke I saw when I got out of the car was Lowndes and that was special too. It would have been great to have shared a Coopers with Peter after it as we'd planned, and given he was a non-drinker that would have made it just a little more special.

As a young kid racing in the rain at Oran Park, I would never have thought I'd have got to this point in my career. I had five Bathurst wins, five touring car championships and three Australian Drivers' Championships, and I often had to pinch myself to make sure it wasn't a dream.

From the time I was a little bloke I always wanted to be the best race driver in the world. That didn't turn out, but to be the best race driver at a time when I was fortunate enough to have driven against such great drivers across the 25 years of my participation – there's no way you would have imagined that, even if I did dream that big.

It was all amazing. I value the records as much as I've valued some of the battles I've had with people like Brock, Richards, Johnson, Perkins and Jones, and then right through the generations up to today with Whincup, Tander, the Kellys, Winterbottom, Courtney and whoever else. I've had some incredible rivalries with people like Seton, Bowe, Murphy, Lowndes and Ambrose. It had been an incredible journey to the point of breaking Brock's record and it really did – and still does – mean something to me.

The end of 2007 was also quite difficult with Todd Kelly leaving the team. We were team mates for five years and had become very good friends. He's a tremendous young guy with a real engineering aptitude which serves him well. He's fast and technically very competent. We spent a lot of time together and I really value his friendship.

> *Skaife's final season as a full-time racer started with pace and ended in frustration. He won the Phillip Island 500 with Tander, but generally had a very tough year. Jamie Whincup won his first title from Winterbottom and Tander, with Will Davison and Steven Richards the only other drivers to record a solo round win. Todd Kelly left the team amid some controversy and Garth Tander was his replacement.*

I did get one more win at Phillip Island in 2008, but that felt more like I was a co-driver, even though my drive on slicks in the wet was a critical phase of the race. I still had speed when I had the equipment, but when you have two cars in a team and one is more than 5 km/h faster down the straight on many occasions something is going on.

Bathurst was half a chance but what a series of stuff-ups. The start, Tander back to last from pole, then we worked our way all day back into a competitive position. We were losing tyres and although Dunlop was trying to tell us there was no issue with the tyre, they were wrong – they were delaminating and failing.

We were battling just to stay in the running. In fact, when I hit the wall we were in front of Jamie Whincup and he went on to win the race. So we had our chances. We'd decided to make some changes before the start of the race just to de-tune it a little bit from qualifying. As it turned out, it was just an absolute dog at Forrests Elbow all day – it just would not turn at the corner, it had such bad understeer lacking front grip.

In the heat of the race, when you come out the Dipper through the left-right, normally you accelerate down to Forrests Elbow and have a quick look in the mirror. There's a bit of a passing spot there and on that lap I just wanted to see where Whincup was. Normally you give the brake pedal a bit of a tap there just to get a better quality feel and a higher pedal. I didn't do that on that lap, so when I got to the corner and put my foot on the brake, the pedal was really long, and I didn't get anywhere near enough speed knocked off it around the right-hand kink. So I was trying to stop it for Forrests Elbow and because it already had heaps of understeer at that corner, when I finally got it turned, it had locked the left-hand front wheel, ran wide, and it was one of those sorts of things when if you missed the groove there, you've landed in some shit on the outside and you'll just keep drifting wide. That's what happened, bang into the fence!

I thought early in the day that my speed was really good and I felt quite comfortable in the car. When Tander and I were on the same tyres earlier in the week, I was faster than him across the top, so I felt like I was driving well.

As a driver I was still feeling OK. My feedback was good, my speed was OK, but I was over it. People like Craig Wilson, who was and still is running Walkinshaw Racing – who I believe have very little understanding about the actual racing in motor racing and the very personal nature of driving a racing car at the highest level – often tended to wind me up further. I was seriously over it and was close to pulling the pin at that stage. Clearly, the politics were wearing me down which impacted on my enjoyment of the sport. It was devastating for me, because I lost my admiration and some of the passion for the sport that had defined me and inspired me for most of my life. I had actually lost the 'Skaife-factor'. In fact, kitting up for the race at Indy, which was just after Bathurst, I remember feeling a real absence of anticipation – no nervous energy at all. Just the feeling of not wanting to be there.

I had a very frank discussion with Tom afterwards and he could see that I wasn't enjoying it. I'd already briefed John Crennan on life after driving and it was really feeling like it was the right time to explore many of the options he uncovered, which is what we were going to announce just after Indy.

That left a huge build-up to Oran Park and the final round, and it was such an anti-climax in so many ways. I was so gutted by the incident with Winterbottom in pit lane – which he came up afterwards and apologised for, even though it was his car controllers' fault and not his – letting him out of the pit bay straight into my car. Then, because I had to start way back on the grid, I got taken out by a goose in the next race.

The final race was OK, but it won't go down in the record books for me as one of my great drives. That was it – all over!

3

WHO DO YOU THINK I AM?

I AM COMFORTABLE with myself and what I have been able to achieve, even if some people aren't. I've worked all my adult life in motorsport and I'm proud that I've never dudded anyone in a deal, I've always delivered to the best of my ability on promises and I've always been up front, honest and forthright. If you believe what you read, this is perhaps a surprising statement, but in that alone you see one of the reasons for this book.

I don't think I'm misunderstood by the people who have a willingness to understand, I am really not that complex. What puzzles me is the number of people who've written and said things about me that are completely false and fed by rumour or, worse still, by malevolence. The past few years, in particular, have been awkward at times because of the conjecture surrounding my retirement and the sale of HRT. But even in that time, I haven't lied to people. I may not have told the full story, but I haven't lied and to me that is an important distinction.

There are times I've laughed about what I've read, and other times I've been so enraged I've rung the journalist in question to set the record straight. I could never be accused of letting a sleeping dog lie.

I also don't believe I should be questioned on my business ethics; like all of us I may not have always made the right decisions but I'm sure I'm not alone on that front. From any mistake in business I've learned in much the same way as I did on the track. As I said, one of the things I can absolutely say with the most robust integrity is that throughout all my years of motor racing and my time in the motor industry, I've always endeavoured to do the right thing, especially for the business or those we were employing or representing. We've been fortunate enough to have done some ripper deals – standout, industry-leading deals in terms of sponsorship or team deals that might have been from a race-winning standpoint, or from a financial standpoint, seen as very lucrative and advantageous: we've always done our best to deliver. If you asked me, 'What's one single thing out of your whole career that you're most proud of?' It is just that – and if you walk up and down pit-lane, some may not like me, but there wouldn't be anyone who could say with any honesty that I've dudded them or haven't acted in good faith in any of our dealings.

I reckon from a straight-out integrity perspective, it's really important. It's such a small business in some ways but it's also a big business. Sometimes it's for sheep stations and there are big decisions and big things that have an impact on your results. But at the end of the day if you can play with a straight bat, and play with a straight bat hard, you can definitely sleep at night.

I don't mean that you wouldn't do whatever you needed to get the best for the team or to try and win a race or to optimise your own performance or the team's performance, but not paying people or ripping people off or having cars or components that are illegal is just not on and I've never been a part of any of that.

I also think most people would agree it's always hard to find the balance between having friends and work colleagues. There's lots of people that have worked with me over the years that might have said 'Jesus, he's hard work' or 'he's difficult to get on with'. But a lot of those people have become really good, almost family friends, people who come to our place for a barbecue. So you may have had an issue and you may have had a blue about something and you may not have been happy about our weekend's result or someone messing up a pit-stop or a car part failing at Bathurst, or whatever the circumstance. There might be lots of aggro attached to all that, but at the end of the day you've only played with a straight bat and you haven't played the man.

My saying with the team has always been that 'it's not personal'. So you can rip into each other if you have to, because I would rather that than people pussyfooting around and holding something in that could make a difference. I reckon that in any business, especially in a small sporting business, when it doesn't happen the right way it is often like a cancer – it spreads and it negatively impacts on everyone or everything. You don't want things to not be spoken about, you don't want things to not be aired. You actually have to bring those things out and be open and honest about the issues.

You need to be able to talk about when you stuffed up to be able to get it right next time. I expected people to be honest with me, and I was certainly honest with them. From any sporting team perspective, I don't think you could ever say that was a negative. You have to be able to say, 'That's just not good enough, you've got to do a better job.' Then get on with it!

A lot of drivers today aren't critical enough of their own performance and probably don't aspire to do things as well as they should. They aren't energetic or motivated enough to maybe have a look at some of the areas that they may be deficient in and try to make themselves into more of a complete driver or professional sportsman. That's part of being a well-rounded, absolutely top-line race driver – it is a very difficult gig. It's not an easy sport and that part of getting all that together is bloody hard and demanding on all around you. It is such a people business that if you don't do those things the right way with your own performance as part of a team, it just doesn't gel and you don't get the desired results.

I've had lots of people talk to the team from different walks of life. The former Melbourne AFL star and TV personality Garry Lyon was one; the legendary AFL player and coach Leigh Matthews was another. Both were fantastic – Leigh said he had the whole Brisbane Lions team and staff assessed to see what sort of personality types they were, and from those findings he was able to understand each person a little more. So on the days that someone was being cranky, he'd think, 'Oh yeah, well he's read something in the papers and he's a whatever sort of profile,' and all of a sudden it was clearer how Leigh should deal with that particular person. On the days that you needed to leave him alone, you'd leave him alone. He won three premierships with those guys, so you'd have to say it was a pretty good approach.

We didn't do that at HRT to the same level but I did something with Dr Noel Blundell, who I'd argue is probably Australia's number one sports psychologist. He does personality profiles on all the guys in the AFL draft, so he's very good on the psych analysis and a very practical sporting person from all disciplines of sport. I had him come and do a lot of work with our guys. In a sense, we did the same thing as Leigh but not in such a formal manner.

Sometimes in the heat of the battle, a lot of things really get accentuated. You end up with the stress of a race and the stress of whatever is taking place – small weaknesses in one member or department of the team could expand to being a major issue. If there's a single weakness the sport brings it out and you can pay a hefty penalty. What may have been a little void becomes a massive opening and it's bloody hard to cover up any deficiencies.

To me, there's a few different types of race drivers and many are trying to jam too much stuff into their heads. You have to be careful of that – you still need natural instincts and raw talent because what you're doing is so finely balanced; one small mistake and it's all over. One mistake can have an everlasting effect. If you're an emotional kind of guy, you need to be able to control those emotions in the car – not get rid of them, but control them. Greg Murphy's the classic case here – he's a volatile guy, explosions, temper outbursts and all those sort of things don't always help him, but when he has it in check he is great, one of the best drivers out there.

Do you have to rein it in when you're in the car? It's a very good question, and I don't know the answer for everyone, but I do know what worked for me. I think you do confine your emotions a bit because simple self-preservation elements kick in, so if you're so aggro and so off-the-planet about a certain thing, then it will change the way you drive the car. So I think your natural reaction is that yes, you probably contain it in a way that allows you to keep competing or keep on driving, and then let it out later. That demonstrates itself best when you pull up in *parc ferme* (French for 'closed park' – the holding area at the end of the race). You always get the best reaction as soon as blokes get out of the car and the helmet comes off, and they might be blueing because they've been running into each other or a bloke didn't put a wheel nut on properly in a pit-stop and he's ripping into someone in the team. That volatility tends to be exposed most when you first get out of the car while things are raw and fresh.

I've always been much more on the 'we, we, we' side, because I've always embraced the level of teamwork necessary to go well. For me it was always a team gig, the people back at the workshop were included in what might have been a weekend's victory. That part of it for me is always top of mind even though the sport often appears like an individual pursuit. What I've been relatively good at is being able to differentiate between a good team performance and/or a good driver performance. So I know on certain days that I may have driven the car as well as I could possibly drive it and got the best result, which may not have been first place. There's been other days when I know that I've made some mistakes when the car could have finished higher. You need to think globally and say, 'How have we gone over the weekend?' The 'we' part of it is the team. And then how did I contribute, did I do my part or did I let the team down? Most drivers probably don't really critique and analyse well enough and they don't honestly appraise themselves with the necessary level of detail.

I've heard drivers who always talk about what a good job they've done personally when it all goes well, but then when things aren't so good, then it becomes about 'we'. It's totally hypocritical if you're being demanding of the team and you're not conscious of how you may not have done the best job on that particular day. So you can't have one without the other and there's certainly been times in debriefs when the first thing is either 'Sorry, boys', or when we get to certain areas of the debrief I've said, 'I've made that choice on that change, that's a stuff-up and I shouldn't have done that'. You've definitely got to cop that when it's your mistake and I actually think it's a healthy thing within a team.

There's not many blokes in V8 Supercar-land today who are that honest with themselves on a regular basis – probably less than a half dozen. But there are different ways of showing that honesty and the intensity to win. Craig Lowndes is a perfect case. A lot of people don't think he cares enough because he can smile even when the weekend has turned to shit. I've never endorsed that, though, because the years that we were together, I saw how fiercely competitive he was, and although there might be a nonchalant sort of happy-go-lucky smile thing going on, behind that is a really gritty competitor. That's one of the great things about Craig, it's part of his fan appeal. One of the reasons we get on unbelievably well – especially now – is because of the respect I have for a bloke who does compete that hard.

A lot of people say that the Lowndes visor down is the switch for him. It's a lot like, if you talk to professional golfers, they have a slight movement before they start their swing. So it's basically 'this is the commencement of what I'm about to do' – or whatever it is.

My one was that I always used to tweak the base of my gloves before the start of the lap to make sure that the stitching didn't roll onto the palm of my hand. I always knew that was the start of what I needed to go and do. And even if sometimes I felt like it wasn't game-on for me, that was still my trigger, and of course I'm talking more about qualifying here. For qualifying too I used to purposely turn the headlights on, even on a lap that I knew there were no other competitors – for me it was basically like: 'Bang! Let's turn it on now, I've got to make sure the signs are there and my focus is to be ultra-committed.'

I think that's a fascinating part of a race driver's story. To me, qualifying is the absolute pinnacle of how well you can drive. It's just so unbelievable to drive a car to the limit so you know that there's absolutely nothing left. Doing a lap where you know there's not one skerrick of road left that you couldn't have been 30 centimetres deeper under brakes somewhere, and you know that you've been so close to having a crash at three or four spots – that's what it's all about, absolute commitment.

So I think everyone has their own little mechanisms of how they may switch on for those things. I've failed in qualifying on occasions where I've over-driven the car and maybe gone off the road – I would much rather do that than come back in after driving the car at 8/10s and say, 'Oh shit, could have been quicker in turn three but I went in there like a girl's blouse.'

That's a totally individual thing, though. There's a lot of drivers who'd be totally the other way. They'd be happy coming in and making excuses back at the team, 'Look, I didn't want to make a mistake, the race is more important.' All the blokes in the team would be going, 'Yeah, mate, good decision, blah-blah . . .' The reality is they should have tried for pole. And for me, there's certainly been times when I've speared off the track, but I know rock-solid that it only ever happened when I was absolutely wringing its neck and trying to get the very last bit out of it.

I've always made the analogy that when you come up to play a seven iron to a 150 metre green, do you play a hard eight iron or do you play a six iron with a fade? It's not exactly like that in motor-racing but it's still semi-like that because if you start, say, a lap like Bathurst, and you drive across the start/finish line and you're absolutely on the job of putting your foot on the brake at the last moment to make the first corner, that whole first corner thing comes at you so quickly that you have to decide on what your policy is prior. You have to decide, 'Do I go in on a traditional wide line and brake a bit early to make sure I make the apex, and I'm going to sacrifice mid-corner speed and be on the throttle, and make a reasonable exit and start my lap solidly?' Or do I start the lap like you won't believe – and I'm going to be so deep on the brakes I'm going to battle to make the corner, the left-hand front wheel's going to be locked, I'm going to turn it in, it's going to hit the curb, it'll fire wide, I'll be on the throttle, use every bit of road, pop it into the dirt with maximum revs, fucking *on* it!

The approach is the difference between a good conservative lap and an outstanding pole-winning lap.

But then you've got to think, as you select gears all the way up the hill on Mountain Straight and then you've got to decide whether that policy was the right one or not. You've got little markers for yourself as to where you pull the gears and you understand yep, yep, this is good, you've got the exit speed out of what you just did . . . I'll stay on this lap, this is a boomer. So do you keep it up? Do you make sure that you brake like a maniac and keep that thought process in your brain for the rest of the lap?

So then you get to the top of the hill at Reid Park or McPhillamy Park so committed you're battling for breath and using every millimetre of track against the fence or rock walls, you pop it into Forrests Elbow and when you come out of there you look at the dash to see where you are – is your lap time better or worse? We can do that now because we have a lap time number and exit speeds for each corner . . . we know where we are relative to our fastest lap. But you know that you might have made more revs at all these places and you think, 'Shit, this is going to be a ripper lap.'

You come on to the straight and then you say to yourself,

'I better not fuck this up.' Then you get a big long run all the way down Conrod Straight to the fastest corner in touring car racing in the world and you think to yourself, 'I'm going to get around here flat and then I'm going to pull this thing up so late,' and then I've got to try to make this second gear corner at the Chase.

Well, that whole process is about whether you still want to back yourself. Do you still want to be absolutely on it – bang, bang, bang! – gear changes down to the final corner of the lap . . . And you see how many times pole position changes at Bathurst in the final sector. Because it might be that you're not the fastest prior to the Chase but you are the fastest after the Chase, because of how you backed your own ability, maintained the ultra-committed policy, and how you analysed it all. You might be driving at 300 km/h down that straight, but it feels like a holiday . . . it feels like it's an eternity. So you're going down the straight, pulling gears, da-da-da-da, arm on the window (trying to be relaxed), and whoooof! Then you've got to get on with the last bit, a flat out 300 km/h corner followed by a complex left/right which is so easy to make a mistake.

It does get a little bit confused with the straight line speed of the cars. I remember the year Mark Winterbottom knocked me off up there in 2007, I think it was like 0.04 or something difference in the lap times. He actually made a little mistake in the Chase and I thought, 'We've got him,' and then obviously he had enough of a margin before that. All I'm saying is that it comes down to how much you want it. But it's only a risk if you over-drive the car and you may be a bit of a goose if you do make a mistake, but at least you've been trying hard. If you under-drive it or you haven't got the best from it and it's not where it should be, that's much worse. The whole thing is about teetering on that edge, and as I said, there's nothing more exhilarating than that part of a qualifying lap.

That's the addictive part of the sport, that adrenalin rush and the sheer exhilaration from getting it right. It's why I talk about cold turkey and it's hard to excise that from your life.

It's one of the reasons I did Bathurst with Greg Murphy at Sprint Gas Racing in 2009.

The past few years in the car were tough; there were periods where I was overdriving. There was pressure to get results and often the car just wasn't that good, but as I said I wasn't going to just sit back and cop it. I was going to work hard to get the car all the way up to the edge, and often I overstepped the mark.

There were obviously a number of reasons why it became a tough time inside the car, and not one factor alone was really in my control at the time.

Despite having some big issues with the car, qualifying at Pukekohe in 2004 when I knocked off Marcos Ambrose in the rain in the shootout will go down as one of the best laps of my life. I took some pretty big risks on that lap and they all worked out. I can remember when I came back in to the pits the guys went off their brain because they knew the level of effort was 11 out of 10. Those sorts of laps, the ones that come together, are simply amazing.

Or conversely, in 2003, there was a shootout run at Eastern Creek, when I caught both pedals (throttle and brake) at turn two and went from first to 10th in the shootout. I remember that day vividly – we were clearly fastest by a long way. In fact, we were almost a second faster than anybody in the first part of the qualifying session. What actually got me that day was that the expectation was rock-solid that we were going to be pole. So sometimes with those, you get a little blasé and I remember thinking before I got in the car, 'Don't think this is a fait accompli, don't rest on your laurels for this one.'

So what I did then is that I almost rebounded the other way too much, I overcompensated for feeling blasé. I remember getting through turn one absolutely unbelievably – it was 8 or 9k faster than Todd Kelly on the entry to that corner, so it was massively faster at that point. And I remember thinking: 'Don't just cruise, make sure you put some effort into this and let's blow them away.' Coming down the straight and maximum commitment at one of Australia's fastest corners – turn one at Eastern Creek – got through there and then got down to the next bit into turn two. The first part of the braking in that section is really important and you must retard the car to the highest 'G' loading achievable because the last bit of the braking area is bad for inside front-wheel locking, but the first bit is really smash the pedal – maximum pedal effort. Because it came through turn one well, it got hard on the rev-limiter in fifth gear down to turn two, I went smash onto the brake and when I did my foot slipped and caught the throttle – I couldn't back it off because I needed all the brake pressure just to slow down. It was actually my own level of intensity that pushed me over the edge that day and I did myself a disservice. I was just trying too hard and it's a great example of how narrow the threshold is and how simple it is to make an error in our game on a highly important lap.

But I don't want people to think it was all about qualifying for me. While that is a very personal pursuit, I enjoyed all areas of motor racing. I loved the testing. I loved getting organised as to what you've got to do for the weekend. I loved going and practising prior to that. I loved getting myself prepared for qualifying . . . I loved the whole lot.

I used to say to the guys, 'Let's not get too far ahead of ourselves, live for the moment – let's go and qualify the car really well and then we'll think about what we do as the next step for the race.' In modern V8 supercar terms, they're big high powered cars, not much aerodynamic downforce, relatively small tyres; and with a control tyre that isn't designed to make them nice to drive, you have to drive the cars back from the limit to get the best from a full race performance. So when you have a more reserved race attitude, the chance in qualifying is to drive a car absolutely its hardest for a very small period of time – sometimes only one lap at certain circuits.

A lot of people have said about me, 'He wasn't that naturally talented,' which I have always felt that some people just didn't understand. The natural talent of going and driving a car on the first lap of a qualifying session, perhaps your first for the weekend on green rubber (new tyres), when you don't know anything about the grip level, is absolutely all about the natural feel for cars. It's about getting the best from something – it's like you're a pioneer, you don't even know what it's going to do when you get to the corner. It's just fantastic to capture and slide it and move it around and be confident in whatever the grip level is. So that qualifying thing definitely turns me on.

Does that mean I had natural talent? On one hand, there is a simple answer. To me, the indicators for motor racing talent are how well you drive in the wet; how quickly you acclimatise to a car; how fast you get a lap time out of a car; things like qualifying where you don't quite know what the grip level is but you can still exploit it. If you said, 'Who are those people?' Definitely Brock, Jim Richards and Craig Lowndes, they're the blokes that you just grab straight away and say, 'Man, they're good, they're very gifted!'

For me, that is always one I was fascinated with. Blokes would say, 'It'll take Mark more laps to do that than Glenn Seton,' and it was absolute bullshit. There would be no one faster out of the gate than us at any practice session ever, and no one who – from a qualifying perspective – was able to grab a car like that. Those sorts of things are innate. People like Ricky Ponting or Adam Gilchrist, their eye and their timing is just extraordinary. To me, one of the things in motor racing which is a real indicator of natural talent is the ability to have it slow down to such a point that you can just tell people things about the lap and the car that would blow them away. Almost metre by metre you can tell people what's going on in all aspects of your performance. My indicator for the guys was always: is it happening slowly?

There are rare sporting people in almost every discipline who can sometimes bundle up all of the gifts and the talent they possess and have a real desire to win. And for me, I look at rugby league and I'd say Bob Fulton was just a standout or Andrew Johns or a Wally Lewis or a Laurie Daley. You could watch them play and they just had so much time, so much natural talent but so competitive. They did things better in the areas of the game than their record shows. They would never credit Laurie Daley as being a great defender, for instance, but he was a fantastic defender even if most people didn't highlight his tackling as a feature of his game.

I think in that way I'm similar and there's other guys who are like that too, like Jimmy Richards. You might clearly have natural talent and you can drive the car very well, but at the end of the day there's quite a few people who can drive cars pretty well. How much do you want to win? How much application are you going to put to the task? How much effort and work are you going to put in to really doing the best job you can possibly do? That level of tenacity or determination is a part of your character and ultimately where you get your best result from.

Fortunately for me, I was always so competitive that I wanted to get the best from myself and the best from the team, so you add that to a core amount of ability and you end up with something. I never had that before motor racing – I was nowhere near it at school – but go-kart racing was my personal signal. Yes, I had a certain level of natural talent. Was I the most talented of my era or just the most determined? I'm damn sure I rank at the highest levels for determination, but I also believe I had the natural ability many people wanted to deny me.

My dad used to say that everyone is good at doing something, and when they are and when they're interested in something, it's very easy to learn it and to apply that ability and to be motivated by it. There's a mate of mine up on the Central Coast who loves horse-racing. He can tell you what race a horse won last, what weight it had on it, what it drew, who it was out of, what it was by, who was riding it and all that, it is just unbelievable. But he was never any good at school. For me, to learn about motor-racing was just as easy as it was for him to learn about horse racing.

Now that I'm a father I probably cheat a little bit because I basically apply the same methodology as my dad did with me. I could go and do whatever I wanted as long as I was doing my best, of which he was always critical. If I didn't have a great game of rugby league, we used to have a blue afterwards, so they were always interesting family times. If Mitch, for instance, wants to be a lawyer – for me it is just 'go your hardest' and the same with his sporting stuff. He plays cricket, he plays football – whatever it is if he is channelled into something that enthuses him, then I'm into it too. I don't think I'm too different to Dad on that score.

Competition is a big void for me at the moment. I'm loving what's going on in my life these days because I've got real diversity and I'm applying my brain to lots of different things. But honestly I genuinely miss the real cut-throat, knock 'em down, drag 'em out competitive stuff, week in, week out.

It's funny, if I go for a run I know that because I'm not competing, it's not as intense. There's just not the intensity there. I've spoken to my manager Craig Kelly and I've spoken a lot to my mate the former AFL star Nathan Buckley about it. Bucks and I are very similar in lots of ways and even in the way that our careers have evolved into the next stage in terms of media work and other things. I don't know where that competition is going to lead me because I know when I take

Mitch out and we bugger around trying to make the kart go faster, there's a bit of that in wanting the stopwatch to signal a better lap time. I want him to go faster – but I'm certainly not going to live my life only through Mitch's pursuits.

There are two parts to what I miss. First it is obviously the driving. But the second thing is the blokey thing and being in the workshop talking about cars, because part of the competitive stuff is 'how do we tweak that?', 'how do we make that?', 'let's buy one of those', 'roll that out', 'let's blow them away'.

What I'm doing now keeps me close to the sport, but it's not the same and that's really why I decided to do the long distance races. I reckon I've probably got four or five years if I want to do that. When I drove Murphy's car at Winton in 2009, I had lists of stuff before I got in the car. I spoke to the engineers ad nauseam, I'm pretty sure at that stage Jeff Grech already wanted to piss me off. It surprised me that he wanted me to come and do Bathurst with them after all those years we spent together at HRT.

When I was asked, how could I say no? There was this itch . . .

4

GETTING INTO THE FAST LANE

My father and grandfather had been involved in the automotive business for most of their lives and Dad raced a lot in the mid to late-'70s and early-'80s. For me having automotive businesses and being around cars was a natural fit. I certainly enjoyed going to the races and watching Dad, but I was also doing all the normal things young blokes do – surfing, playing rugby league, everything you'd do growing up on the beautiful New South Wales Central Coast.

But I was always turned on by how the business ran and how it worked with motor racing. In those days you could start karting when you were 14, and that's when I began. Dad and Barry (Bo) Seton were good mates and Bo was preparing some cars and doing some engine work for Dad's race cars. So we were close as families and obviously Glenn and I were good mates, even though he is two years older than me. He was riding motorbikes before I was riding motorbikes, he was driving go-karts before I was driving go-karts . . . I sort of followed him through those phases.

I tried to pick up on some of the little loopholes of getting involved in motorsport based on what Glenn had been learning, and it helped give me a leg-up. In my second race meeting I won a race in the rain at Oran Park and, on that day, I felt from an ability standpoint that this was something I could do. You knew if you'd played a good game of rugby league, and on that day I knew I'd gone alright. So that was the start of a little fire that started to light up and evolve and take over my life.

I'd ridden a lot of motocross bikes but I knew as soon as the four-wheel thing happened that my ability was better served there. So that was an interesting snapshot into how young people operate. I've always been interested in how these things work and where natural talent lies and now I'm interested in it with Mitch, because it's a similar evolution – it's like being a football scout, identifying aptitude and working out if you can apply it.

My family worked really hard in the business to afford not just the karting but then the junior category stuff – none of it was cheap. Dad came to as many races as he could, but he couldn't do all of them. So we enlisted the help of a seven-times Australian senior karting champion, a great bloke named Don McLean, to give me a hand for the last couple of years of karting. We had a great relationship and I learned a lot from Donny.

The first step after karting was when we went and bought a Torana XU1 sports sedan and ran in Sydney events at Oran Park and Amaroo in 1984. Dad and I did most of the work with Bo Seton helping out with the engine and some suspension set-up. Then the following year was the launch of what was the biggest one-make series in Australian history. Ford, Motorcraft and Goodyear put a one-make Ford Laser series together and it was open to KA and KB Laser models. The deal to buy a car was a special purchase price through any Ford dealer. You got your car and your kit of parts and then had to go and have a roll cage and harness fitted, but essentially it was a very cheap way to make an eligible race car.

At the first race meeting they had 56 entries and they could only start 26. In those days there was more money to win a Laser series round, $3000, than to win a touring car championship round, which was quite staggering. We won a few races – in fact we made money, and that was the only time in our racing career up to that stage that we genuinely made money from running a car.

We were running well in the first year, won the series the next year and in September 1986 I moved to Melbourne. Barry Seton had spoken to Fred Gibson, and Fred was looking at how I was going. He was watching my progress and I was racing not only in the Goodyear series in NSW but also in the Motorcraft series in Victoria. Dad and I would drive the truck overnight and we'd go down to Melbourne, do those races and drive back on Sunday evening to be back at work on a Monday morning.

They were really tough times because of the amount of

effort required, but it was also a great period of my career. We were working bloody hard, but the results were good too.

Glenn had by now moved to Melbourne on a deal with Fred Gibson to essentially replace Garry Scott as a driver. There was a lot of change going on for Fred: he'd restructured the business and moved it from Sydney to Melbourne, they were swapping from Bluebirds to Skylines and there were plenty of other things happening too. Glenn started out driving the front wheel drive Nissan Exa with Fred's wife, Christine, and then the Bluebird a couple of times.

All this change happened because Howard Marsden, who managed Nissan's motorsport investment in Australia, was moving to Europe to do the same thing there and Fred was going to take over the local Nissan motorsport operation. Fred worked pretty hard to get a lot of his people in Sydney to move to Melbourne with him, and that included Barry and Glenn. Barry was really brought in to run the engine program and Fred was keen to put a young guy on with George Fury, who was the team's lead driver at that stage, and it worked well.

1986 was when Glenn started with Peter Jackson Skylines – it was the DR30 prefix car – and he made an immediate impression which was good for all us young guys. He was obviously quite fast and he was doing a really good job. It was a funny period for me because there were glimpses of really good stuff in the Laser, and I knew that Fred was taking particular interest and I knew that Barry was also talking to him about some of the races and sort of prompting Fred to keep an eye on me.

It didn't bother me that Fred was paying attention, the

real pressure for me at the time was really just for me to do my very best; whether it was Dad standing on the pit wall or Fred Gibson looking from up on the hill at Amaroo Park, it wasn't really anything other than me needing to do the best job I could do for myself. I've always been pretty hard on myself, not just as a driver but in every respect. It doesn't matter what it is, if I haven't done a good job of it I'm angry with myself.

So that was an interesting time. There were some really good drivers in that Laser series – Mark Gibbs, Peter Dane, Steve Williams, David Brabham, Ken Douglas and Jim Zerefos were all really good production car drivers. We all started out as pretty good mates and many of us were actually preparing the cars together in Barry Jones' workshop in Sydney, often alongside each other.

A lot of them were very experienced drivers of the day in those sorts of cars. Underpowered front-wheel-drive cars on standard road tyres are quite hard to drive because you have to flow them and keep the momentum up to set good lap times. Being front-wheel-drive they have a quirky nature in the way they handle and respond to driver inputs.

I was desperate to do the Victorian series as well as the Sydney one and I remember sitting in Dad's office calling every Victorian Ford dealer to get the money to come down to Melbourne. Without that money we simply couldn't afford to do it.

In the end, a guy called Ron Kaplan was the only one to show any interest. He was at Stillwell Ford and the only deal he said he could do was to match whatever money I could win on the track. I had to run full front of the car signage and everything, and if I didn't win any prize money I wouldn't get a cent. The Sydney series had fantastic prize money at $3000 for a win, but the Victorian Motorcraft series was only $1000. We won every round in Melbourne, though, and I kept on sending invoices to him and he laughed because he thought it was only going to involve having a sign on the car from a young bloke from the Central Coast and it wouldn't cost him anything. At least he could laugh about it, although it turned out to be quite expensive in those days for that class of racing.

I remember being a little bold at the time and I said to Dad, 'We'll go down there and if we win we'll be right.' You probably shouldn't ever go into motor racing and think that the only way you can make it financed is if you win. But it worked that time for me. There were plenty of times we went out on a limb, but they were all a little more calculated than that one.

In the second last round of the series in Sydney that year at Oran Park, Peter Dane fired me in the wall coming out of BP corner coming on to the straight. I'd passed him up the inside off the dog-leg into BP and he ran into the right-hand rear corner as we exited onto the straight and fired me in the fence – I was so angry I couldn't speak to him. In fact, we don't speak even to this day. The first hit to the fence hurt it, but I was stuck in the middle of the road when another guy ran up the back of it and it was just absolutely destroyed.

There was one more round to go and we were leading the series prior to the incident and Dane was second, but the car was ruined. There was lots of aggro at the time as you can imagine – I've never handled that sort of stuff very well and I was always up for a fight. We spoke to Ford and told them we couldn't go racing at the next round and couldn't finish the series and they sent me a body shell. In one week we totally stripped the wreck and built a brand new race car. We went out on a limb to get on the track, but it was nowhere near the stretch or risk it had been to do the Victorian series.

A guy called Bob Riley, who used to run the Mitsubishi Ralliart team and was a really good mate of ours, a mechanic who was working for us at the time called Dave Fergus, Dad, a mate of his Les French and myself all got together and built the car in a week; we got a lot of help from Barry Jones who was a master at preparing series production cars. It was a massive drama getting it all ready, but we took it to Amaroo Park and hosed the field. It was one of those situations where the level of energy and the level of effort was through the roof – it was so important to have it all together and get on with it.

There were little symbolic things like that through my career that made such a big difference. It would have been easy to not bother, to just blame a crash and sit out the final round. I've been lucky to have so many good people around me who've shared my enthusiasm and motivation. We put the energy into it because we wanted to go back and beat Dane and to win the race, but it really was all of us that wanted to do that, not just me.

As I mentioned Dad did quite a lot of racing but he stepped away from that when I started kart racing. It wasn't just financial, it was about a time commitment with the family and we had quite a big automotive business at the time. We had different franchises, we were wholesaling tyres all around New South Wales – it was the biggest tyre dealership north of the Hawkesbury River so it was quite a big gig. Dad was just flat out doing the business part of it. Mum worked in the business and basically held it all together. I was off doing kart racing or car racing and my sister, Lisa, was doing a lot of dressage competition with horses. There was not a weekend where the F100 wasn't towing something to some venue and it was a really busy time for all of us.

I can never remember a time where we were just hanging around with nothing to do, and it is pretty much the same for me today. It felt like if you weren't busy you were going to stagnate. Treading water was not an option. Mum and Dad worked very, very hard and it was a very successful business in those days. Dad had pretty much stopped his own driving and he was pretty keen to help me, but he was also super hard in terms of expectation. If the car wasn't presented properly, if there was one element of it that wasn't organised, if there was one bit that was average, he was off his head. We always aspired to make the car as good as it could possibly be – there's a lot of that that's still in my make-up today.

Dad – or 'Skaifey' as I affectionately call him – is an extraordinary man, very clever and very demanding. He has a heart of gold and he can be the softest most loving guy you'd ever meet . . . or the crankiest, wildest prick imaginable! (Sometimes within an hour.)

At most of the kart meetings it was just me and Don, and Dad would lob at as many events as possible. I remember being at the state titles and Dad arrived late on the Friday afternoon just to see how we were going. The kart had silver wheels on the front and black wheels on the back and he was just off his brain! He just ripped into Don and me like you could not believe.

He said, 'We are in the fucking tyre business and can't even have the same coloured wheels on the fucking thing!' He was off his head!! Don and I were just passengers in that conversation. We didn't laugh because we certainly couldn't laugh at that point, but we do laugh about it now. But that was just how it was – if you were going to do it, you had to do it right.

Where my dad was different to others was that he was a very realistic guy. If I didn't quite have it (i.e. didn't have enough ability) he would have been the first one to say to me, 'Boof, you are wasting your time going to Melbourne. You're driving pretty well and if you want to do a bit of racing in Sydney that's fine, but you're probably better off hanging out with me running a couple of tyre stores.' That is the sort of guy he is – he has never bullshitted to me and never told me something that he didn't believe. Sometimes the truth serum may have been hard to digest but . . .

Most parents love the thought of their son or daughter competing in whatever their sport is. In motor racing you see it all the time. There are plenty of dads who are living the dream through their kids but I don't think that was the case with Skaifey. I reckon he thought I had a bit of talent and he didn't want to see it wasted, but it wasn't about him. There was some pretty lively debate about my performances. If I was going to do this he wanted to make sure I was committed, and it was the same back when I was playing rugby league, working in the workshop or whatever – he wanted to know that I had done my best.

Both Mum and Dad were keen to teach both my sister Lisa and myself the importance of hard work. When I was a mechanic in the workshop I could charge out more on a daily basis than any of the mechanics in the place, provided I hit certain targets. That meant, for instance, I might have had to do 13 or 14 wheel alignments in a day and Dad used to run a book so he could keep track of it all. If I came back to him at the end of the week and I only charged 40 hours out, he'd say, 'What were you doing during the week?'

Overall, from a general motorsport perspective, Glenn and I were quite lucky in that we came along slightly behind guys like Tony Longhurst and Neil Crompton when the superstars of the day were in the twilight of their careers. Moffat, Bond, Johnson, Richo, Brock, Grice – almost the whole era of unbelievable drivers were all getting to that stage in their careers. Allan Moffat had Gregg Hansford in his team, Bob Forbes had Crompo, Gibbo had Glenn and myself, Frank Gardner had brought Longhurst along and Brock was really good at giving young guys a drive – Brad Jones, Mark Larkham and David Parsons . . .

It used to make me laugh – at the time there was all this industry talk asking, 'Where are all the young blokes?' The classic is, and it remains the same today, that there is only any use in bringing on young blokes if they can beat the older blokes. The reality is that it's like finding a superstar young AFL player – you don't take Matthew Lloyd's spot or Nathan Buckley's spot in whatever sport unless you earn it.

Glenn and I were pretty lucky in terms of the generational change, but remember in 50 years of Australian touring car racing, there have only ever been 57 round winners, so that

Above left: At Nan and Pop's house on the Wyong River (Central Coast, NSW) aged 18 months.

Above right: With Lisa, my sister, when we were five and three. She's always had a great smile and is still lots of fun.

Below: Nan and Pop – Joan and Herb – who were both such an important part of my life. I spent a lot of time with them as a young bloke and we had a great relationship.

Above: What about my dragster! Dad always bought bikes for me to grow into.

Far left: Off to school in Wyong. Could I pull my pants up any higher?

Left: With Lisa at Oran Park watching Dad race in 1974. I always wanted to be a race driver and Lis wanted to be a fashion guru.

Below: Standing in front of a GTS Monaro that Dad was doing some work on at the time.

Above left: Coming up to the bridge at Oran Park in 1984 in my only drive in the Seniors. This is the circuit where I had my first racing win ever.

Above right: At Newcastle with Glenn Seton on the left.

Left: In the Laser heading Peter Dane up the hill at Amaroo Park. They were great days with lots of hard work and some great rewards.

Below: Glenn Seton and me in the workshop with the HR31 Nissan Skyline in the background. Take note of how the colour schemes used to be applied.

Above left: Joining Brock at Bathurst in 1997 for his first retirement run there. We were very unlucky not to have won his final race.

Above right: In 1998, replacing Brock at HRT.

Below: One of my best mates, Neil Crompton, and me in 1988 when he was a works driver for BMW and I was with Nissan.

Above: My first touring car win and shared with Jim Richards, who is one of my best mates. We had some great times on and off the track.

Left: On the podium at Oran Park with Craig Lowndes, a great rival and mate.

Below: The first post-Lowndes race meeting with HRT after he defected to Ford. It was one of our strongest performances ever.

(John Morris/mpix)

(Chevron Publishing Archive)

(John Morris/mpix)

(John Morris/mpix)

Opposite top: This is the scene of the biggest crash of my career, turn one at Eastern Creek in the rain. Fortunately, the car spun and made contact backwards – probably saved my life!

Opposite middle left: In the Formula Brabham (also known as Formula Holden) at Eastern Creek – it was a great car and a great track.

Opposite middle right: The GT-R at its first Bathurst. The car was still fragile at that stage and we had to pace ourselves all day.

Opposite bottom: Our white car outside the workshop in Dandenong, signalling the end of the cigarette era and our Winfield sponsorship, and bringing about tough times for the team.

Above left: Qualifying at Bathurst in 1997 with Brock – pole position and the start of the next phase of my career.

Above right: In front of Parliament House in Canberra. The track was our first crack at circuit design, but unfortunately the race was staged in the middle of winter and got caught in typical politics.

Below: A great first corner battle at Barbagallo in Western Australia with Paul Radisich and Russell Ingall.

Left: The press release photo announcing my ownership of HRT.

Bottom: Bathurst 2005 was a big win for the team, and the crew assembled here is a real who's who of the top guys working on Holdens.

Opposite top: My 2007 win at Eastern Creek moved me one win clear of Brock in the ATCC. I would love to have had a drink with him to celebrate.

Opposite bottom: Rob Starr and me having a quiet one after the Bathurst win in 2002.

(Justin Deeley/inetpics)

V8 NEWS
SKAIFE MOST EVER WINS
38 SUPERCAR/ATCC ROUND WINS

(Justin Deeley/inetpics)

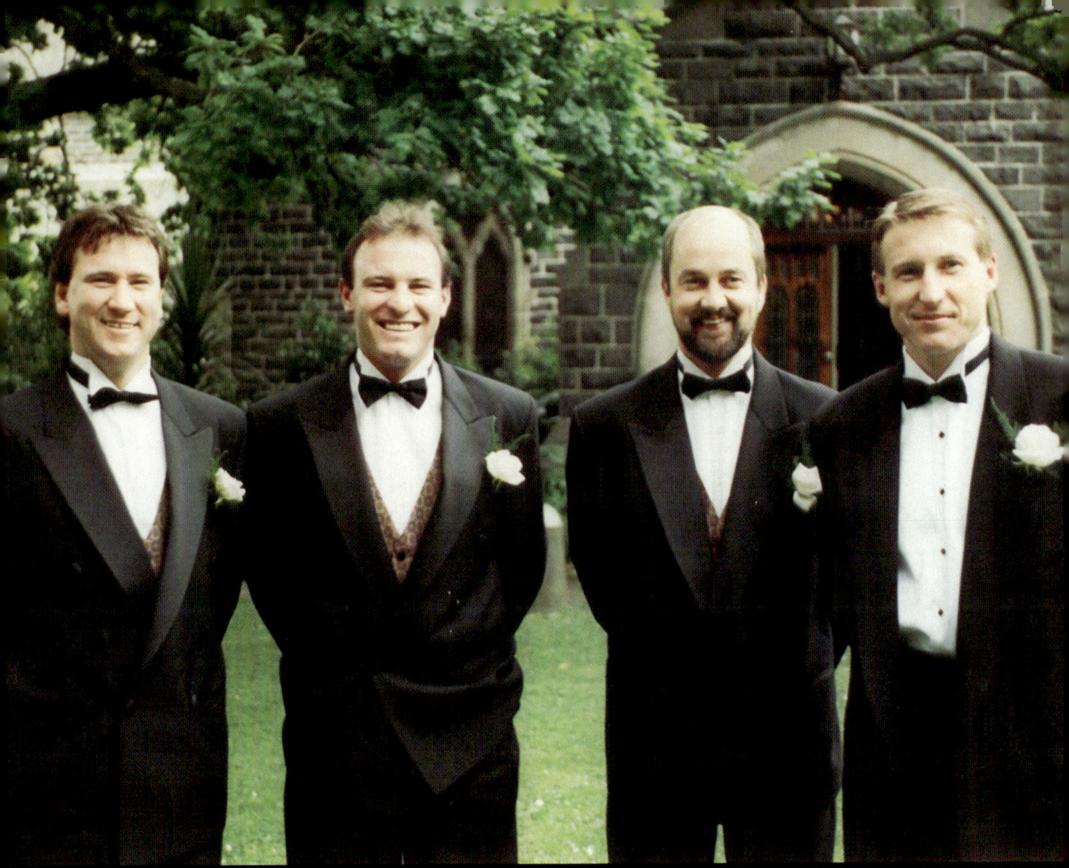

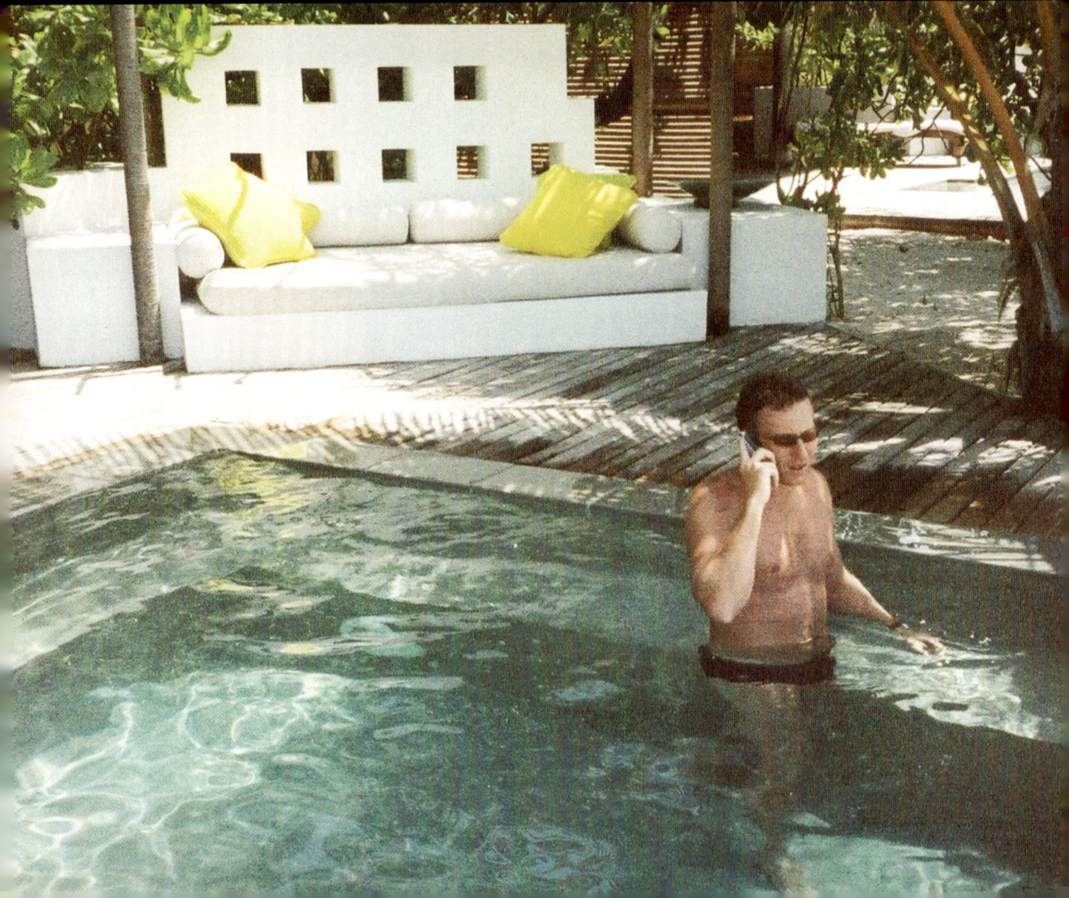

Opposite top: Gavin Wand, Anthony Tratt and Rod Smith were my groomsmen at my first wedding.

Opposite bottom: Even in the Maldives the phone never stops. This was in the off-season leading into the 2005 year.

Above left: Having a couple of glasses of personality with one of my best mates, David White from Channel Ten.

Above right: In Shanghai with Craig and Meredith 'Moo' Kelly, prior to our first event in China. They are two of my closest friends and we have had some fantastic times together.

Below: A rare holiday in Europe without any race commitments, at Portofino in Italy.

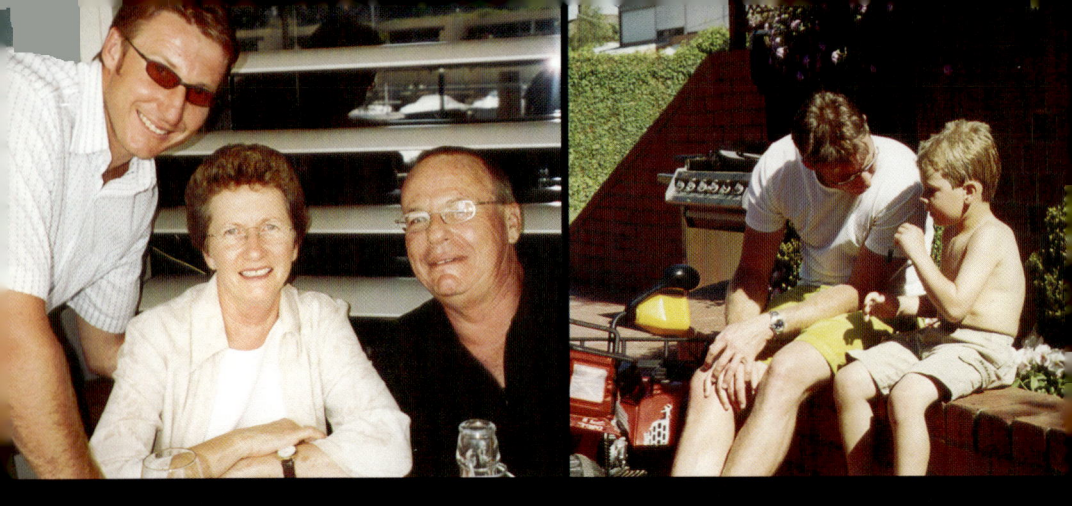

Above left: Enjoying lunch with Mum and Dad at Kingsleys in Woolloomooloo, in Sydney.

Above right: In the Kellys' backyard having a quiet chat with my godson, Max.

Below: Fred Gibson with Mitch and me in 1997. The Gibsons (Fred and Christine) were like a second family to me.

Opposite top left: With Mitch at my wedding to Toni. Hugo Boss made him a special suit to match mine and those of Craig Kelly and David White.

Opposite top right: Dancing with Toni at our wedding in Byron Bay. Doesn't she look stunning? She is such an important part of my life.

Opposite bottom: Relaxing at Toni's and my home in Melbourne.

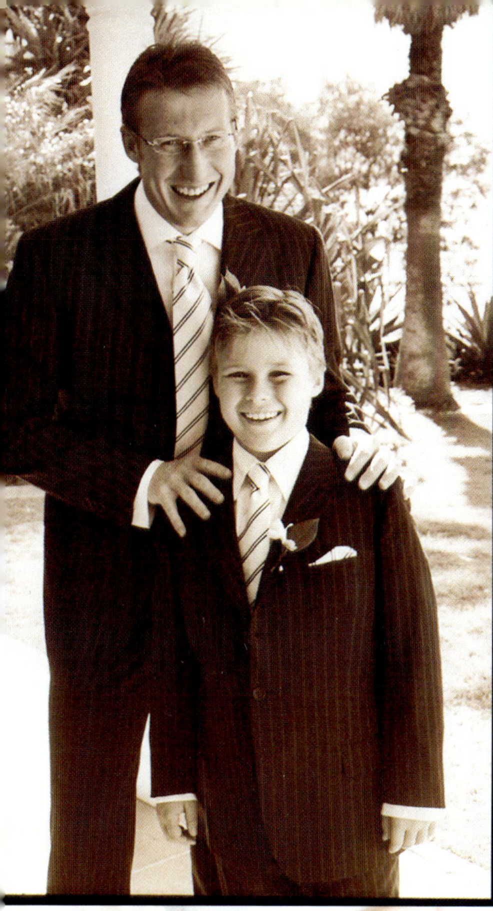
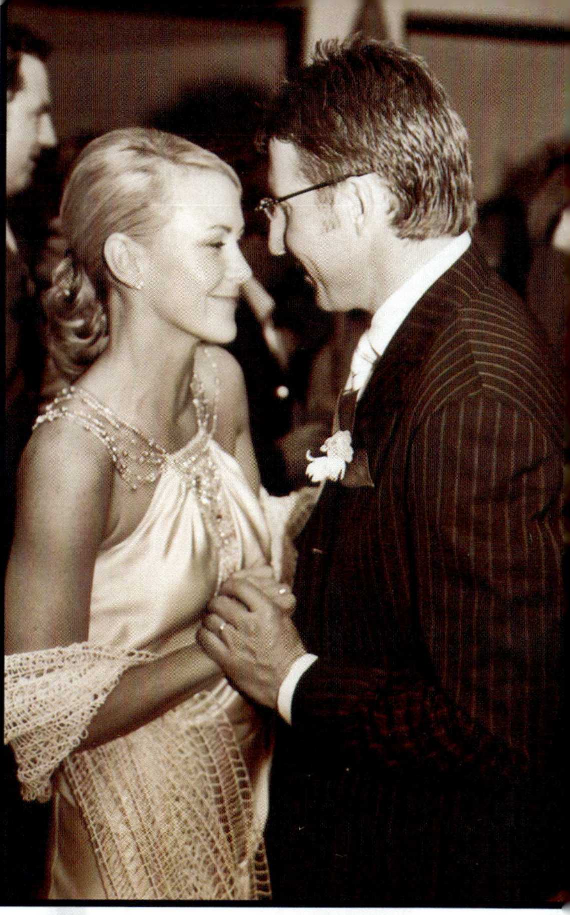
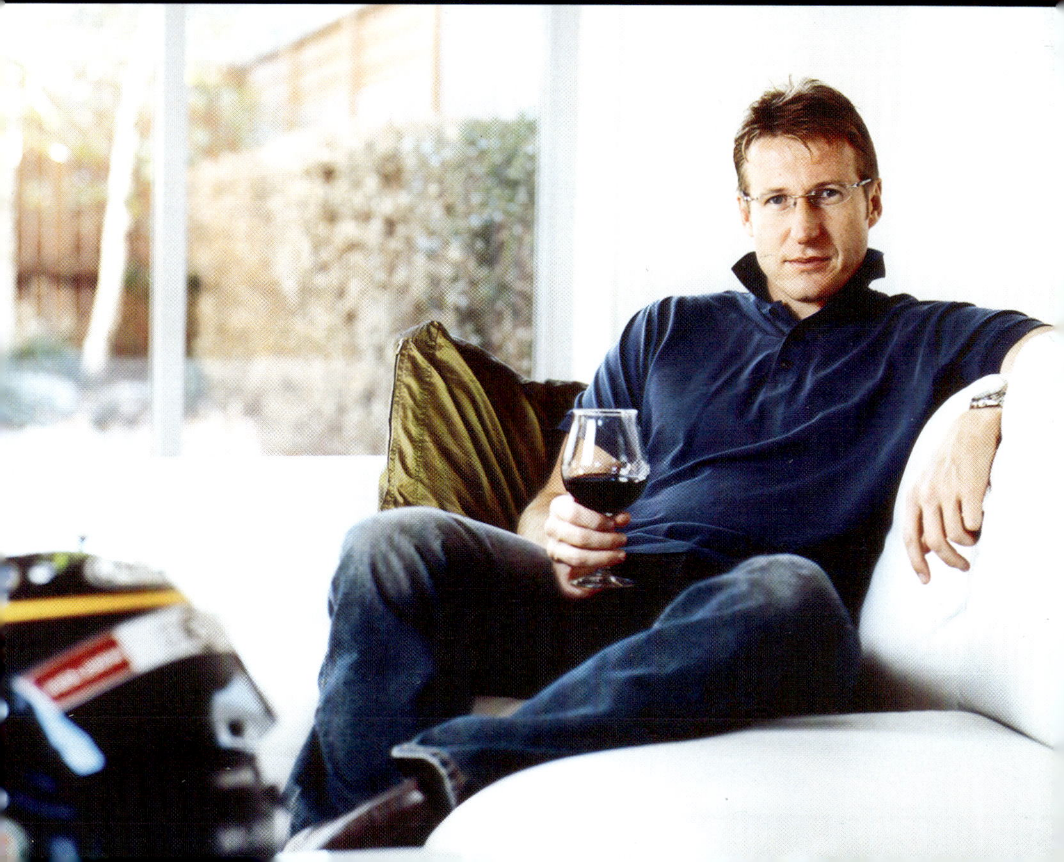

Above: This crash in 2006 was the end of my worst-ever day at Bathurst. I cannot ever remember being more disappointed at a motor race, although Bathurst in 2009 gave it a push for different reasons.

Below left: Preparing for the final run on board the HRT car.

Below right: Test drive of the Nissan Le Mans sportscar in 1990.

(Justin Deeley/inetpics)

Top: Mitch in his first race suit helping me sign autographs.

Middle: Mimi giving me a cuddle.

Bottom: Tilly helping me to prepare for the final race at Oran Park.

Above: James Courtney coming in to wish me luck for my final full-time race, with John Crennan in the background. Crenno was a massive influence on my career and remains one of my closest friends.

Below: Tilly, Mitch, Toni and Mia at Oran Park for my last run as a full-time driver.

basically means one new driver a year is a winner. Then you think, who were the real winners? Who has *really* come along and how often do they come along? After Glenn and myself, for instance, it wasn't until Lowndes in the mid-1990s. After Lowndes, Tander maybe, Ambrose certainly, the Kelly boys and then Whincup and Winterbottom (Courtney and Briscoe focused on overseas endeavours but are genuine stars). When you look at the generational change, it is probably once every six or eight years that you actually find someone special.

So there were plenty of young blokes getting a go at the time, as some of the older drivers were looking at finishing up in the seat and running a team. This is what Fred was doing, but the reality was that it was never easy finding your next talent. And even if you did, you had to have patience with them, even if that young driver didn't have any patience of their own . . . such as me. I wanted it, and I wanted it immediately if not sooner, even if I had to move away from home to do it.

Having had such great support from my family and others on the Central Coast, it was a big thing to move to Melbourne to try out for a professional career. When I moved south in September 1986 I was basically on an arrangement with Fred where I got $200 a week and did whatever had to be done around the place in the hope that I'd get a drive of something moving forward.

It was a busy time for the team and Fred's business in general – we were doing a lot of road car work. I lived at the Setons for probably about a year, and Barry and his wife Bev were great in how they looked after me. Coming from the Central Coast and not knowing anyone was quite difficult so to have a nice family experience was critical. I also formed a really good relationship with Fred and his wife Christine and their family, and even to this day I am very close to them.

Glenn and I trained together all the time and we worked in the workshop together. The desire to learn all things automotive was really strong at that stage. Even though I had a background in the trade, that was more focused on retail, whereas this was genuine automotive development and I was really enjoying the challenges.

The level of talent around the place was amazing – guys like Andy Bartley, Trevor Jones, Ian Walburn, Wyn Ellery and in addition to Barry Seton in the engine department were absolutely the best of their day. Young blokes like Peter Schaeffer, or 'Pete Alphabet', evolved too – I watched him become probably Australia's best fabricator because he was willing to learn and the team provided an environment for that to happen.

I was welding and making stuff and on the lathe and doing things that I wouldn't have been able to do if I was at home. That was all great, but I felt the racing part was going too slow. I was also doing a heap of road car development work so I was always driving something. I raced the Nissan Gazelle in 1987 while Glenn ran second in the championship in the DR30 Peter Jackson Skyline. 1988 was such a shocking year for the team when the new Skyline came along – we had to put all our effort into sorting that out and it slowed me up a bit in terms of transferring into the main outright category.

In fact, 1987 was a very progressive year – CAMS put together a two litre touring car series. We – that is, Fred – bought the Gazelle back from the Nissan dealer John

Giddings who'd bought the car, and he made it into a Peter Jackson car and we went on to win the championship. As an intro into Fred and Nissan-land it was a pretty good start on the track. There were some really supportive people at the Nissan Motor Company in those days, like Steve Markwell, Paul Beranger and Lee Miller just to name a few, and there were obviously some really good results.

I'd entered my first Bathurst prior to that with Peter Williamson in a Toyota Supra but we didn't make the start of the race after he had a big crash in practice. The record books have 1987 listed as my first Bathurst because I actually made the race, but I thought it was going to be a very short race. Stopped on my first lap, it couldn't have been a worse start. The car ran out of water, so we came in and put some in it and then went all day and we finished 19th. It was a great car to learn in – it wasn't big on power but it was nicely balanced and easy to drive.

There were other big events throughout that time, like at Amaroo Park where they used to have the 300km race – the CRC 300 – which was one of the endurance races of that era. During practice in the rain in the Gazelle, we were second fastest to Jim Richards in a JPS BMW M3. So there were good times in that car where you could show whether you were driving all right and whether the car was any good.

But things were starting to change inside the team. George Fury was the lead driver and Glenn Seton was the number two, and I was pretty much number three, but I had to wait for the opportunity.

Fred said that hopefully something would come up. I was around the workshop all the time and working on the cars, and I was willing to do whatever was needed to secure a drive. I was doing a lot of work on their development cars at that time. They had the Nissan Special Vehicles Division and it was evolving into a strong model line-up and we were doing a stack of work on various types of cars. In fact, we created a complete other division of Fred's business, concentrating on road cars and specialty engineering services and that was great knowledge for when I later joined HRT with the HSV connection.

At the end of 1987 Glenn had almost won the championship, Jimmy just pipped him at Oran Park's final round. Then 1988 was a shocking year, as I said. We had a new car – the HR31 – and it was one of the most unreliable and difficult cars ever. It was heavy over the front with a big inline six cylinder engine, and the car was a dog. Glenn was with Anders Oloffson at Bathurst and they completed one lap, while George Fury and I did 17 laps. So the factory Nissan team was out in 17 laps. In hindsight, change was inevitable.

The Ford Sierras were coming on and the BMW M3s were still going well. It was a time when Phillip Morris weren't as happy either, so they pulled money out of us and it was just Nissan Motor Company as the principal sponsor. Ken Potter and Carey Turner from Phillip Morris went to Glenn Seton and they set up their own Sierra team in Peter Jackson colours. There was a lot of disruption, but it's important to remember that, under their own steam, Glenn and Barry had gone out to set up a new team. There was no pushing from anyone inside Gibson Motorsport, it was all about external forces and opportunity. Some of the staff left with them and meanwhile we were busily trying to improve the HR31. And, as I said, it was a genuine dog; it was a really difficult car to get right.

I'd been down in Melbourne for two and a bit years and was pretty hopeful of getting a full-time drive, but Fred never said to me that I was going to replace Glenn. We didn't ever have the discussion. I had a small inkling that there might be an opportunity but I didn't know what Fred was going to do. At that stage Glenn was established as one of the very best in the class and Fred wanted to replace at that level, which pretty much ruled me out. There were only a couple of drivers available at that level – Jim Richards and Allan Grice. Getting Jim Richards was a real coup, but we lost some really good people who went with Glenn. It was a seriously tough time for the team.

I think in my heart of hearts I probably needed another year and the exposure to Jim was probably the thing that helped me to get through that period and to understand it. When he first drove the car at Winton he wasn't any faster than I was – we went to Amaroo Park for testing at the start of 1989, because that was the venue for the first round, and we both did a 52.3. I remember it as clear as day; there was nothing in it in terms of speed for one lap. But Jim was ultra professional in the way he went about things and had a special ability at the time as he did for most of his career. If you gave him another set of tyres and pole position was a 51.9, he would have done a 51.89 to be pole, because that's what he did. I wasn't ready to do that. It was another year on at least.

George was a very good driver, but like me he wasn't quite Jim Richards. In that era George was certainly in the top handful of guys. But Jim just had this incredible natural talent in how hard he drove the car, and that is what people don't understand. I have said it a hundred times, the 'Gentleman Jim' thing is one of the world's great urban myths! I remember Fred saying to him when he joined the team, 'You drive the car as hard as you can drive it – if anything breaks, we'll fix it.'

That was carte blanche, and Richo would drive the wheels off the car. He'd brake harder than anybody else, he'd come in with brake temperatures higher than anybody else, all the shock travels were higher than anybody else, he'd use more kerb – he would just smash over things, he was an animal. He drove it so hard, but that is what it was about. Probably the only other guy I saw in that era who was driving it really hard like that was Win Percy in the HRT car.

This is where people get this whole thing wrong about what the team actually requires from a driver – it is not about keeping the car straight, it is about sorting it out and going fast. Jim was in my opinion the number one driver in the world for touring cars at the time and he was a great bloke. He was so competitive and he just gave it his all, all the time, and for me it was a great learning period. We didn't have data until the end of the following year, so you couldn't layer a lap across another lap and see where you were at to compare your speed trace versus his. What happens with young blokes at that stage of development is that you don't actually know – you might be over-driving it in some spots and under-driving in others. Jimmy was really good at grabbing the right corner emphasis and prioritising the right section – where there was time to be gained: when you had to do a really good job at Hell Corner to get up Mountain

Straight, he'd go and do it. He was on another level, he was just outstanding. He used to say, 'Skaifey, you've just got to think about it!'

To begin with, I don't think I understood just how good he was. Remember, it doesn't matter what car it is, you can only drive it to the limit of its grip and you can only drive it as hard as that car can be driven, so when he first came along he wasn't any faster than George or myself for one lap. We thought he was good but that was about it at that stage. Not that we were downplaying it, but he was complaining about some things on the car that we also were; it wasn't like we were getting any information out of him that we didn't already have, he just consistently drove the wheels off it.

We had some very clever technical people at that time and Jim grew with the car as it evolved. It probably didn't show up until race meetings, but he'd go and do an exceptional job and qualify up the front and whenever Richo was near the front he was bloody hard to beat. He'd put the car in positions that the car shouldn't have been – he drove it absolutely to its maximum.

When he first came along, as I said, the outright speed wasn't unbelievable; what was unbelievable was his ability to drag something extra out of a car at race meetings. He basically went on to win the 1990 championship in the old car; it was a fantastic job because it was nowhere near as good as the Sierra in the day.

Sure I'd hoped that when Glenn left I could have got the drive, but the door was still sort of opening for me and closing for George. Not in an immediate sense, but clearly there was a succession plan that Fred was working on and I was working hard to get a full-time drive. The team ran three cars at certain race meetings that were reasonably cost effective. That was a little bit frustrating for me because it didn't happen immediately, and as a young bloke, clearly without a great deal of patience, it was difficult to hang out for a little while until a full-time gig materialised.

But by the end of 1989 Jim was ultra competitive and we won the Sandown 500 together and we finished in the top three at Bathurst, which was the first of four visits we'd have to that podium together. In 1990 it had become Jim and myself as the factory drivers for the Nissan Motor Company.

By that stage the cars had developed and were fantastic – they were Sierra-beaters at places where it wasn't just about horsepower. Amaroo Park, Winton, Oran Park, Mallala, Lakeside – at those sorts of non-horsepower places that really required good set up and chassis balance. We were a real shot and I was getting closer to Jim all the time.

We were together and against each other lots of times throughout that year and there were plenty of firsts for me. I out-qualified Jim for the first time at Lakeside in 1990 and I thought that day was as good as I had ever gone. As a young bloke you've always got to firstly demonstrate that you're fast, that's the number one item. The second part of that is how you evolve experiencing things and how to use that speed effectively. Jim and I worked very well together, we've got a great relationship even to this day, and we had it from day one. He never lied to me about things that I asked him, and you've got to remember that in those days with no telemetry, no data acquisition, to ask your mate whether he got through that corner flat out, where you're braking for that corner or whatever, was very intrusive and I relied on his honesty. He could have said whatever he liked – but he didn't.

Jim was comfortable in his own skin as a person, and that's the first aspect of how he was able to help a young guy. The second part of it was he was very comfortable that he could drive the cars better than anybody else, and there was a level of security that he always felt from his outright ability. As time went by, when I'd just started to nibble on the door and we were close on the track, that actually made it better for Jim because he had to work harder to beat me and I was certainly working hard to beat him.

But never in all those years did we have a bad word with each other. It was a remarkable relationship, great mates, and I've never met a more intensely competitive person. Learning from him, and eventually getting to a point where I could compete genuinely with him, was pretty special.

With all the resources that were behind me, Fred's team clearly provided a lot of immediate support for me to operate at absolutely the same level as Jim, which was what everyone wanted. Andy Bartley used to say the relationship had a bit of Senna and Prost about it, but it was a little different because we didn't hate each other. It was intense, but there was no aggro about it. We were desperate to beat each other which was fantastic, and that's one of the things that drove the team forward so much. It was kind of funny to find myself 10 years later on the other side of the age ledger, although in fairness Craig was a little more evolved when I joined HRT than I was when I went up against Jim. But I still had to prove myself at HRT the same way I did when I got my break with Gibsons.

Nothing was a given – pole at Sandown and Bathurst in 1987 helped, but I was still the interloper to Lowndes who was entrenched. There were also some difficult personal things with that move, because there were some of our ex-Gibson guys at HRT who we may have fallen out of favour with, whether it was because they wanted to leave or I wanted them to leave.

On the track I clearly had to earn my stripes again. Craig had all the competitive stuff of Jim, all the natural gifts of Jim and we had to go out and compete. It was bloody good even if it felt like I was starting out again.

While some of it felt the same, there were different elements. We knew at that stage that the new car – the GT-R (codenamed R32) – was coming and it was a massive project; there was not a part on the car that was the same as the old car and we'd just got the old car to be really good. We understood the potential because Fred and I were going to Japan quite a lot, so we saw the GT-R over there and we knew what it had. Typical of the Japanese, though, there were a lot of things that happen in their world that just made it all a little bit harder. Because it was a Skyline it had to have an inline 6 cylinder engine where a V6 was clearly better for racing because of the better weight distribution – a V6 was obviously a better option but it had to be an inline six, the same thing that caused us all that drama with the previous model HR31. The Skyline boss had determined only an in-line six was going to be fitted to his pride and joy.

So we were critical of some things immediately, certainly critical of their invoicing because the cost for some of the components was out of control – $18,000 a turbocharger, I remember clearly. That meant we needed to do a lot of parts manufacture ourselves, we couldn't afford to do it any other way. I was so excited by the thought of the new platform we were going to use, but I also knew the workload that was in front of us to develop the GTR – 'Godzilla'.

5

CLIMBING THE PEAK

It was one thing to make it to the top, another to capitalise and to really make it. I knew that with the GT-R I had a great opportunity, even if it meant I eventually had to beat Jim Richards.

As I said earlier, we engineered and built a lot of components and we 'Australianised' the GT-R for 1991 and the car was just fantastic, we basically won everything. There was a lot of conjecture from other manufacturers that we were too dominant and the car was handicapped significantly for the following year. We did a deal with Winfield that was probably the most lucrative motorsport sponsorship in Australian history at that time, and we needed to give them a return on their investment – and both in terms of on and off the track, I think we did. We've already spoken about winning both the Australian Touring Car Championship and the Australian Drivers' Championship on the same day, but we also won Bathurst and with the car in that handicapped configuration – it was a massive effort.

Importantly for me, I was learning heaps and getting better with each race meeting. Fred always had the feeling that driving open-wheel cars improved your skill sets – he was absolutely right. When you drive purpose-built race cars, you can tune more things and you get to a stage where you demand more of the car. I suppose throughout my career that's been one of my trademarks – demanding more of the car and translating that into lap speed.

These cars were, in terms of lap speed, faster than touring cars and as I developed greater technical skills we were able to be more critical of the touring car which further helped its development. It made me feel like the touring car was a taxi – guys like Ross Holder and Andrew Bartley hated me getting back into the touring car and complaining about all its faults.

That was a really good part of my career, partially because I was running the road car business on one side of the factory with two or three guys and that was successful enough to fund most of the open-wheeler effort. I was also learning heaps because in those days there were a few good operators in open-wheel land. I had two guys, Pete Schaefer, who still works at HRT and worked for us for 20 odd years or more, and a young guy, Scott Owen, as well as some mates of mine – Anthony Tratt, Rod Smith, open-wheeler specialist Harry Galloway and Ross Holder from the GT-R program – and a small crew of us that would go away with Dad and Fred also helping when they could. We worked hard on running it cleanly and efficiently which ultimately was successful for us.

I enjoyed those weekends. There wasn't as much politics and there wasn't as much media hype which allowed me to concentrate on driving and working with that group of people as best we could.

That was just at the time when data acquisition was starting. Ross Holder who was, as I mentioned, normally in our Touring Car team also started coming along and we started lifting our professionalism in all areas. We had a ripper time. There was good competition and there were some very good teams with strong funding. Mark Larkham with Mitre 10 was spending a bucket load of money, they were doing an excellent job. He had good people around him: Greg 'Pee Wee' Siddle was running the program and a young Sam Michael, who is now essentially running the technical side of Williams F1, was looking after the engineering.

We were already working hard before the open-wheeler program came on stream, but I can tell you we were just eating, sleeping and breathing motorsport running the two operations side-by-side. I calculated that in 1991 I spent 115 days in a racing car of some form, which was just incredible. Obviously there were no testing restrictions back then.

There were certainly times when there was a risk I could overload on motorsport. Motorsport can be all encompassing, and perhaps it wasn't all that healthy. But you end up getting so caught up in your own little world that sometimes you don't see the forest for the trees.

It was a big thing for me. I'd moved to Melbourne at 19 not knowing anybody, really having to dedicate my life to working hard to get ahead. Five years later, we'd won Bathurst, the Australian Drivers' Championship and the ATCC and we were on the road and going all right . . . but you had to use all your energy, brainpower and effort to get to that point. I wasn't going to blow it by a half effort.

It took sacrifice, and that included my social life and other activities. Sometimes I would have loved to have gone to the footy or to have gone out and had a beer, or my other favourite passion, chasing girls – but I didn't. I wanted to succeed and it was pretty difficult to be a normal bloke. I don't know if I could have worked harder or dedicated more of my energy to making a career in motorsport.

It felt like a real kick in the guts when they changed the rules to what has now become V8 Supercars. For the team at that time, Nissan Motor Company were like friends of ours. Leon Daphne was the managing director – we would be over at his place playing tennis with his wife, Kerrie, and it was great. He was always at our workshop, and we had a great period of time with him but we just couldn't believe it. It was very difficult for a car company that had been so successful to suddenly not be allowed to go racing – it was very strange. The new rules were clearly targeted at creating a Holden and Ford battle; in short, the new race cars had to be based on Australian-built road-going, four-door cars with pushrod V8 engines – Nissan didn't have one of those. In fact, no-one other than Ford or Holden did, so it was quite clear what the agenda was, and that was a Ford and Holden only affair.

It wasn't until really late in 1992, after we'd won Bathurst, that we could seriously start to think about what 1993 was going to look like . . . we didn't even know what sort of car we were going to drive. I went to Europe and did a couple of F3000 races and in the midst of all the changeover we basically grabbed Bob Forbes' old Commodore to get ourselves going. But it wasn't a great time, especially knowing we'd have to start from scratch.

A lot of people were saying, 'That team is only any good because it's running Nissan GT-Rs,' so we were pretty motivated to prove them wrong. There was also some thinking that 'Mark is only winning because he's driving the best car' – all the normal knocker mentality.

So we had that old Commodore and we started buying bits from other teams and suppliers just to get it ready in time to go testing. We only got it all together after rushing to build two fresh cars for Richo and me, which is why the Amaroo Park podium at round one was so satisfying. We had started later than everyone else, we had no intellectual property to draw on and the car was just pieced together, and the knockers said we couldn't do it – it was *very* satisfying.

We struggled through developing the cars for the rest of 1993, gradually building the Commodore that we wanted and we came out in 1994 and won the championship, but then slipped a little bit in 1995 as things began to get tough for the team in terms of replacing Winfield as the major sponsor. This time it wasn't CAMS that got us, it was the Australian government when it banned sponsorship from tobacco companies. Looking back we probably didn't handle it the right way. I remember trying to do a lot of it myself but I was only 28 and still learning. We went to a new factory and we did a huge amount of things to show potential sponsors that we had all the infrastructure required and that we were the best team. But the cost base was so high we had to use our capital to go racing the next year.

So it was a white car at the start of 1996 with no major sponsor. We had a couple of commitments from corporates that didn't materialise and those sort of things were very disappointing. The people handling the Sega sponsorship failed to make their final payments and as a result we had to scale the team back massively. It was a time in our lives when, again, I probably worked harder than I'd worked for a long time, and I also thought that, within that period, I probably learnt more about motorsport than at any other time in my life.

It was a cruel period of time. I mean, we went from 35 people to less than 10 and we were multi-tasking and doing a bit of everything. I now realised the marketing department was as critical as the engineering, and the commercial realities of the sport and sponsorship had hit hard.

6

THE BEST OF TIMES AND THE WORST OF TIMES

I WAS WORRIED about my future in 1996, but for the two previous years I'd been approached by John Crennan (Crenno) and Tom Walkinshaw who wanted me to come across to HRT. So I always thought there might have been a safety net there for me. That's how it turned out, but it didn't mean we were just going to give up on Gibsons.

We did everything humanly possible to keep that team running at the front, but when it became obvious there was nothing more we could do, I sat down with Crenno. We agreed early in 1997, that with Brock retiring at the end of that season we'd run a changeover program.

If I'd gone there in 1995 we may have won another championship because clearly in 1996 their cars were so much better than anything else. By the time I got there for Bathurst in 1997 I had to really make sure that I took the opportunity of being with Peter and doing a good job.

Pole positions at Sandown and Bathurst were fantastic, but importantly I fitted in with the team. There were a lot of ex-Gibson faces there, but there was a lot of conjecture about whether I would or wouldn't settle in, and only time would tell. It all worked out even though it was a nervous period. Sometimes you don't know what the next phase of your career will look like; that was certainly one of those times for me.

It was also a time where you have to have a bit of faith. When I went there I was fast enough, but I probably wasn't treating the car properly as a race car. I was qualifying really well yet I ended up finishing third in the 1998 championship. In 1999 we won more rounds and more races than anyone else and still finished third. There were double points for certain rounds and that hurt me with bad results at Clipsal and the Queensland 500, which had replaced the Sandown 500.

For me, it was important to beat Craig in 2000. When it was obvious he was leaving the team, it was critical that we maintained car number one, and that meant I had to win, and there was plenty of pressure to make sure we did that. The cars were great and we were driving the cars really well. Competition between us was fierce but it was a really, really good time for the team.

At that stage, I felt like I had total support from the team and things were very good. 2000, 2001 and 2002 will go down as my best memories of motor racing without the drama of all the motorsport business aspects – I was purely a race driver. It was a very well structured and sound business that ran the race team. John Crennan, Jeff Grech and all the technical and engineering guys were outstanding – definitely the best team in the country.

It was all about momentum, and we'd been picking it up since I went to HRT – the 2000 title was the culmination of that. Rob Starr came across to work on my car that year and that worked immediately. Richard Hollway for continuity was looking after everything from an engineering standpoint, and we had a really good handle on what made the cars work. Garth Tander was an emerging driver, and in 2000 he was the one I had to beat rather than Craig, who was a bit up and down over the season.

Then it just got bigger. 2001 was better than 2000, and then 2002 was an improvement again in terms of results. I had four round wins, including Bathurst with Tony Longhurst in 2001, and won the title from Russell Ingall. But 2002 was amazing: we won the opening five rounds, but it should have been six in a row and then ultimately seven. I love the history of this sport, and I am acutely aware of records. It is one of the things that makes it all special – and you know from earlier in the book that missing that round win in Perth still winds me up.

My five round wins in a row equalled Allan Moffat in 1977, but in 1985 Jim had six wins in a row on his way to the championship – I would love to have equalled that record and then had a push at beating it at the next round.

As I said before, 2002 was clearly a career-defining year – our operation was on top of the world. We knew some changes were coming in at the end of the year, some really big engineering changes under the Project Blueprint program, but we were confident we'd be OK. Then it all started to come apart as TWR's (which owned HRT) financial issues began to strike us.

But there was more to it than just TWR's dramas. Ford was effectively given a leg-up by Project Blueprint and AVESCO (Australian Vee Eight Supercar Company) changed the points scoring system to reward consistency over race wins, and the way that our dominance had been used by rivals to try to level the playing field made a big difference to the way we went into 2003. So we had two major things – when Blueprint came in, we had to change the front suspension layout plus other technical aspects, and we were in the process of changing the engine to the new Aurora specification. The new engine was totally different – not one component was the same as the older Chev-based spec – and as the official factory team we were compelled to use the latest GM/Holden units.

In 2003, the best win for Holden Racing Team was Clipsal 500, the first time we rolled that VY-spec car out. There's no way in the world that in all that change and with all that drama you could expect to get it all done and go and win one of the most difficult races of the year.

Even though they were tough times, I felt pretty positive about the future. The deal was done for me to buy the team quite early, but it wasn't handed over until June. You wouldn't believe some of the names that were sniffing around at the time, and I honestly believed we could retain the HRT culture because the staff were now stable and that was a huge part of the DNA. But again, you also wouldn't believe the crap I read about it all. If I'd had to read one more time that I only paid a dollar for the team and we were losing key personnel, I would have gone off my brain!

In hindsight it affected me a lot. I wanted to leave Jeff Grech alone to run Holden Motorsport (HMS), and working with Crenno I wanted to try to ensure that the activity and the race relations connectivity with HSV was as strong as it had ever been. I wanted the guys in the workshop to feel like things hadn't really changed. I worked very hard on not coming in and turning it upside down. So that part of it was difficult. There were great times in that year, though – we won the Sandown 500 and the Clipsal 500 and we were in with a big chance to go well at Bathurst until the door came open and the officials forced us to pit to tape it closed late in the race.

We were still in the running for the title at the final round even though it was only a slim chance, and that's when one of the worst incidents of my life happened. Russell Ingall's actions will live with me forever. There's a couple of things about that incident that are important to clarify. I was trying to win the series and if I could catch and pass Murphy I was going to finish second overall for the year. When I got to Ingall he was holding me up, which was just ridiculous. From a racing standpoint, I've always prided myself on being a hard but fair racer, so when I got up the inside of him at turn nine and took that position, he forced me off the road after the corner was finished when driving in a straight line, which is clearly not how we play the game. You'd think that elite-level drivers should be able to drive in a straight line without running into each other!

I'd never been so angry in my life and even to this day I get angry just thinking about it. Seriously, if he pulled up I would have dragged him out of the car and belted him because he deserved it. I wanted to express my anger, so I waited for him, but he pitted – not that I knew it then, but he gave my pit crew the bird as he drove by the team in pit lane – and he seemed to take an eternity to make it back to me. I offloaded my helmet and waited, and when he finally appeared I was well and truly steaming and I visually let him know what I thought. When he pointed his car at me, that just made it worse. The TV footage and the photos make me look like some kind of mad man and to a certain degree I am embarrassed by the whole affair, but I was so angry. For me, it was the most unsportsmanlike thing I'd ever seen.

When I made it back to the pits I wanted to continue the argument, so I stormed into his pits looking for a fight with someone . . . it wasn't a pretty look.

What I was mostly surprised about was when Peter Hanenberger – Holden's boss at the time – saw me afterwards, because I thought I was going to get a full-on grilling from the boss, but he just came up and gave me a hug and said, 'Mark, you only react like that when it means so much to you,' and he was in tears as he made those comments. I felt the level of support was fantastic at the highest levels of Holden. Peter and his wife, Ingrid, always gave me solid, loyal support. They remain good friends to this day.

It was dubbed 'Race Rage' by the tabloids, and in hindsight I wish I'd handled it differently. But it did matter to me – the result of the weekend mattered, and the rights and wrongs of what went on mattered too. In my view, it was no coincidence that it was Ingall's teammate – Ambrose – who was leading the championship at the time, but at least the incident got more media coverage than Ford's first title since HRT started its run in 1998.

So 2003 was a year where there was a lot of change. We were running two engine programs side-by-side and then from 2004 we had to run the new engine which was still underdeveloped. Our installed power package was 30 or 40 horsepower down. But understandably, we were the factory team and as I said before we had to run the Holden Motorsport engine, which had previously been called the Aurora. Not the greatest year for HRT!

2005 was clearly a much better year. We were back on the road to having the engine problems fixed, we were second at Sandown after a front splitter failure and a fantastic wet weather race with Lowndes. We were able to win Bathurst on Todd's birthday – it was probably one of my best drives ever up there too. Walkinshaw was coming back in to do a management agreement with the team and by 2006 he had taken over HMS, purchasing the business from Holden and supplying us with all the components to go racing, as well as engineering and R&D services.

There were some development items that we were working on in that period that made the cars better. 2006 was one of my better years. I equalled Peter Brock's record with a round win in New Zealand and went on to win a stack of races but for one reason or another wasn't able to turn them into any more round wins – the reverse grid system turned some of the weekends into lotteries and that cost us. In Perth, for example, we qualified on pole and won two of the three races but lost the overall win because of the results in the reverse grid race. We won the final reverse grid race ever from the back of the grid – I had to battle with Lowndes near the end of it and it was one of my best drives of my career, but even that didn't get me across the line for the weekend's overall win.

We started that year well, though. At Clipsal we outqualified everyone by 0.4 of a second and were absolutely super strong in the races but I crashed at turn eight, one of the biggest crashes in my life. The car was fixed overnight and it was a ripper, we came all the way from the back, got right through to eighth or ninth and we were going to finish in the top five, and we crashed again at the same spot (turn eight) with Murphy. As the year went on, there were so many places where we went really well.

At Bathurst I felt on top of my game and got pole position even though we were out without even completing a lap. There were a heap of those sorts of races where we did a really good job, but it wasn't as satisfying because as a complete season we didn't win.

Then we rolled into 2007 and that was also a really good year in terms of speed and we were able to break Brock's long-standing round win record at Eastern Creek. I remember we had a very big pre-season briefing at the workshop and basically the guys thought only Tander, Lowndes or I could win the title, because even though the pointscore favoured consistency, it was less so than previous seasons and you had to win the races again. There were great times in 2007.

My final win at Phillip Island in 2008 was pretty special, quite emotional. Not that I thought at the time that it would be my last win, and perhaps even to this day it won't be if I can keep coming back for the endurance races. Many people had written us off, but I did my job that day. I said then and I'll say it again – Garth did the best job on the day; he drove very, very well. Getting back to the pits on slick tyres in that race was important, but I didn't win that race – my input was that I didn't lose it. It was important for Garth to go and pass Whincup late in the race, so I had no problem with Garth taking most of the kudos for that win; that's just how life is. At the time it was good just to bounce back and get some runs on the board leading into Bathurst. I think it meant a lot to all of us at the time.

After that, Bathurst was just horrible, and that was perhaps when what was going on in my head started to crystallise. As a race driver you always know there's a finite span to your career – it will come to an end at some point. I knew it was time, so a couple of weeks later after the Indy race meeting, I announced my retirement from full-time racing – not racing in totality, just full-time. At that stage I was still the owner of HRT, but I had plans for that too that took a little while to become public.

I had three rounds for a farewell tour, and one of those was in Bahrain. So that left Symmons Plains and Oran Park, fittingly also at that track's last ever round of the championship. I have so many good memories of Oran Park and it's a track I always enjoyed. Perhaps I, like many, had dreamed of a final round win, but that was unlikely when all the circumstances came to play. The car simply wasn't good enough, and even though I put my heart and soul into it there was nothing I could really do.

It couldn't have been a worse lead-up to that final race and I remember with all the hype and all the activity that there was no other scenario for me other than pressing on with it. The car was a shit-box in qualifying, really bad, I think I qualified 16th. The pitstop incident with Mark Winterbottom, where he came out into the fast lane into the side of my car, was just unbelievable, and that put me back. And then Michael Patrizi decided he was going to smash into the back of me coming up to the bridge in the next race – guys like that just amaze me, pointless contact on the first lap and it ruins the race. That made two shockers with just one final race to run on Sunday afternoon.

I enjoyed that last race, although I still made a couple of little mistakes and should have done a better job. I would have loved to have rounded up Ingall to make it into the top 10, but I had damaged a tyre when I locked up while passing someone 10 laps prior and I was battling just to stay in 12th.

I was in tears on the warm-up lap after seeing Toni and Mitch on the grid, and it was incredibly difficult to compose myself for the start. But in the end, if you put it into context, you're just a sports person who has done hundreds of races and I wanted to go and do a reasonable job in my final event, which fortunately I was able to do.

To me, that was close to the real Mark Skaife, just one last time.

7

THE GOOD AND THE BAD

Most of my career I've had to deal with as much negative press as I have positive. Most of the time it hasn't really bothered me even if I haven't liked what has been said – in that sense I've always been happy to cop what I rate as fair criticism – in terms of the media, I mean stories that have been well researched and tell both sides.

Any high-profile sporting or business person has to accept that there will be people who'll criticise and judge what they're doing. But what I've always felt strongly about is when something is clearly wrong or when it's been misreported. Sometimes there's been a real judgment error in terms of how people have assessed what I've been doing, and occasionally some have been on the receiving end of some mischievous information. I've never agreed with people who have misused the media for political advantage. It bothers me.

In recent times, there have been plenty of one sided stories doing the rounds, and we'll get to those later, but it isn't a new part of my life. I guess I had to learn to deal with it quite early in my career, especially with the rumours about Glenn Seton back in the 1980s. I was accused of all sorts of mischief back then – that I somehow forced him out of the team.

There was not one semblance of fact in any of that. Actually, it was almost the total opposite. Glenn and his dad, Barry, were close with Ken Potter and Carey Turner from Philip Morris, and they did a deal to run a Ford Sierra team in Peter Jackson colours. I was disappointed in them doing that, and the way they went about it, to the point where we had a real rift between us for a while. I was upset from an ethical standpoint. Fred certainly told me the ins and outs of what had taken place and I felt like it wasn't upfront. It commercially affected the team that I was with and from a technical standpoint it had an impact too.

So I looked at it and thought it just didn't seem very right. When I first came to Melbourne I was living with the Setons and then went and got my own place, so we were pretty close before that happened. Then for a fair while it wasn't very nice between us because I struggled with what had taken place. But life moves on and in reality we were never going to carry that on forever because we've been such good friends for so many years.

It wasn't like people suggested at the time. I didn't jump over his body to steal the drive; in fact, Fred went out and got

Jim Richards to replace him and that was the right thing to do. The team needed a superstar to replace Glenn. Jim was at the head of the list of available drivers and the deal was done. I think they looked at Allan Grice as well, so I wasn't much chance of getting the drive. In my eyes, while it delayed my elite level drive a little, it was good for me overall. I was exposed to Jim Richards, who was the best touring car driver in the world at the time. I learned so much from him and I got to benchmark myself against the very best.

Fred and I had some pretty heated discussions about what I was actually doing. I was working very hard for the race team and for the Special Vehicles department at that point and I thought I deserved a little more back. I was doing a bit of test driving but I was very eager to get to the highest level and race the cars in the championship. So although I had long distance endurance drives, I felt like I was treading water a bit and patience has never been a real forte of mine, so I wasn't happy about not getting some of the opportunities that I thought should have come my way. Fred explained that there was a lot of work going on in the background so I was happy with that and I was happy with the amount of involvement I was having, but I wasn't happy that I couldn't drive at that level straight away. I could see the guys like Neil Crompton and Tony Longhurst and Glenn who were getting some opportunities and it was pretty hard to wait.

So contrary to what some were misreporting, there was never any Mark Skaife pushing Glenn Seton out. His leaving didn't open doors, it wasn't done because he didn't like working with me – it was purely a commercial decision by Glenn to set up what became a pretty successful race team of his own.

At the time it was announced Glenn was leaving, I think it was pretty easy for media and fans to turn around and blame me, but it was wrong. I didn't go home and punch walls when I was reading all that shit, but I do remember being angered by it. Stuff like that has always affected me because I want to set the record straight, but you can't always do that. I've often picked up the phone to a journalist to say 'what's going on?' I don't think it's healthy for anyone to have the wrong information out there. That time was my first real exposure to negative media and I remember it very clearly; I also learned a lot about dealing with people and the media through those circumstances.

Ten years later, I couldn't believe I had to go through the same crap with Lowndes. When I went to HRT, Craig was the golden boy. There were a lot of ex-Gibson people at HRT and the dynamic was different when I went there, and not just because of Lowndes. Having previously managed Gibsons, I went into HRT as just a driver and it took me a while to form new relationships with a lot of those guys. They could see how eager I was to drive a car and to get the best out of it – they knew I'd give it my all.

Those who knew me understood what my approach would be like, and that from a competition point of view there was never any doubt that I suited the HRT ethos. The open question at the time was how was I going to fit in and how was the team atmosphere going to change with me, rather than, say, a Greg Murphy, who'd previously driven for the team and had been a chance to replace Brock.

Even though John Crennan came to me, there was a lot of conjecture about whether it was going to be me or

Murphy with Lowndes in 1998, and in the end they went with me, after I'd run the endurance races with Brock at the end of '97.

In 1998 Lowndes out-raced me, fair and square. We out-qualified him with five poles in a row at one stage, so our speed was good, but it was my first exposure to Bridgestone tyres and I concentrated too much on what the car was like for speed and we probably didn't make a good enough race car. By the end of 1998 Lowndes and I joined up in the VT together and we put it on pole at Bathurst. We should have won that Bathurst too, so things were gelling pretty well.

Then 1999 was a cracker year for me. We won more races than anybody else but didn't win the series. My relationships with the team and other key people were going really well too. I was doing a lot of work for HSV with Crenno and I was working hard in the workshop. While we were probably a little unlucky in 1999, in 2000 we did a really good job and won the series. Once we unlocked what was required in terms of consistency, it all started to come together for me. Rob Starr played a big part for me in 2000 after he was on Craig's car in 1999, and I think Craig felt like there was some support going my way rather than his.

I'm absolutely 100 per cent sure, though, that at no stage was there any intention to try to usurp Craig. It was all about me doing the very best job I could. Of course, I wanted the best resources and the guys around me – who wouldn't? But I still had to do the job in the car, and with all that happening we were able to go and win the series. This type of thing happens in every race team – every driver is demanding the good guys and the good gear.

So there was a lot of the conjecture about Lowndes. John Crennan's probably got a slightly different view of that because he said from day one that Craig was quite taken aback by how much effort I was putting in, but I don't think that had anything to do with Craig leaving the team. I suppose you'll have to wait for Craig's book to find out the answer to that.

My role in the team was to win races, to do the very best I could. That's a selfish thing in one way but it's also a team thing in another way, and how Craig coped with that was up to him. It was easy for people to be very simplistic about what was a complex situation, and because Craig went to Ford the emotions were quite high at the time.

From where I sat, it looked as if Craig had started to pull away from the team well before he announced or even decided he was going to leave. He was clearly unhappy – it was obvious to pretty much everyone in the team. It made sense that they'd look to me for some answers on the track.

There were some leaks about Craig leaving and it all got out of control. But I was staying and they had to give me the support I needed to win the title; not that anything was done to stop Craig winning. If HRT was going to win, you would rather it was with the driver who was staying over the one leaving. I know that both John Crennan and Tom Walkinshaw wanted to keep Craig, but once it was obvious what was happening there was nothing more they could do.

It worked out well for both Craig and me. If he'd stayed with the team there's no doubt he would have had more race wins than he did with Ford, but from a brand perspective it was a pretty good outcome. He effectively became Ford's front man and I actually think it raised the profile of the sport. It made it a Skaife versus Lowndes, Holden versus Ford battle in the style of Brock versus Moffat or Brock versus Johnson. So I actually think that from a helicopter view it did everybody a bit of good and I think if he had his time again, he'd probably make the same move. Whether he went to the right team and did the right things within the Ford camp is another thing altogether, but again that had nothing to do with me.

People knew that I'd always be forceful in making sure that the truth was preserved and if there was a rival opinion on something that I didn't think was fair or justified, then I certainly would have pushed back.

Motor racing is not an industry with a lot of secrets. People tell you things like, 'This bloke's been saying that,' or 'He's been doing this,' or 'This sponsor wants to move from here to there,' or whatever – you just don't keep secrets for long once a couple of people know what is happening. Pit lane is just a mongrel of a place and it's a lot about the competition and the ferocity of it, and in some weird way I think that is culturally essential. It's quite a difficult thing to explain, especially when it is you who is in the firing line, but there's a lot more 'playing of the man' in this sport than in most others.

Our game is harder to keep in the media because once the season is on we don't compete every week; sometimes we have three weeks off and other times it's four or two. So I actually like some controversy hitting the papers because it keeps the brand and the sport going from a momentum standpoint. It's about rhythm and regular press. In cricket there is a huge amount of personal sledging and drama. In

AFL or NRL, blokes on the field are genuinely belting each other to upset a rival and they say stuff to each other and all that ugliness gets played out during the course of the game.

Our ugliness spreads from blokes who are sitting in cars with helmets on that run into each other or do bad things in terms of gamesmanship. Then that spreads through the pit lane to other combatants and to other people. When you're out of the car, all the sporting part's gone and it can be a full-on wildfire – if there's drama between teams, between drivers, between the administration of the sport and some team and *whoof*, up it goes. It can just blow up.

A team would do anything to have the fastest car and some have stepped beyond the regulations and will then push against the administration to explain that the car was within the rules. That is not a refined process and it's not necessarily nice; it's also not necessarily a legally well-handled protest. It can be Larry Perkins in pit-lane telling the chief technical director that he's a useless wanker, or more severe and public than that.

Where we get it wrong as a sport is how we handle that sort of thing and it builds the aggro and often has the makings of an implosion. Whatever the issue is, whether it's judicial or technical, it tends to just get wound up in this massive drama all the time and that's the culture of the game and you're never going to change that. It's endemic and a lot of it is integral to the competition and the severity of competing at the highest level.

I simply cannot stand it when it becomes all about self interest over the best interests of the sport. I've seen some fairly pointless slanging matches which are not positive, and those involved often forget we're actually in this game together. Yes, we all want to win, but at what cost to the sport?

For one reason or another, I haven't always been able to tell everyone exactly what is going on. Some things are private – other things may be commercial in confidence. What has always amazed me is how certain journalists just don't bother ringing to check something. I don't know why that is – I've always tried to be open with people, but some people just see me a different way.

That kind of started early in the Gibson days. I think there were times the team's aspirations of professionalism and the way that we operated was slightly aloof and maybe people felt less comfortable to come and talk or 'encroach' on our area. For us, though, we were just super-serious about going racing. I would have my race face on because I needed to do a job, and there were also times when I was not only driving the touring cars but driving the openwheeler on the same weekend. I didn't have time to sit around in between races and do bugger-all. I was out of one car, do a debrief and then drive the other car, do the same thing. It meant I was really consumed by the racing and I think that the blend of my personal endeavours and the team's overall functioning created an aura where people felt we were not easy to access, and some people didn't feel very comfortable dealing with us.

There were even silly things that built on that perception. We were the first ones to bring a motor-home to the track, but it wasn't to build a barrier, as our critics suggested.

We did it because by the time we finished work and made it back to a hotel we could never get dinner. We stayed in some fairly ordinary spots in Australia. So we actually organised our own people to come and cook for the guys at the right time – it was cost effective and it kept the team together.

There were times when I'd go back to the motor-home to have lunch or to have a shower before another race or something. It did demonstrate that we were out of the normal picture a little bit. We didn't purposely go out to make our area a sanctuary, but the nature of what we were trying to do just pushed us that way. But at the same time you could walk into Brock's garage and they were less concerned about the look and how professional they appeared – everything was much more of a garage mentality rather than an exhibition. Now every team has a motorhome or catering area to look after the entire team, so we were really just raising the bar.

I can understand how people took the view we were trying to alienate them, but it wasn't deliberate. The GT-R was a polarising car in this country – it had so much untapped capability.

I've never seen anything before or since in motorsport that has created such opinion and almost professional jealousy from everyone else. A lot of other aspects as to how we operated at the time, like scrambling radios, 100 per cent came from Fred being able to talk to me and Jim about how much boost the car was running and we genuinely didn't want anyone to know. There were lots of days when we'd run the car with less boost and we'd have to drive the wheels off the thing to make it go all right, because Fred sometimes didn't want to show the car off for what it really was. He was already understanding the industry's reaction to the car and was forecasting further handicapping.

In the end we had massive penalties, like a 1500 kg minimum weight and our boost was limited – the whole thing was just a total nightmare for the team to preserve the GT-R's winning credentials or capability. We had the biggest sponsorship deal in pit lane with Rothmans and Nissan Motor Company was bringing a lot of money in too, so it was a high stakes game of making sure that we did a good job.

I did start to protect myself a bit, and there has been a public and private Mark Skaife, although I think as time has gone by they have merged a bit. I was very much my own person away from the game and very much a spokesman for either a car company or a sponsor, or a driver desperate to make his way in the sport. Often those things don't necessarily go together and are difficult to manage.

I used to go to a race meeting to drive the race car, and there were all these other expectations on me in the way that people looked at and judged me. I didn't care too much, and that came a lot from the purity of me wanting to drive a race car versus all the other things I should have been doing – like signing autographs or what others have perceived I should have been doing. First and foremost my job and my desire was to win races. If there were times I needed to put more time and effort into that, then so be it. It wasn't me purposely being cranky or not being available for media or saying, 'Sorry I can't sign that autograph mate, I'm about to get in the car and qualify.' None of that's been personal – it's about the absolute objective of going and driving a car and remaining focused.

I wasn't into game playing, so when we were talking in 2001 and 2002 about racing parity between Holden and Ford, I was absolutely certain, as I am to this day, that there was no issue. We were doing a good job and the Ford teams weren't – it was that simple.

Fred Gibson came from nothing in Ford-land and he put Craig Lowndes in a second-hand Stone Brothers Falcon and rolled out at the Clipsal 500 in 2001 as the lead Ford, and that was a very clear indicator to me as to how poorly the other Ford teams were travelling. If you can tell me the other Ford blokes were doing a good job when that can happen, you simply can't know what is going on. I thought that the Gibson/Lowndes thing was absolutely the team that was coming to challenge us. I knew the quality of the people they had behind them and I knew Craig's ability, and I thought rock solid that they were the outfit that were going to give us the most trouble – and they'd come from nowhere.

But then Marcos Ambrose came along and he gave Stone Brothers purpose and direction. He had ability and raw speed and he gave the team something extra. This game is all about speed; it's not about whether the cars finish or whatever. If you're not fast, go home. What they saw with Marcos was absolute raw speed, absolute commitment and driving a car at a level that they hadn't seen for a while. Every car is beautiful if you drive it at 8/10ths – if you're not complaining about what the car's like, you're obviously not driving it hard enough.

You can go out there tomorrow at a practice session at Phillip Island or Bathurst and pick six or eight blokes who are just driving the car fantastically with a massive level of commitment. You can see it in the way the car moves around in the fast sections – perhaps even how brave they are. You watch Lowndes sometimes and you think, 'Wow, he is trying hard,' and it's great. It looks like you are right on the edge of crashing, which is how it has got to be. As soon as I saw Ambrose I said to our guys, this young bloke is seriously fast.

He was using every little bit of road, every skerrick of braking room. And the Stone Brothers team moved with him. He went off the track in practice because he was searching for the limits and that is how you have to find it: overstep and then come back. You don't necessarily have to crash to find the limit; what you'd normally do is find three or four times in the day that you've arrived somewhere under brakes and put your foot on the brake a bit deep and you run wide. That's what normally happens and most people don't see that, but you keep pushing until you find the limit with your car on that day.

You get signals back before you actually leave the road and you vary how hard you push depending on the circuit and the level of risk. At a simple circuit like Winton, if you fire into the sweeper too fast you go off the road, but at Bathurst going too far can have pretty severe consequences, so finding the limit there is a bigger risk, but it is also more rewarding. These are the tracks I love, the ones with consequences, as Brock used to say. You don't want to damage the car but you do want to push it to its limits.

I see some of the young guys actually drive purposely for the fence in those second gear corners, because it's easy to look committed in the slow corners – you can drive it up to the fence and rub it but you might as well just park it; it is just crap. If it is somewhere fast and you give the mirror a bump then you are seriously committed – Ambrose was like that and that's why he's doing so well in NASCAR these days. It was a great battle we had and I really enjoyed it.

Ambrose came along, and I saw immediately that this kid was trying hard. I watched the body language of him driving it and knew he was definitely going to lead them down a path where they were going to go better. And then you started responding to the level. That's what I did at Gibsons – we were driving a car so hard that we were driving the wheels off it. As I've mentioned, Fred used to say, 'Just drive it as hard as you possibly can – we'll fix the car.' And it's a great lesson. It's like a Sebastian Vettel in Formula One. You grab a kid like him, arrow him in a shit-box, he drives it at 11/10s, he pops out at the end with some good results and he's demanding of the car. He'll come back and say, 'This isn't good enough and that's not good enough,' a big list of things. He'll say, 'You better fix those, boys.' All of sudden you're into it. And that's exactly what Marcos did at that time.

So it was interesting, and if you just apply the two lines of thinking: Craig Lowndes in a brand new team can come out and be the lead Ford in his first race, and a kid who's never driven a touring car comes along in a Stone Brothers car and wins pole in his first race. Do you reckon the rest of the Ford teams were troubled by these two new boys on the block? I'd say yes!

Even before Project Blueprint came into play, Ambrose and Stone Brothers had unlocked something in the Falcon that others hadn't found. At Sandown in the final race with the AU Falcon, Ambrose dominated. I had to go to the back of the grid and I finished second in that race. He won the race and our lap times were exactly the same for the whole race – and that was at the peak of HRT. In fact, I drove around behind Jason Bright for a while because he was trying to beat Murphy for the second in the series. The Falcon was absolutely competitive before Project Blueprint came into play and that's why I believe Blueprint was so hard on the Holden teams – we were punished for doing a good job, not for having a genuine car advantage.

So while people thought I was lying at the time to protect our position, I believed in what I was saying. As I've mentioned, I'm genuinely proud of the fact that I've always played with a straight bat and even in the last couple of years, I certainly wasn't lying to people as to what was going on. I used to say to my wife Toni or 'Ned' – my manager Craig Kelly – that I'm just not going to lead people up the wrong path. I'm not going to tell people the wrong thing. If someone asks me something that I don't want to answer, I'll just say, 'I'm not going to answer it.'

It was hard not to correct stuff and get people on the right page about what was really going on, but a lot of it was confidential legal stuff that you just can't do anything about. Other parts were commercial-in-confidence and it would be breaching agreements to deal with some of it, so I was restrained about a lot of what I wanted to say. With certain journos at that time you could help their understanding, but others were a waste of time. I could do it with guys like Peter McKay from *The Sydney Morning Herald*, Paul Gover from News Limited, Michael Lynch from *The Age*, Bruce Newton from *Wheels Magazine* among other publications, and Phil Branagan from *Motorsport News*, because they were concerned about being right, not just having a good story. Clever journalists would say, 'Mark, this is what I think is going on – am I OK to go with that?' So they weren't really asking me, they were trying to get the right read and effectively rolling out what they thought, and as long as it wasn't too far away from reality, I let them go.

Others, though, were just way off. There was one article in the *Herald Sun* around my retirement that was so far from being correct it was just ridiculous. There was a picture of a house or 'mansion' they said we'd lost before moving into an apartment, and it was actually the house that we were living in at the time. This was a case of certain people misleading a journalist. I knew who was feeding them and I knew why, and I just had to have patience.

I suppose in general my rapport with the media has been good overall. You sometimes have to accept the good with the bad, as long as over the long haul the correct messages are relayed; that is, that the public receive accurate information. Clearly the media messages have an impact on the motorsport fan base and although our Holden (and, previously, Nissan) fans are always loyal, the Ford fans could be pretty harsh. On a positive note, one of the great things about those last three rounds in 2008 was how many Ford fans came up to me. It was truly flattering, and to me it showed that while a lot of people following the sport are colour blind, there are a lot of people who really understand what's going on.

What happens with me is that there is an intensity to beat the opposition in the media, to beat them with marketing, to beat them on the track and in every aspect of the sport. You're not going to be liked if you don't let some bloke into your hospitality area with the wrong T-shirt, and we've done that. There have been people who think they can arrive at an HRT hospitality suite wearing a Ford jacket – no way! That level of real mongrel in me waned a little bit so you probably do let people in a little more, but you'd let them know you thought they were wrong to do it.

Glenn Seton is a seriously nice bloke, but that mongrel Mark Skaife didn't get rid of him. Craig Lowndes is a really good bloke too, and again I played no part in his departure from Holden. The GT-R was a dominant car, but we didn't deserve to be treated the way we were – Jim didn't make those comments on the Bathurst podium without reason. HRT was the dominant team of the early-2000s, but it wasn't because the parity system wasn't working, it was because the Ford teams weren't doing a good enough job. But that doesn't make good headlines.

I always felt like it was easy to paint me as the devil; perhaps I've got a personality that can rub people the wrong way. I've certainly learned that a lot of journalists don't like being told they've got it wrong, and I did that on many occasions. Even today when I've stopped full-time racing they keep going on – in the lead-up to Bathurst in 2009 I read how some people were saying I was compromised, that I'd learned things while working with the Seven Network that as expert commentator would allow me to make the Sprint Gas Commodore better, and that I was stretched too thin with the Car of the Future and other things . . . it was a crap story and nothing more than mischief. Again, though, it showed there were a bunch of people who just don't and never have understood what makes me tick.

Perhaps if I was able to let a sleeping dog lie, I wouldn't have reacted so strongly. But that was never going to happen.

As a sportsman you only have X amount of fuel in the tank and by the time you get towards the end of your career, the energy feels a bit lower and it has a cough and a splutter every now and then. You don't have the consistent level of intensity that you might have had in the past, and that was how it began to feel in 2008.

You need to enjoy what you're doing, and you need to have enough energy and motivation to take it that little bit further. Can you lift again for it? Can you generate enough enthusiasm and commitment? There were times in my last year of full-time racing when I was very happy – if you can out-qualify and beat Garth Tander at his home track in Perth, then you're obviously going all right. But I didn't consistently have that feeling: I didn't actually have the drive to want to be fitter, to want to be at the workshop as long or as late.

There were certainly times in 2007 and 2008 that I was upset in terms of the cars and their speed and reliability, but it was more than that. It was about the pure enjoyment of racing, the love of wanting to be out there and doing it, and that was fading. Footballers talk about the recovery from games being a factor in their retirement; that as they get older it takes longer mentally and physically to get up again. There was a little bit of that. As the sport continues to grow and gets more competitive the threshold age is certainly going to decrease.

Sometimes it was more enjoyable for me to do a board presentation to find a new couple of million dollar sponsorships than hanging around at the gym getting ready for the season. No one can change that for you; that is just a natural thing. I know it will sound trite, but I also wanted to spend time with my family, with Mitch and my two girls, Mia and Tilly. I even remember driving to the track sometimes on a Saturday morning wondering what they were doing . . . or I wished they were with me or I was there.

I'd never had those feelings in my life before. I'd never headed off to the track without my head being filled with ideas and thoughts about how to make the cars faster, or thinking about how I was going to put it on pole or a way of beating the other blokes.

Even at the end of 1999 when Belinda, my ex-wife, and I were separating, or at the end of 2002 or the start of 2003 when the team was up in arms, or 1995 when the cigarette sponsorship money was stopping, I was able to keep my focus on the task. It was what I lived for, and if you ask Fred Gibson one of the things that he was always blown away by was that I was able to jump in the car and drive and operate at a level that no one else could, even with all that shit running around in my life. That is when you are 100 per cent committed in race driver land, and when you start thinking about other things the signs are getting quite obvious and the commitment wanes.

That was always a pretty good barometer for me. And that's what I said when I retired. I wasn't enjoying it as much, and as a consequence of not enjoying and not getting the best from myself, it wasn't the real Mark Skaife in the car and that was really the indicator for me not to do it any longer on a full-time basis.

It contrasted amazingly with my time back in the car for the endurance races in 2009. For me, it just clarified that I'd made the right move. I stepped away at the right time for me, which is what I always said I'd do.

8

WINNING IS EVERYTHING

When the time arrives to stop doing something that you've done for a long time, and loved doing for a long time, you sit back and take stock of your life. For me, the second half of 2008 was about taking a good hard look at myself, I knew my passion for racing was diminishing, but by the same token I needed to know where I stood in the world.

As a commercial entity, in essence, what was 'Mark Skaife'? I'd been a racing driver and a team owner, but what was life going to look like when I stepped out of full-time racing? To be honest, there was only ever a slim chance that I'd totally walk away from the driver's seat. I talked about that at my retirement announcement, but not being in the game week in week out was going to be an entirely different affair.

That announcement on 28 October 2008, at Crown Casino in Melbourne, was the result of many things. As I said, my passion had started to wane, but there was also a study that I'd commissioned my long-term friend, mentor and former boss, John Crennan, to complete for me. This was a snapshot of my working life and of my brand. It was what we called 'Skaife Next', and in logo-land we added four arrows to symbolise what he determined.

John is one of the smartest businessmen I've ever met, and his work on Skaife Next was as good as anything he'd done with HSV. It gave me clarity and confidence to face the future without the 14 or 15 race meetings a year that had been my stock in trade for so long.

In terms of the four arrows – or my 'brand pillars', if you like – there was clearly a very strong motor racing element, but that was coupled with an involvement in the general automotive industry, so that was a second arrow. There was my emerging work in media as a third part, and then the less tangible and more personal aspects, which was the fourth element.

It's kind of funny how it all evolved, and not that I knew what was really happening at certain times in my career, but there were a lot of key steps that helped my brand evolve into what it is today. I certainly became quite brand aware in the 2000s, but up to that stage it had really just grown itself almost organically.

The really heartening part of what we discovered was that even without me sitting in a racing car, I had a strong future in front of me and that made it much easier to make the decision to retire from full-time racing. It sent Ned and Boxy – my managers Craig Kelly and Tony Box – into overdrive back at ESP (Elite Sports Properties) headquarters as they worked out how to leverage all the elements into creating a new business direction for me, and they worked wonders. The next thing I knew I was with Seven as an expert commentator, a radio man with Triple M, I was on the board at V8 Supercars with specific projects, I was designing racetracks with IEDM, and I was also involved in some books.

As a young driver you rarely think of anything other than where you'll get your next drive and will it be good enough to win races. At that stage your personal brand is inextricably linked with your racing brand or the team for which you drive. I became a part of Gibsons after a few years running my own deal as Mark Skaife, and eventually I began to grow as Skaife again, albeit with a strong HRT connection.

Also as a young driver the opportunities in terms of personal sponsorships don't really come along that easily. As young guys are forging their careers, I often advise them not to worry about media training or hairstyles – although some of them should do more of the latter and not for their career – or the ability to generate income away from the track. What you have to do first and foremost is go and drive the car well – become a part of the team you are with and get the best results possible. The opportunities to make money, build a career and develop your own personal following come from winning races; it's quite a simple formula. Don't, under any circumstances, make decisions purely on money – winning is everything.

I've always believed that if you look after all the right things, money will flow later, but it should never be the primary goal. It's all about establishing yourself from a credibility standpoint, establishing some of the brand pillars that come from your own character – how you go about your racing, what sort of person you are, all the things that end up being part of your personal brand.

Some things come naturally, but all of those aspects need to be developed over time. There is no point, though, if you're not winning, so first and foremost you must be in a team that can win. What happens with race teams and drivers is a little bit different from football clubs, for instance. It's probably a little harder for footballers to develop a brand profile because there are so many people of such diverse character, but with race teams there are not many at the elite level. There are 30 V8 Supercar drivers and more than 650 AFL level footballers, so it's easier to be seen as a driver than as a footballer simply because of the numbers.

For me, absolute loyalty to my team was a key, and what we were doing as a team had to be complementary to what I was doing as a person. I was never going to get involved in a situation where a personal sponsor wasn't absolutely in line with the team – I was never going to wear Adidas boots when the team was with Puma. I did some personal services agreements where I had my own deal with team sponsors to do additional work for them, but I was never in negotiations with anyone that was not totally in synch with the team's bank of sponsors.

But it also worked the other way, and Xbox was a classic example. I had a personal deal with Xbox and we ended up bringing it into the team as a sponsor. The same thing happened with Fosters and the VB brand. A lot of those things tend to come out OK if you're willing to work hand in hand with the team, and I ended up with some pretty good arrangements with team sponsors for work over and above my contractual responsibilities. I was also lucky to have blue chip sponsors who were extremely credible to work with.

When guys don't operate like that, you start to see conflicts in sponsor agreements, whether it's rugby league, cricket, motorsport or AFL, and it can be ugly. It happens a lot with media arrangements where players sign themselves up to a TV network and, because of that lock-out deal, then can't be seen on another network. If you do that too early, you'll really hurt your personal brand because you won't be seen as much, and you won't be able to grasp other media opportunities. Personal sponsors don't want to be involved with someone who can only appear on one of the commercial networks if that someone is just a bit player – if you are a superstar, it's different, because you can make so much money out of being exclusive and you already have your reputation and support. Irrespective of your allegiance to a particular network, the others are forced to give you coverage based on the merit of your result. They must show the winner cross the line.

A lot of those aspects are really important to have your brain around and do them in the right order and with the right intent and loyalty to your team. When you own the team, you don't seek personal agreements as often. That certainly happened to me when I bought HRT, firstly because I was too busy to take on any extra commitments, and then whatever money we could find we were putting into the team.

I think the transition from the young race driver forging a career into a paid driver with a team is often awkward. To get to that stage you've probably had to fight and scrap with the best of them on the track while working to build a name. You'll probably have also had to sign sponsors to keep growing, although there are a few who have enough money to do it without that part of the arrangement.

So, you've been pitching yourself out on the open market. Seeing potential sponsors, asking for money and telling people how good you are. You believe you're a brand, but at this stage you're far from that. You're on the path to being a professional athlete, but you aren't there yet and this is where motorsport is different to most other sports. It takes a lot of money to get to that stage – much more than any football code – and you've had to pimp yourself around a lot.

I got through most of my career without a manager as such, and even into my early years with HRT when I did take on someone, it wasn't for them to get involved in my racing. The reason I ended up doing a management deal initially with IMG and then with Craig Kelly's business – Elite Sports Properties – was their ability to generate outside ideas that weren't limited to motorsport, such as outside media and other commercial arrangements. Even things like merchandising and memorabilia and associated apparel – which we'd never done too much of – these were things I couldn't do on my own.

We were churning out memorabilia at one stage, and it was very good. Even my first book, *Diary of a Champion*, wouldn't have happened without ESP. It was Craig's idea and he did the deal with Ali Urquhart from HarperCollins. It worked so well that she hunted me down for this one, even though she'd changed publishers. The other great thing management did for me was being very critical of how I spent my time – Craig was very stringent on having the correct work-life balance that we could achieve given how busy we were.

Craig plays the game the same way that I do. We can say anything to each other without getting belted in the dial because we're mates, which is good because I don't think I'd want to take one from him. But it's important, as I've said before, to be able to be straight with people. He's very good at what I call simplifying things – he's a very bright guy and strategically he's a genuinely smart bloke, especially at getting me to prioritise things and trying to make it basic. He is good at saying 'no', which is important too.

John Crennan has always said the hardest word in the English language is 'no' – it's the hardest one to roll out. I've been able to use Craig to filter opportunities when it's needed; sometimes I use him for that because it means I can say no without damaging a relationship.

Craig has also been clever at not getting involved in my motor racing *per se*. Any of the stuff outside the box of motorsport, he is very much hands on, but for the things inside the sport it's always been me – and that isn't just because I don't want to pay him 20 per cent of everything! I've always handled my own driver agreements even though it has often involved some hard discussion – but I still believe I'm the best person to handle that because I know the business. It was a hard discussion when I had it with Fred Gibson and it was a hard discussion when I used to have it with John Crennan. If you have the policy of wanting to win the races, which I always did, it almost goes against the grain for the team to pay the driver too much money, because then you're not spending it on the cars or team infrastructure. But, at the same time you know you only have a prescribed period of time to drive cars or be involved in your sport, so you want to get an earn commensurate with other leading sporting people in the country and more than the other drivers up and down pit lane.

Like all things, commercial deals and money stuff leaks. There is always a lot of chat and conjecture as to who is getting what and where they're getting it from. I think probably a lot of that came from Lowndes leaving Holden and getting signed directly by Ford and there was a lot of speculation as to what sort of money he was being paid. Rumours, as ever, flowed freely. We were hearing figures in the million dollar range, and while I don't think it was that big it wasn't far away from it.

I knew what other top sporting people in Australia were being paid and I would have thought a top line driver – Skaife, Lowndes or Ambrose – lined up against a Nathan Buckley and James Hird in the AFL or Andrew Johns and Alfie Langer in Rugby League should be line ball. That said, motorsport has some other unique properties that need to be considered. In our case, we were just one of, say, 30 drivers representing every aspect of the sport. There was a percentage of ambassadorial work, a percentage of media and so forth, and we had to share that load between fewer people than any other elite sport in the country. Also, we have a truly national following which places additional demands.

At the peak of my driving career versus the absolute best

AFL guys or best Rugby League guys, we would have been line ball on salaries, which at that time I think was pretty fair. They probably have less longevity in terms of the tenure of their career at their best, but ultimately we have a higher risk, so at the end of the day it half works.

I know that I was underpaid at Gibson Motorsport for a long time. It wasn't necessarily on my radar, because, as I said, I was so focused on doing the best I could with my career and essentially driving at the highest level to seek a full-time opportunity, seek a result and then earn a motorsport career. My modus operandi was not to worry about money – that would come if I did a good enough job. Everyone likes to earn good money and I was no different. I was well paid but I could have earned more than I did at that stage. I think I did an OK job of managing the balance between chasing money and race wins in that phase of my progression.

When Lowndes made the move to Ford, one of the things I was very critical of was that it led to a lot of guys in pit lane being paid way too much money for their ability. The escalation was staggering, and it turned the drivers into the biggest cost centre inside a team when it should have been the engine bill or some other engineering aspect that would make the cars go faster. I'm very critical of the manufacturers for making that happen – they were the catalyst for how that rolled out. The increase in pay for average drivers was dizzying and counterproductive to the future of the sport. I'm pleased to say now that arrangements have to be through race teams and the manufacturers can no longer spend crazy sums on personal exertion deals with drivers.

I guess a lot of teams would sit back now and wonder why

they spent the money they did on some of the drivers; the results they got didn't justify the spend in many cases. It wasn't just a question of how many races did that bloke win for you for $400,000, it was also what sort of feedback did he give you, did he lead you down the right path in the development stakes? How many days were they at the race team helping out, how many other sponsors did they help sign up, and then all the other stuff that happens, like apparel or merchandise. Did that roll out of the back of the truck because they had this bloke driving for them? Honestly, there were so many deals that if they did the business case they would be very, very negative. I've heard figures of $800,000 a year for a bloke who has barely won a race in three years – staggering.

Conversely, guys like Lowndes are worth their weight in gold, but there aren't many like him. He sells T-shirts and caps like no-one else and he does the job on the track; he also brings sponsors and helps reinforce existing relationships. He is quite unique and I would have said he's earned every cent he has been paid.

Even back in the Laser days I loved the business side of the sport, which means I had passions in each of the three areas that matter for motorsport – the cars, the competition and the business. I got as much pride out of how well the businesses were running at times as anything else. Coming from the background that we had with automotive businesses, I have basically been hanging around cars and doing work on cars and selling tyres forever, and that was a very good grounding because it meant I knew very clearly how to account for my racing, how to apportion my time.

One of the things Dad and I had was an arrangement

where we'd never prepare the race cars during business hours, so effectively customers came first. Then we'd work till whatever time of the night to get the car finished and be back again at 6.30 in the morning. Dad and I had a lot of things going on. Second-hand tyres was one: a bloke would buy a set of tyres but the two rear tyres might have 80 per cent tread left on them, so we could paint them and sell them to people as second-hand units. We went halves with all of those and a lot of that cash was paying for fuel money to go to Amaroo Park or wherever the next race was. We also had a deal going in the workshop about me being a mechanic and how many hours I could charge out. Clearly we were working hard and Dad was obviously funding the majority of it, but my wages and anything else I could earn was being fired at the race cars.

There was a lot of that with Dad, and they were very good business lessons to go through. You didn't just have to be organised financially, you also had to be on top of it from a time perspective too. Even the simple thing of going to Melbourne for a race meeting required effort over and above loading the trailer and heading off. After a race in Melbourne or Winton, we'd pack it all up and drive back overnight to be at the workshop on Monday morning to serve customers. It was hard and it was demanding but they were great lessons, and to me those sorts of things have served me really well. He was very hard and rigorous but also very fair.

So then in Fred-land I found it very easy doing the stuff that he wanted me to do, because hanging around the workshop doing a heap of different sorts of work was great. But because they weren't road cars, they were race cars, everything we did was up a couple of notches above in terms of the presentation of the work you had to do. I found the non-timeframe thing interesting – up to then everything was by the hour; now you had a whole day to put a fuel tank in a car if you had to and you had to do it very well. It just amazed me.

The guys used to say around the workshop, 'What are you running for?' It used to blow them away, because I'd run down to the other end and grab that thing, and run back. It was just mad.

When we embarked on the road car program for special vehicles with Nissan (SVD), I was working incredibly hard and it was different again, and this was before I was even a full-time driver for the team. We were working with Nissan motor company on all the areas of the car that they wanted to improve. There was a huge amount of work and there was a lot of R&D work we were doing that was really good. The quality of the car that rolled out for sale was exceptional.

Fred and I are very alike in that we really want everything to be done as well as we can. Fred's presentation of everything was absolutely mint because that was just the way we did it. The road car program was pretty much the same. It had to be right, it had to look the part . . . but it also had to make sense on the money side too, and I did a lot of the business cases for him on the development and the supply of components.

We were importing Bilstein shocks from Germany that we ended up sea freighting out of Hamburg, lobbing them in Australia and dragging them out of the boxes. At the same time we were freighting all the front struts, brake components and front hubs from Japan. We'd then put the Bilstein shock in a brand new front upright, with a brand new coil spring, a brand new front hub, a brand new front caliper and rotor and hand it back to Nissan Motor Company and they'd put it on the assembly line for Nissan SVD. We did the whole lot and sometimes we'd do 50 sets a day.

The business case at the time gave me a few lessons in foreign exchange and I was constantly dealing with Gibson Freight. I was watching the markets and anticipating it to hurt as the dollar fluctuated, but we ended up being pretty lucky because it worked the right way for us. At the end of the day we made a lot of money out of that part of the business, which funded the race team in both Touring Cars and Formula Brabham. A lot of the money we made was churned straight back into those programs, including running a third touring car at some places in Nissan Special Vehicles guise. You can look back on it with rose-coloured glasses now, but it was bloody hard work. It was excellent.

This was a time when I got my first serious lesson in branding. We were running what I call the barber shop car in 1990, and when we rolled the cars out in 1991 we'd moved away from the paint scheme because it was so limiting. We needed extra sponsors, and with the barber shop car there was nowhere to put any extra signage – Nissan basically owned the doors and then with the hatching of the colours there was no way to write something over it. They owned the whole livery or colour scheme without paying for it.

So we had to go to a more basic livery and, to keep Nissan happy, we picked up the European Nissan colour schemes, which were the same as the Le Mans program at the time. We changed things around and Nissan accepted that, but I wanted black wheels which they didn't want. We tested three or four different colours, but I originally sold the black wheels to Fred on the basis that we wouldn't have to paint the wheels so much because black was going to be good in terms of serviceability, which clearly it was. But we didn't have to service them for too long because Nissan hated them and ended up convincing us to go back to white. Don't worry, though, Fred gave them an invoice for it, so that was fine.

But I started to understand a little more at the time about corporate brands and how far we could push. And, in some cases, whether we could push at all. Changing that paint scheme was important to us, so we had to handle the process properly to make sure it happened.

The road cars ran white wheels too. In fact, when that car was first launched it was a grey wheel with a slight red tinge in it, which actually made it look pinkish, so in the end we went back to white for that too. Paul Beranger was the guy who was overseeing the whole thing from Nissan, Ross Holder was looking after the mechanical engineering, and a guy called Stefan Lofhelm was doing a lot of interior stuff. I was in the deep end of the pool and paddling like crazy until I could swim properly.

In the race shop everything was designed to be light and super-safe, all well made with machining, welding and fabrication that was just beautiful. But over the other side of the workshop we had to meet Australian Design Rules (ADRs) and validate the engineering integrity. We had to make sure a car could do 100,000 kilometres, for instance, without a front hub failure, or meet the brake proportioning test, or have a front strut fitted without the shock knocking after

20,000 kilometres over typical Australian roads. I'd never been exposed to anything like that before.

Blokes used to arrive at our workshop in Wyong and say, 'My shock absorber is rattling around and it has a knock,' and you'd just fix it. In the race shop, though, you had to be part of the design, part of the validation, part of verifying from a durability standpoint, and you had to determine whether it was all going to work. I'd sold more tyres than most people would see in a lifetime, but now I was worried about noise levels and tractability, whether the tyre was suitable for that particular car and even how the tyre would wear over time with the camber that we wanted to run. We never had to worry about that when racing because you only ever think about how fast they go, so it was a completely different mentality.

I was pretty proud of what we did with the special vehicles. There was a white Skyline, then a red Skyline, and then a silver and black Pulsar with a limited slip differential (LSD) in it which was interesting in itself and took a bit to get working well. Ross and I had a brain wave – it had very limited front shock absorber travel and we buggered around with everything to get it to behave with that diff, but everything we did was too stiff and it rode too harshly. So Ross Holder thought we should cheat and put a long bump stop in it, shorten the body of the shock as far as we could to get as much travel as possible, and then use the bump stop as part of the suspension. At that time, bump stops were really only used to stop metal from hitting metal, so this was quite a novel approach. We had a heap of different ones we tested and we ended up with a BMW long bump stop which is about 85 mm long, we fired it in and we made it ride beautifully. It was a clever solution and not too uncommon today.

I drove one of these Pulsars on Nissan club day a little while back and it still rode absolutely fantastically.

As you can imagine, we were required to do a huge number of rigid quotations for Nissan Motor Company. We had to document everything to the nth degree and we had booklets for each of the mechanical aspects. We had to verify things like the build of the front upright and the way that the whole front suspension was delivered back to Nissan. We had photos, engineering manuals, all the torque settings for things like caliper bolts, for instance – Nissan even had a paint mark over them to verify that they'd been tightened up and someone had checked them. All that sort of stuff was really pretty good – it worked well with my mindset.

So that business part of it was fantastic. When Fred and I finished up I was running the workshop, so when I went to drive for John Crennan at HRT, I asked him very early on what else I could do – I knew I'd gone there to drive the car but I also knew that wasn't going to be enough. I couldn't just hang around and be a race driver. He fully understood when I said I wanted to keep my brain active, so he got me to do some work with the product group at HSV, trying to work out new models and future directions and other little bits and pieces. I knew I had to earn my stripes there a bit because I'd had open slather back at Fred's, but as time went by we really hooked up and I enjoyed being able to bring something extra to the table.

I'd also started to become more involved in the commercial dealings with sponsors before I left Fred – all post the

Winfield deal, which I didn't have much to do with initially. In fact, that sponsorship came from a really great mate of ours called Graham Ferret who'd had lunch with Des Hancock from Rothmans. Graham convinced Des to come down and have a look at our operation. Fred did that deal with them pretty much within a week. It was worth $3.5 million at the time and it was the most lucrative motorsport sponsorship ever in this country – even to this day it would be a pretty good deal for most teams at the front of the field. Des was a tremendous guy – very clever and articulate – loved a beer and a smoke!

I was hell bent on making sure they got a return on their investment. Even just the workload for everything going from blue to red was massively important. And we had to roll it all out before the season for a photo shoot at Eastern Creek. Winfield was also spending a lot of money with speedway and drag racing, but we wanted to be the pre-eminent Winfield runner and that meant we had to make everything perfect. I think we did that too. From 1992 to 1995 we worked incredibly hard, then tobacco sponsorship was banned.

In 1995, there was a lot of conjecture about how we might be able to work around the new laws but the rulings from the Government were very well drafted to include 'accidental' and 'incidental' coverage of anything related to a cigarette brand. We looked at the options and explored a Pack Leader type of arrangement that Alan Jones used with Philip Morris, where the branding was carried in a much more subliminal manner, but we thought it was all a bit sleazy and a bit of a risk. We were just going to run the car with a lightning bolt on it because that was an identifiable trademark for Winfield, but

I'm sure that would have been considered incidental. Marlboro did a similar thing at the time in some places that it had to run Formula One and it worked because of the strength of that brand mark. But I think we would have always been in the firing line had we tried something like that.

We'd established ourselves as the number one team in the land, but we were in trouble. Other than the Tooheys thing that I had going, and a bit of money from Shell and Holden, there was pretty much nothing else going on. What I learned at that stage was not just the value of marketing, but also about having the right blokes doing the work for you. We always had the best people in our workshop, but we didn't do the same with the suits.

It was a harsh lesson to learn. Now I'm not saying there was anything untoward, because there are plenty of stories like that in motorsport, but we just didn't have the right people to get the right results. Their intentions were pretty good, but in hindsight it just wasn't effective. It's a little bit like a real estate agent coming to sell your house – with some of them you'll have a good experience and they'll deliver you a sale at a price you like with minimal drama, while others will be an absolute pest. A guy like John Crennan would have delivered a replacement sponsor or sponsors to keep us at the pointy end of the field. There may have been a reduction in costs and reduction in overall sponsorship income, but it still would have kept us there.

That was a part of the business that we were not good enough at and it was actually one of the biggest lessons I'd ever learned. In that 12-month period I learned more about motorsport than I had in the previous 10 years. It was pretty simple for me – I knew how much money we had and we spent every dollar in making the car go fast and win races, and in terms of business it is the simplest model in the whole world. In reality, motor racing is only a spending business, so when all of a sudden we didn't have the bucketload of money with which to go racing, it was quite a stark reality. That's why I reckon today the marketing is more important than the engineering stuff; if you don't have the money you won't win races. You generate income from sales or sponsorship or some of the other commercial aspects of your business, like selling components – all of a sudden that just took my focus. I'd been working on the wrong end of the game.

I had pretty much half the money we needed locked away from Tooheys, but then there was a change of policy and personnel and a restructure inside Tooheys and it all fell over. Then we ended up doing a third-party deal with the Sega group and they defaulted, which cost us $400,000, and it was just a series of nightmares.

As I was getting my head around all this, I was starting to understand my personal brand a little more. I'd been approached by a guy called Peter Johnson from Tooheys a few years earlier about whether I'd want to do a personal deal with them. I knew at the time, which was in 1993, that Fred wasn't that happy about that because it was like I was seeking my own monetary gain away from the team. Even the signage that I put on the helmet was a bone of contention. We didn't have formal agreements as to who owned my helmet; in fact, I blued like you wouldn't believe because he sold everything to Rothmans – even my undies had to be red. That's how the colours of my helmet came along, because the red and the yellow are the Winfield colours. As it was, I said I wasn't going to do it, but we ended up having a compromise on what the helmet looked like.

A lot of those deals I started to ark up about because they were affecting me, and then the Tooheys deal started to fire up and it started to generate some leads. Fred got a little bit antsy with me at one stage because I went on to be chairman of the Formula Brabham Association. Brian Shead (a veteran open-wheel racer) was the secretary and the category was struggling, it didn't have good enough television. We had Channel Nine doing it at one point, and we were looking for a better television deal from them plus a sponsor and I went and sold the series sponsorship to Tooheys. The classic thing here was – and the other competitors don't even know this – but when I sold it to them for the series they couldn't pay for six months, so I went and got a $50,000 overdraft on my racing business and funded the prizemoney for everybody else until the Tooheys money was paid. To keep the series going and have a reputable series sponsor was really important, so it was the Tooheys Australian Drivers' Championship and they came through as promised.

So those sorts of things were the start of me generating income outside the team, exploring my own pull in a marketing sense. It did start to bring some conflict, though. I went and drove for Mazda in the 12-hour race in 1994, and Fred said, 'You can't do that because we're with Holden,' and I said, 'I haven't got an arrangement with Holden,' so I went and did the race. Those sorts of races were interesting because I got paid well by Mazda to drive the car and it was a time when a lot of little opportunities were starting to evolve and clearly Fred and I had to have some rules around that. We absolutely never had a falling out about it and I know at some time he would have had to speak to Holden about me driving a Mazda, but the fact was, I didn't care if he had to do that.

When I went to HRT I certainly learned a lot more about commerciality. John Crennan was half a dozen steps in front of everyone else in terms of how regular commercialism could be applied to motorsport. He had a very sound understanding of business which he applied to the team and that's why it was successful. My driver's agreements had lots of stuff locked away in a much more detailed and diligent manner than I'd ever seen before. Restrictions over snow skiing and motorbike riding, for instance, were in place to limit the team's risks.

As we came into the Holden Racing Team, we started to win some races and my brand was gaining momentum – the additional media stuff was coming together because I was doing some work with Channel Ten outside of motorsport. I'd done a deal with Crown Casino and a deal outside with Mobil and I was doing TV ads for Holden. There was a lot of stuff that was starting to bubble up – then the Xbox sponsorship happened and we were doing television commercials for Xbox. I was doing a stack of work for VB and for Gatorade too – it was all happening – and a lot of that was done with proper agreements and proper methodology: how we could use the car and who had the rights on that in terms of being able to use those images and intellectual property (IP).

My first Tooheys deal in 1993 was for $30,000, which was about 1/5th of what I was being paid as a professional race driver, and after winning the series at that time I was probably as well paid as anybody else. Brock and Johnson would have been generating more money for themselves, but that was more as a consequence of owning their race teams, not just driving.

I remember the Tooheys deal very clearly. I had to do six appearances for them and they set something up with some other blokes they had at the time as sporting ambassadors and they'd call on us to do corporate functions. We'd all front up in our Tooheys gear and they did a really good job of promoting it and using us. They were pretty active and the sponsorship manager, Peter Feenan, and a great girl called Susie Crowe were just outstanding. They activated those things really well – they were good at using you properly. Sometimes those sorts of sponsorships are laborious, but they did such a good job and it was all good fun.

The success with Gibsons and the Tooheys stuff was pretty high profile which was great. There were a couple of really good Channel Nine things too, although Network Seven had the rights to the series. I did a couple of interesting motorsport things with Darrell Eastlake and Anne-Maree Sparkman who were reporters on Nine's *Wide World of Sport*, that were good for my profile over and above our normal demographic.

I wasn't always comfortable in front of a microphone, but Darrell taught me a lot about that as a young bloke. He was a great family friend and he taught me not to be a blonde bimbo. He always said these are the sorts of answers you need to have in different situations. Basic media training really – TV news is different to other TV formats, which is different to radio, which is different to the press. Above all else, he said, when you're saying it, you need to say it with conviction, and when you do it you can't just be the non-answerer of questions. You can't have that political answer of not describing anything and you can't do it in such a way that doesn't express an opinion.

Motor racing is big business and these days even the guy who is 28th in the field is very capable of being interviewed and coming across well. They are better at it than any other sport in the country, which is because the commercial considerations to get to the very top are quite different to other sports, and that is what gets noticed. It certainly matters when Tony Cochrane goes out knocking on doors for more money for the series.

Yes, the number of elite athletes in our sport is smaller than many others, and in reality the elite of the elite has always been quite competent at all facets of sport. But I reckon the guys at the front of the field in our game have always been quite savvy. Moffat, Brock, Johnson, Bob Morris, Jim Richards, Allan Grice and Colin Bond were all pretty good compared to other sportsmen of their era. We certainly have more consistency on that now, from the top end of pit lane to the bottom, but they were always good at the top.

A harsh lesson to learn, though, was that simply being the best was not enough. When the tobacco money disappeared we found some pretty lean times. We found some extra money from Holden through the Motorsport Manager John Stevenson via a second-hand car program called Network Q, which was a big development and used car initiative that General Motors had utilised in the UK. They were sponsoring cars over there too under that banner, so Stevo did the same deal with us. Clearly they were endorsing Fred and the whole team, but they were endorsing me too.

Things got so bad for us in 1997 that something had to give. I'd spoken to John Crennan and he'd spoken to Holden and they were all very supportive of me coming across, especially Kevin Wale, who was Holden's marketing director and is now the president and managing director of GM Shanghai in China. I still see Kevin and his wife, Marilyn, when they come back to Australia, so it was great not only to get that endorsement back then, but to know that I did a good enough job to not let him down, or anyone else who trusted me at that stage. Both Crenno and Kevin wanted to get me to HRT, so I suppose in hindsight it was always going to happen, even if I'd resisted for a while.

From a personal branding perspective, joining Brock, and then from the public's perspective replacing Brock, was a big kick. So the way that rolled out after I came in and did a good job for those couple of races was a real significant part of how the thing with HRT unfolded. For the following year Lowndes was coming back from Europe, I was coming in to replace Brock, and it shaped up as a sensational combo.

But it wasn't just Brock: having John Crennan's endorsement was important too in terms of being seen as a Brock replacement, but that had a life of its own as well. Whenever I did a speaking engagement in those days – it wouldn't matter where it was – the MC would introduce me as the replacement for Peter Brock: 'Here's the man who replaced Peter Brock at Holden Racing Team.' So that was just people's perspective at the time.

Even though I'd been pretty successful in my own right – being a two-time Australian Touring Car Champion and twice winner of Bathurst kind of had its own authority – it was very flattering in a way to be seen as Brock's replacement. Peter and I had always got on really well and to have that feeling of replacing him in the works Holden team was pretty special – he was more to the sport than just a race driver and I never thought I'd be able to replace him entirely in that sense. He was clearly Holden's 'golden boy' and for me to pick that mantle up was both an honour and a challenge.

But as I said earlier, the single most important thing in this game is winning. If you're doing that, everything else sorts itself out. So what we had to do after making sure we did a good job in those two endurance races was to beat Lowndes in exactly the same equipment, and I knew that was going to take absolute resolve and everything I could give.

The competition with Lowndes was very, very healthy and good for the team. Holden were very keen to do things with me too, and Ross McKenzie, Megan Stooke and John Elsworth who were all in sales and marketing at Holden were fantastic in terms of developing more of the Skaife brand within their campaigns. So when all that control freak stuff appeared in the TV ads, it was both a good pitch for them and an integral part of my character, or so they believed. The first line of the ads was 'I'm a control freak' and I wanted to tone it down to say 'I'm a bit of a control freak', but they wanted a strong statement. I don't think I'm a control freak as such; I just like things to be done properly. When I trust you, I'll let you do it your way . . . maybe. They saw it differently.

We did two or three TV ads that were quite strong and personal ads, then some came that were much softer. There was one with a kid which everyone thought was Mitch but wasn't, there was one in a classroom, another in a park with a young bloke playing soccer, and also one where I had the wrong car in the car park. They were made over a period of time and they were really well done – McCanns was the agency and they had a lot of Holden involvement, in terms of making sure that the whole branding thing for Mark Skaife and Holden was done really well.

There was a fair lesson in all of that because I was clearly doing a lot of stuff for Holden with ads, appearances, things with dealers, launches and conferences, and through the whole process my brand was growing too. We also did a lot of other stuff that never went to air, like an amazing Calais piece that we shot in Chapel Street in Melbourne for a dealer launch of the new model. It was me getting changed out of a normal shirt and jeans into a business suit, and coming out onto the street in the dark in the latest Holden Calais. Australian Business Theatre did it and it had some amazing lighting and a heap of tracking shots of the car in Chapel Street. The quality of it was first class; it could have gone to air as a television commercial (TVC).

I was also doing a lot of HSV work. I remained on the product group at HSV which guides new product development and I was doing a lot with the media as a consequence of that. John Crennan used me a lot at the dealer launches to endorse the cars and I was genuinely doing a lot on the cars themselves, developing bits and working with the engineers. It all made sense to me – I was busy, I was playing with cars and I was winning races, and my personal brand was growing as a consequence. The biggest single thing I learnt at that stage was that those things are cooperative, it all goes hand-in-hand. If you said to Holden, 'I want $100,000 to do an ad for myself,' they would have said, in John Elsworth speak, 'You're a goose, go away!' But what it did for me from a branding standpoint was fantastic and it was a two-way street, and very much a reciprocal arrangement. I did the very best I could for Holden and they did a really good job with me.

But there was always a balance between what I did for HSV and Holden. John really wanted me to be the face of HSV as well and I had to work very hard on maintaining both my role with Holden and that with HSV, but it was also good because of the linkage between the two. When I was doing SS Commodore ads or ABS ads or Holden Equipe ads I was very much doing that for Holden, but there was high-level engineering and high-level corporate work for HSV. It was connected. John led that all very well; he's assisted greatly with my involvement in the car industry.

From my overall brand point of view, they all happened at the right time. There was lots of other stuff that came off the back of it too – we were doing Xbox, Gatorade and Mobil TVCs. There was just a massive amount of activity. But it didn't just happen all on its own. Craig Kelly, John Crennan and myself carefully mapped it all out; we had to make sure I didn't get overexposed, or attached to inappropriate products. What sort of partnerships would we enter into, whether it was Hugo Boss with HSV or various things for Channel Ten or Crown Casino? A lot of thought went into all of it.

There was a lot of high-level relationships that we managed really well and that was quite a hard period because I'd convinced John when Craig Lowndes and I were together that we needed someone to manage us – in essence both of us needed to manage our diaries better and manage our outside-of-racing activities so we could continue to do a good job on the track. So it was a very interesting period of negotiation with HRT and Holden. Craig Kelly was just setting up ESP and IMG had approached me for a management deal and that was where we started, which was a tough call because Craig and I were great mates. I felt reasonably comfortable when I first started with IMG because doing deals with mates has never been my go because they have such a potential to blow up. IMG seemed like the sensible thing to do at the time.

Chris Giannopoulos and Martin Jolly from IMG were across all my dealings, but James Henderson was doing most of the work. We headed down the track of a tighter agreement with HRT in terms of what I had to give them off the track and things were reasonably good. It became clear though that there were some real differences from where I wanted to head, and Craig Kelly seemed much more in synch with me on that front. I ended up switching to him after a transition period with both involved, which has worked well. The first thing we did was working on a system for saying 'no', and Craig was great from that perspective.

We had a form that people had to fill in if they wanted me to do anything commercially, and between Craig, John and myself, we'd work out what to do. Was the money reasonable, was the image right and was there any chance of bringing it from personal-land to team-land? In reality, though, we were really just too small for IMG, and I remember John saying once that the entities didn't combine very well, they just didn't link up properly based on the dimensions of the business.

John was clearly marketing savvy and we were reasonably organised in terms of what we thought was good and bad and we were probably difficult clients in some ways for IMG – fussy and small. There was basically no extra sponsorship that came from them. In fact, things like the CUB deal which ended up as my own deal that went into the team, IMG had very little involvement even though it was on their watch. So when the IMG deal started to crumble, we went across to Craig totally and then I basically began to row my own boat with Ned.

A lot of expertise, time and effort is required in sharpening the way you want your brand to appear. I remember having a real heart-to-heart with John Crennan, Ned and myself at one point in 1999 when we agreed on who our partners were, essentially, and that these were the only the things we were going to do. We'd only do this number of appearances and the rest of our efforts would be concentrated on winning the series and generating the best outcome for the team. It meant that the next three years were the best three years we'd ever put together because we put a big barrier around things that just weren't worthwhile. It had been starting to get out of control at that point, so we needed those guidelines to keep it all together and to prioritise the demands.

It was no different to any other top sportsman, the demands are massive, and if you don't organise yourself well, if you don't have control of your diary, you'll get into trouble. That was when I started to block away some time for myself: the day before and after every race was just for me. No appearances, nothing – one day clear prior to and post the event. Those shutdown times were critical for my on-track performances. It didn't matter if the boss of CUB wanted me to come and talk at their lunchtime function on the Thursday; if that Thursday was a block-out day, it was blocked out.

This was done in a way that I had enough protection around me not to be the bad guy. Craig and John understood that they could say no for me if I didn't. Often if it was a bit difficult for me from a sensitive sponsorship perspective, I could just say, 'I've got to get this ticked off for whatever reason,' and Ned or Crenno could go back and say no, which was excellent.

That was in all the phase where we were really working my brand profile, building a business that could stand the test of time. It was all cleverly done, but how we maintained that profile afterwards and what we did to continue the on-track success was probably better than that in terms of its overall execution.

I'd already been forced to change my view on the business of racing once, and now I was needing to do the same again. When I entered the game I thought it was an engineering business, then when the Winfield money was blocked I learned that the business of bringing in the sponsorship was the top of the tree. Now, with John Crennan, I was discovering that bringing in the money was all about brand. I would say he is the best brand person I've ever dealt with and I've been involved with lots of high-profile companies with very clever marketing directors and managing directors and product planning people with the best ad agencies in the land to support them.

The best niche automotive brand in the country was and probably still is HSV, and that was John Crennan. Anyone can build a good car, but not everyone can sell them or build a brand statement the way he did. HSV was hugely successful, and it wasn't about whether it was a good car or not, it was about people wanting one. John was instrumental in making sure that he had good 'car people' around him and on parts of the business that he didn't really know. From a straight-out engineering perspective, he had the Walkinshaw engineering empire to back it up – guys like Ian Callum on design and locally John McInerney on engineering. There were a lot of really good guys that were part of the business. John had a feel for the market and he was very good at picking out who to listen to and then what to react to.

We used to have this thing called RAC (Retail Advisory Committee) with our top ten dealers, for instance, and they're really clever guys and a lot of them were at the coal face of car sales. The job of the RAC was to get involved in the various HSV product lines and opportunities, to help fine tune what we were doing. We'd run them through proposals, schematics, projections, and then get them on-site to sit in the car, and they'd give their feedback on all sorts of things – whether it was a seat, a steering wheel, a road wheel, a paint execution or whatever it was, and John's real talent was listening to them and working out what really mattered. He was very good at picking out the stuff that he wanted them to pick out, grabbing it and heading into the market. On stuff he didn't agree with, he was very good at parking it.

So we'd moved all of my business stuff outside of motorsport to ESP around the end of 1999, my work office was at HSV, and with Ned a lot of opportunities started to open up outside of my direct driving. The most important thing was for me to be winning, so I concentrated on that while he worked on the other bits.

So that early focus was essentially about maximising my racing performances to the highest level. If you think about those years from 2000 to 2003, we were at the top of our game and the results were great. We won three titles and two Bathursts in that era, and there could easily have been another one of each. On the track, the whole thing was fantastic. But off the track that all changed in 2002.

9

LIFE ON THE EDGE

I REMEMBER VERY clearly John Crennan and I having some father and son chats – our relationship was very much like that, which is interesting in itself. Without taking anything away from my own father, I've found a lot of father figures in my career. Outside of Dad and my family relationships, guys like Fred Gibson and John have been very important to me.

John and I had some real lengthy discussions about where we were headed and what was going to happen, especially once I'd hit 40 and had to start thinking about life out of the driver's seat. This all really started in 2002 and obviously copped a rocket with TWR's financial issues in England that were going to engulf HRT. I remember a two-hour meeting with Ross McKenzie at Holden about going and doing some

Harvard Business School courses and what GM could help me with in terms of external business seminars and projects and things that may develop other opportunities; from a total business perspective, not just automotive. So we were already on the case of thinking about what the next stage of post-driving might have looked like.

To be absolutely frank, a lot of that thinking was totally about me going on to be managing director of HSV when John stepped down. That was the whole thinking of my racing and my workings within HSV and the roles that I was playing: eventually to take over the running of HSV – that was the 'next stage' of my life. Or so we thought.

TWR's financial issues in the UK changed all those plans. First of all, we had to find a way to save HRT, and by that I don't mean there was ever any risk of not having HRT; it was about keeping the integrity of what we'd all built – of maintaining the culture in a sense. We'd all worked pretty hard to build something special and I felt that had to be maintained and protected from the vultures that were swooping. I'm sure some of the people looking at HRT would have done a good job – Roland Dane from Triple Eight Race Engineering, for instance – but I didn't want the team to change too much.

I'd seen some tough times in the few years leading up to that period, and much of it I bounced back from quite well. One of the things that happened that was never in the 'life guide' was my marriage breaking down with Belinda in 1999. All the work I'd done and a lot of the money I'd earned was tied up in the divorce settlement. That was one of the most difficult times in my life, and although I was earning good money I was working pretty hard for it.

If you were doing a good job on the business side of racing and were getting results on the track, doubling your driver's salary was more than possible, and we were doing that. If you think what Craig was supposed to be earning from Ford at the time, you'd understand there was a lot of money at stake – it was seven figures.

But that period at the end of 2002 and the start of 2003 was a really testing time. John and I said it was like watching a train smash, it was just an incredibly destabilising time. I'd done a deal with him for another five years and the TWR collapse was very unfortunate in that a lot of things conspired together to affect Tom Walkinshaw's business in the UK. Unlike John, I wasn't really that close to the TWR UK part of the business. Craig Wilson was running it in England and I knew that he was spending a lot of time on the phone to John in those days trying to sort out the future of the business.

I don't think the whole story has been reported very well and there were a lot of outside forces that caused what happened. There were changes in automotive policy and TWR had been doing some big projects for car companies that didn't eventuate – not really because of anything they had done. TWR was trying to sell its stake in the Arrows Formula One team and one of those deals fell over because a large proportion of Arrows was owned by the banks. They'd also bought a huge engineering development facility in the UK based on the work it was going to generate from the auto makers, so they had large outgoings and then a few projects that were all on the go didn't materialise. The wash-up was a massive cash flow drama for them.

I knew just from discussions with John that things weren't looking that great. We'd just done a deal with Hugo Boss to do a big HSV promotion with a launch of one of our cars. As I said before, as we left the Hugo Boss building and Craig Wilson was on the phone to Crenno, at the end of that phone call, John said, 'I don't think this is going to be very good.' When it all came out that TWR was in receivership Holden went to the UK to ensure that TWR Australia, which was trading as Holden Racing Team, wasn't part of the receivership action.

From our side of the ledger, though, it really rocked the boat. There were people doing due diligence on HSV and HRT. Holden knew that, as part of the regulations, they couldn't own a race team so they needed a long-term ownership plan for HRT that didn't involve them, and as I mentioned there were vultures swooping from everywhere. It was a really weird time because the team which had been rock solid was now being destabilised from the other side of the planet. Suddenly guys who knew they could pay their mortgage were wondering about their future; there was a feeling of insecurity for the first time. Because I was the face of HRT, it was a really interesting and very tough situation. So many of the guys were coming up and saying, 'I've got a mortgage,' 'I've got a baby,' 'What's gonna happen with my family?', 'Will we all have jobs?', 'What's going on?' I felt that, if I could, I had to do something.

John, Jeff Grech and I had lots of very serious meetings about what needed to be done and how we were going to go about it, there were lots of options from Holden in terms of who was trying to buy HRT. Even Peter Brock was involved in one bid with another set of investors.

At the end of the day, Holden's view was that HRT (the race team) and HSV (the special vehicles operation) were joined at the hip and that needed to be maintained. They spoke to me privately about all of that before we negotiated an outcome. I'd been thinking about it, but these discussions convinced me it was the right thing to do. We were using the tagline 'race relations' at the time to talk about HRT and HSV, but it was more than just a piece of marketing spin – the connectivity was so important and that all needed to be linked with Holden. Holden had arranged with the receivers to acquire all of TWR Australia, so they were in control of what was going to happen. They had a temporary hold on HRT that AVESCO allowed, but they had to off-load it by a certain time.

Ray Borrett, who was looking after Holden's racing operations, was very keen to form some sort of engineering business that supplied services to teams like Holden Racing Team, and that could come out the back of what was HRT. The goal was to run four or six cars out of the engineering side of HRT, and then to supply others with components. Basically, he wanted to have a central services engineering company that could supply the teams running Holdens. From HRT's point of view it was not a very good plan as it split the business in half and relied on a manufacturer-owned operation to supply the teams. Even things like HR and OH&S policy had to be under strict Holden controls. The flexibility, dynamics and emphasis on HRT was changing.

Ross McKenzie at Holden was a critical element in keeping the Holden–HSV–HRT triangle together, and he was good at making it happen. To make that work and maintain it, as

I've said before, we needed this Collingwood-type scenario where we had strong leaders in the roles of president, coach and captain. In our case that became three separate entities and we needed to keep them together, and Holden was saying that under their plan Jeff was going to run Holden Motorsport (which was formerly the engineering and development arm of HRT) supplying services to other teams, but primarily HRT. No-one really knew at that point what was going to happen with HSV, but either Tom would maintain the ownership of it, if he was still in a financial position to do so, or Holden was thinking of buying it. Either way, John Crennan would still remain at the helm of HSV.

We were coming to arrangements with Holden to buy HRT, but the way it was all working was so convoluted and difficult to get your head around. There was so much brain power focused on just keeping the team alive. I was doing everything I could to keep it all together, and that meant trying to keep the culture of the place intact, trying to keep Jeff Grech where he was, trying to keep John as our high-level business person, and trying to keep the staff treated in the same way and with the same vibe that they'd previously enjoyed.

That was very hard and if I had my time again, we would probably have made some different decisions immediately on all that, because essentially what I bought was only half a race team. HRT needed to have the engineering business inside it and, without the engineering business, that particular race team was hard to keep absolutely meshed together, but in addition, there were lots of other outside influences. John Kelly (Rick and Todd's father) had bought the other

TWR licence to be the second supplied team and Kees Weel (who owned PWR Racing which was going to run as Team Brock) had come to an arrangement with TWR prior to its collapse to be the third supplied team, and that meant immediately Holden Motorsport had three teams it needed to supply. When you have different business people, like Kees Weel, John Kelly and myself, all expecting a certain level of service from Holden Motorsport, that was always destined for drama.

The creation of Holden Motorsport as this so called central services business to cater for three top teams was strategically and structurally flawed. We can all be geniuses in hindsight, but there's no way it could have worked and that had the biggest impact on whether HRT could be successful or not. It was a business model full of holes which were exaggerated by car company policies, high overheads, and future management agreement issues.

Everyone said 2003 wasn't much of a year for us, and maybe it wasn't because we didn't win the championship. But we won the Clipsal 500 and the Sandown 500 and we were 1.2 seconds behind Murphy when the left-hand rear door opened at Bathurst. We could have won the three biggest races of the year and we did win two of them. It was never going to be easy, no matter what anyone said. I'm quite volatile about this because getting all that complex racing world together and just to keep the team running was a massive task, and not many businesses would go well straight after an unplanned restructure of that magnitude. That was the first part; the second part was if you're going to take over a business which has just won five championships in a row, you're always going to be on the slippery slide going backwards, because you're not going to win another five in a row – that's a fact of life – no modern day sport would allow it or could sustain it.

The third part was that Project Blueprint was introduced at the start of that year, and what people don't understand is that a lot of technical work had to be done to meet those requirements. So, as I've said before, we had the biggest single engineering project that we'd ever encountered in bringing the VY Commodore in to conform to Project Blueprint, to theoretically bring the Holden and Ford racing models closer together, which was crap in itself because as far as I was concerned there was no technical or speed gap anyway. HRT was just doing a good job. We had a new engine, all-new front suspension, new aero kit . . . we were basically racing a completely different car. To think there was not a single part on that engine which was the same as the old one is incredible. The all-new front suspension layout was the same as the Ford and we had to design a whole new front end, then understand how the front geometry actually worked – it was totally different to how we'd been previously running with the McPherson strut layout. Then there was the aero stuff, which was different again in terms of how it made the car work or react at certain speeds and certain corners.

So if you just take the business part as a drama and then the car part as a massive technical issue, either one of those on its own would have been a huge job. Putting them both together was a nightmare. If Project Blueprint had come along with no ownership change at all, there was no way we were going to continue at the same level of dominance as before, because, as I've already mentioned, even the point score system had changed. So whether it was the point score, the car drama or the business being changed in terms of its ownership, there was a lot of work being done to deal with HRT's dominance. It was more about us than Holden.

2003 wasn't a bad year, but because of the engine program, 2004 was a nightmare. As the factory cars, we had to dedicate our cars more to the new engine program, which on the dyno had reasonable power, but it was so far down on installed power it was crazy – and there is no easy fix for that. I could show you graphs that clearly show how rough it was. I made a presentation to the whole of the board at Holden showing them that the engine dyno figures were almost exactly the same engine-to-engine, and then showed them the differences in the car. In some places we were 10km/h slower on the straights. Denny Mooney, the then Managing Director who is an engineer, and a great supporter of the race program, was just blown away by the disparity of performance from rig to road.

There were also new rules put in place that had minimum weights put on reciprocating components. We were developing engines that accelerated better, so the lighter you could make those reciprocating parts in terms of inertia, the faster you could accelerate the engine. You didn't actually make any more power, it just got there faster. That's why the Murphy lap at Bathurst in 2003 was so unbelievable. He had a qualifying engine in with all the lighter reciprocating parts – all supplied by Holden Motorsport – and he was more than a second quicker than anyone else. As I write this prior to Bathurst in 2010, that time still stands today as the fastest-ever lap up there. It is kind of like a target that we all set out to better at the start of the weekend; all motor racing fans talk about who will win the race and will anyone knock off 'that' lap. The engine performance on Murph's lap in 2003 is still better than today!

Our engine at that stage was the gun engine, but they were only making 1200 or 1500 kilometres. So when we had to start running a heavier crank shaft, for instance, the installed acceleration was worse. We had all these new components plus a level of restriction on us from a technical standpoint that we'd never seen before. At some places the engine performance was shocking. Jason Bright or Greg Murphy could be faster than us in cars that were supposedly two development steps behind ours, but because we were the factory team, we couldn't really run whatever we wanted. We had to sacrifice engine performance because of the factory team status and we had to use the latest GM technology.

In the third Holden Motorsport supplied team run by Kees Weel, Jason could have won the championship in 2004 in a VX Commodore modified to VY specs when we were in the latest VY. That's the pressure of essentially being a factory team and the onus was on us to operate with the latest gear. I've never been a good loser, so you can imagine the amount of blues I had in that time with people making high-level technical decisions for us. But a lot of that was about trying to keep the culture and the place operating in basically the same way and, honestly, I should have had much bigger dummy spits to not have HRT part of that business model – number one – and for HRT not to be compelled to have that gear in the car. It was just a joke; we should have been testing in the other teams, not HRT.

I don't think that period was affecting my brand as such, although I'd personally taken a back seat to the team, the team ownership was adding an extra string to my bow. Let's not kid ourselves either – no one really owns Holden Racing Team because Holden owns Holden Racing Team, that's the fact. While I was the 'owner' of the team with a large debt and management responsibilities, I was really only a caretaker, because the whole of intellectual property rights and the use of the name is totally owned by Holden. It's a bit like some land ownership in the UK or Australia where you own a 99-year lease. I didn't even have access to the merchandise sales stream at the tracks to help support the funding of the team, which was another issue.

But, as I said, it didn't hurt my personal standing, even though we weren't winning at the same rate. There were a couple of things – including the Ingall thing – which probably didn't help me in some ways, but in others it was OK. I'm not sure I had my head fully wrapped around my brand at the time because I was more looking at the team rather than me as an individual. I was the driver, I was a part of the team and I owned it and I was concerned about how HRT was evolving. My emphasis had shifted to HRT and it was all encompassing.

I was involved in everything to do with the team and I suppose there was a bit of a lesson in that too. In hindsight, I should have more heavily delegated and probably appointed immediately an MD or someone similar to handle certain managerial parts of the business. But what happens is that you're just so committed to making it all work and to keep it all going and to ensure that there's going to be longevity there, that Mark Skaife in a sense didn't matter as much. But while I didn't feel like it was affecting me in the marketplace, it probably affected me from the media point of view a little bit, because I was probably more short with the media and I certainly wasn't as easy to get a hold of, because I was busier than I'd ever been. I was less open to requests, which probably changed some of the relationships and the dynamics of the relations with media outlets as well.

As I mentioned earlier, my lack of desire to offset some of the team management wasn't necessarily because I was a control freak; a lot of it was just making sure that we could operate at the highest level in every area. It was about the marketing of the business and the way that it ran from a commercial standpoint. It was bloody hard. For example, when we did the initial Mobil sponsorship deal, it was under a 10-year Holden arrangement, but we had to renegotiate every three years on what the monies were and what sort of bonuses were in place. It was all things. In one sense, motor racing teams are not complex, because they're primarily spending businesses with maybe between a dozen and 20 invoices to manage, but they're hard to keep running because they are large numbers and from a cash flow perspective they vary quite a lot from month to month with higher costs associated to certain parts of the season.

There are peak periods of cost – the early part of the year and perhaps the month before Bathurst. You have to cash flow forecast to cope with those humps. We'd grown up with that and knew about it from day one, but when they're big numbers you've got to stay on top of it – it certainly wasn't like running the Lasers 15 years earlier. I used to know the number every month, $432,000 – it was *bang-bang-bang-bang-bang*, month after month, that's what it took to run Holden Racing Team in 2003. And there were times when I knew that a particular sponsor bonus may apply to a certain race or to a certain position in the series, which you pretty much continually needed. You hadn't banked on it, but you knew in the back of your mind when a campaign was going to cost you a little bit more, and you'd take the risk that you'd get the result and earn the bonus. You might have got a new development item that cost $100,000 and you're down the track of getting those things put on the car and hoping a little bit that it's all going to work out. That is how motorsport works. For instance, I got a $300,000 bonus from a sponsor to take Peter Brock in 2004.

There was a lot of pressure that I felt was very much mine, and I accepted that as team owner. It becomes your ultimate responsibility to keep people employed and the whole thing ticking over. You've got such great relationships that you'd never want to go back into the joint and say, 'Listen guys, it's over and out.'

Like I was saying about the reaction when Ingall knocked me off the track, a lot of my dramas were because of the total exposure to the total problem. If it was just me as a driver, I certainly would have reacted the same way, no doubt, but the way I felt was that it affected me more severely, it affected the Holden Racing Team, it affected our result in the series, and I didn't have the buffer that I previously had. If John Crennan had been at that race meeting that day, I would have come back and the first bloke to meet me would have been Crenno and we would have had a heart-to-heart about what my reaction was going to be. He might have said to me, 'Skaifey, settle down I'll handle this.' He might have said. 'Go to the motorhome', or 'Head to the truck and don't come out for an hour'. Whatever he said, it certainly wouldn't have been 'Head for the Stone Brothers garage and have a fight with a few blokes.' Which is what I did. That was probably one of the biggest things that I felt exposed from; I felt like there wasn't the layer of protection that I'd previously had.

It was a massively different world for me on every score. I felt very exposed and I felt like I was right at the coal face of whatever drama there was. One that really comes to mind is when Stone Brothers Racing got caught with an electrical infringement, and I was really vocal about it. I remember saying that they should have had a holiday for it, meaning a penalty which stopped them racing for a while.

I don't know how long after it was, maybe two or three months, but we got pinged with an extra resistor in the wiring loom on Todd Kelly's car. We were doing our debrief back at the workshop after Indy and one of the guys from V8 Supercars called my engineer Dave Swenson to say that there was an irregularity. Dave immediately went into a tailspin and he couldn't work it out straight away. But he went through it all and found that a supplier through HMS of a part of the wiring loom had made an error: there was a little sensor and they'd put the wrong fitting on the end of one of the tails and it had an extra resistor in it.

Dave couldn't have been more apologetic to me; he didn't know that that was the case. I can assure you that every tail fitting we had was checked within 15 minutes and we would have had 30 or 40 of them that were all wrong. I knew there were areas in our agreement with Holden where if we were ever caught for any technical infringement, they could pull the pin, and if that happened then the whole thing could be over. I knew that it was a naïve mistake – we certainly weren't intentionally cheating but we had broken the rules. I had all the technical guys – Dave, Jeff Grech, Rob Starr and Richard Hollway – in the room and writing down a plan of how we were going to handle it, who was going to communicate with who and how we were going to explain it – for them to write me the document as to how it happened and to get the bloke who made the part to make a statement was imperative. I really didn't care at that stage what happened to him, but we had to make sure we could save the business if we had to. It was just an incredible action list of crisis management.

Number one, we had to confirm to people that we weren't cheating and we needed to protect our team brand – for everyone connected with us, especially Holden. I thought it was going to come back on us as a team, but it was also coming back on me.

That was seriously one of the worst weeks of my life. I had to do a press conference about it because we'd qualified in the top three at the next race meeting at Symmons Plains and I knew that as soon as the questions about that day were starting to close up, the next question was going to be about the irregularity. We'd already been to the stewards and we'd already done all the hearings and we'd basically been cleared of any intentional wrongdoing, but then the media questions started to roll out. Todd had lost his podium from the Gold Coast and we couldn't hide from it, even though Ambrose had been allowed to keep his win from Queensland Raceway.

There had been three or four races between the Stone Brothers incident and ours, but I'd been so vocal I could easily look like a hypocrite – I had to choose my words carefully. I was privately very proud of how the team handled the incident and I got through the media conference being able to explain how it happened. It was a clear example of how many hats I had to wear. As a driver and team owner, I couldn't avoid the questions and I needed to front up in the way that Darrell Eastlake had taught me.

We had to be on the front foot, be open about the error and admit the mistake. We couldn't be 'holier than thou' about it, we needed to be humble and hope it went away without too much harm. We obviously had to make sure something like that couldn't happen again, and while that was critical, so too was saving the business. We needed to minimise the harm. Real damage control.

I know that I did talk to Ross Stone about it privately but I can't actually remember what was said. I think Ross was actually at the press conference, so I clearly had some work to do there and I did it to the best of my ability.

It was a great example of how life had changed from a pure 'grab your helmet, come along and drive the car' to basically being ultimately responsible for all things to do with the team. Even in those days, a Dave Swenson or a Richard Hollway were technically capable of explaining what had gone on, but they wouldn't have wanted to front a press conference with blokes attacking them – it was something I had to do no matter how tough it was. I have heard it explained as the burden of leadership, and it really felt like a burden that I didn't need when I had to keep racing cars.

There were plenty of other times when it was tough too, and blending the business with my racing was often not that easy. In 2005 some of the arrangements that we had with Holden Motorsport were under scrutiny from the Touring Car Entrants Group Association (TEGA) who ran the technical part of the sport, and AVESCO which ran the business and commercial aspects of it. That was when Tom Walkinshaw had completed a management agreement with Holden Motorsport and then subsequently acquired Holden Motorsport. The questions were being raised around the linkages of the racing licenses between Tom, the HSV Dealer Team which was owned by John Kelly, and my Holden Racing Team. As time went on, Tom and I did a deal together but there were constantly issues about whether we were actually in compliance with the Teams' Licence Agreement (TLA). I'd spent a lot of money on legal costs to ensure that we could operate the way that we needed to in the best interests of the business.

The sport is owned 75 per cent by the teams, which was TEGA, and on certain issues all the team owners have a say by way of a vote in what happens. I know there were teams that voted to wipe us out of the sport in 2005. It was so weird that rival teams could hold so much power; it was and remains the ultimate conflict of interest. Some of those teams thought they were going to get Holden's money they were paying me and that was the only reason they were doing that, which was crazy. It's actually one of the major reasons why I was losing faith in the industry and faith in the sport. I just couldn't believe that anyone would vote to stop myself and Holden Racing Team racing. It just blew me away.

It was a secret vote because I'm sure they'd never raise

their hand in the air when I was watching, but it doesn't matter what the voting process was, the reality was that people could do that and I was shattered. What I couldn't believe was that people could be so naïve about what we brought to the sport and then so vindictive that they could effectively vote to iron out the number one racing team in Australia. But even through all that drama, I was still driving well at times. Bathurst in 2005 was absolutely as good as I've ever driven, then in 2006 Bathurst we qualified unbelievably well, although we crashed out the first lap with the clutch problem. But we were still right there in the game, and I wasn't making mistakes that were costing us anything.

When I was operating at the right level I felt like I was driving the car as good as I'd ever driven, especially at those big race meetings. But I could feel that it was getting harder, it was taxing me more and I wasn't as committed to it as I was previously. I was probably a little bit more inconsistent too. Then in 2007 I remember one night talking to what I used to call the 'life committee', which was basically Craig Kelly and David White, about how long I could keep driving. I figured at the time a couple more years would have been enough, so I started to think about that for a while and had a couple of conversations with my dad and also with Toni. At one stage I contemplated taking a year off, just to concentrate on running the team, and come back and drive another year later. But Dad didn't think you could have a sabbatical and come back and operate at the level that we were at or at the expected level based on the competition improving.

One of the things that was worrying me a bit was that I felt like I was too desperate to win, and a lot of times I was in contention to win races and I either made a mistake or got caught up in the wrong circumstance somehow. When you get a bit too desperate to win, the opposite seems to happen. You seem to find ways to lose races – it's almost like you've forced the issue too much, a bit like a tennis player making too many unforced errors.

I felt like the real me wasn't in that car at times, but it is all a bit fuzzy now. I knew there were times where it was an unbelievably good drive and I knew there were times when I had a shave on a Monday morning I was thinking I had to do a better job than that or I wasn't going to be able to keep doing it. I obviously had to be responsible to the team since I had such a significant stake in its future.

For most of my career I think I'd been between 95 per cent and 100 per cent Mark Skaife – I'd been pretty consistent for a very long time. Then you started to see an 80 per cent result, which probably came from trying at 110 per cent. I could think of 20 races right now that I should have either won or been on the podium, but which either didn't end up there or I finished further down than I should have. Often in that era the car wasn't that good either.

I used to say that when Russell Ingall was driving with Perkins or Garth Tander was driving for Garry Rogers, sometimes they were picking it up and carrying it. There were too many times during those later years when that was going on for me. Bathurst in 2005 was the ultimate case of picking it up and carrying it and in that instance we were able to win. For most of the race it was lap after lap after lap after lap, qualifying laps, and that is hard to do – it was at an incredibly high level. There were times when I didn't do a good enough job in that era because it was so hard to keep carrying the car when it wasn't right. One race meeting it worked, the next it didn't, and I ended up spearing off the track; that's what happens when you are racing on the edge – expecting too much from the car and yourself.

The politics of V8 Supercar racing is hard work. The best politician in pit lane at the moment is Roland Dane and he's getting results; he does a very good job. He's 100 per cent committed to it and the difference is that he's just operating as the owner of the business, he's never driving the car. I always felt like the race weekends for me were always easy because I could come along and just drive the car, and the purity of that was almost like my relaxation time. But what was definitely getting to me was that people in pit lane knew that I was busy in the car and that a lot of the negative politics would take place while I was doing that.

Yes, I was on the TEGA/AVESCO Boards, but I shouldn't have had to deal with some of the crap that was thrown at me while I was preparing for qualifying, for instance. I couldn't believe that people wouldn't want to line up and have a conversation properly about it on a Monday morning. A lot of the personality attacks just kept coming at me; the Tom Walkinshaw issues, for example, were relentless. There's not too many guys in the world whose views on racing are as similar as Tom's and mine – the engineering influence, the way of going about doing a good job for a race team. Tom had a very good understanding of motorsport and was an ex-high level driver who actually understood.

But he was mostly on the other side of the world and the information that was getting to him was polluted. What was clearly not going to work was people from outside HRT telling us how to run the show. But even though Tom was based in England we used to try and talk once a week, but even that was getting harder. Whenever Tom would come down to Australia, we'd spend a couple of hours together, we'd talk about the world and we'd look at the business. It was Tom's idea to shift the Toll money across to our team when Garth came over because he genuinely wanted HRT to succeed and he wanted to take some pressure off me from a commercial standpoint, in terms of reducing my need to hunt out extra sponsors. A lot of his actions were genuine and designed to help.

But even with that in place I was struggling with motivation, and that led me down the track of talking to John Crennan quite directly about my future. At that stage I didn't know how long I had left in the driver's seat, but I knew we had to have a clear and analytical view around my driving future and what other opportunities that may lie ahead.

What I spoke to John about was not just the team – it was the whole box and dice, including HSV. I didn't train anywhere near as much as I needed because I just wasn't motivated enough about it, and that was a bad sign for me. When I got to the race meeting, my energy for going fast was still there and I felt sometimes that it was actually quite a dangerous feeling, because my level of competitiveness and my desire to drive the car as fast as I could possibly drive it was up there, but I knew I wasn't as prepared as I should have been. I finished some qualifying sessions with the thought that I had gotten away with it. *Man, that was close.* Some of those laps were just fantastic and other ones weren't.

Qualifying at Bathurst in 2007 was just unbelievable; it was as good a lap as I'd ever done and it was good enough for the front row. Being close was almost not the norm at that stage.

Consistency was always an absolute key to getting the best results. If you have a look at my 2006 results, the amount of mechanical failures we had that year was just unbelievable. There were lots of races where we should have just bolted. We were smashing them at Oran Park and in the lead at lots of other places and simply didn't finish. There was always lots of drama and innuendo about how all that was going because Rick and Garth in the other HSV team were finishing all the races. There were times when our red team was very worried about what was happening in the orange team, about why there were differences in the reliability and speed of equipment.

There was a lot of chat inside the team about what was going on, and there were a lot of people from outside our camp who were saying it too, and as you know 40,000 Mohicans can't all be wrong. I wanted to win and I wasn't content to settle for a lesser result just because of the way the points were structured. Others were able to settle for an OK result so long as it was near enough, and good luck to them, but it wasn't fun for me to worry more about finishing rather than winning.

At my peak I was really good at picking out trouble spots and evaluating risks. My engineers used to tell me when I could start to back off. I remember at the GMC race at Canberra, the last race there, we just bolted! At places that were difficult like that, I found I was less likely to make a mistake if I just kept on pressing on. I mightn't have been quite as deep on the brakes at the two spots which carried a greater risk than others, but the rest of the lap was like I was racing hard with an Ambrose or Lowndes, because I found that was a better way to keep it flowing and keep my concentration.

Across the course of 2005, there were times when I got the lead or established a lead by driving the wheels off the thing for a certain period of time, and then I could back off and look after it. At my peak that was always a big part of my driving. You even got to the point where if you made a mistake in a qualifying lap you could tell the guys almost exactly how much time you'd lost, because you just had such a feel for it. And they could measure it later, and sure enough you'd be spot-on. I know it's a bit clichéd, but when you're at one with the car and understanding what's going on, it's really an incredible feeling. But that wasn't happening as much as I would've liked in those later years.

I think you can still be an owner-driver provided you have the right structures and personnel in place and we clearly didn't. You couldn't do it the way I was doing it. You have to build the right people into the right areas of the business, to put people in place to complete certain tasks and manage parts of the operation – you don't see captain-coaches in football anymore because the game is not that simple and has become more professional. If you think about me coming back and just driving the car with Greg Murphy in 2009 at Phillip Island and Bathurst, it was just a walk in the park. I brought my helmet, I made comments about the car from an engineering standpoint, signed a few autographs and jumped in the car. It was refreshing and easy, certainly easier than anything I had done in 2008. I found my love of racing again and I was enjoying myself and I think I did a good job.

I could have enjoyed Bathurst with Greg a lot more, though. Seriously, of all the Bathursts we've been to, that's the one that got really away. We went there thinking it'd be nice to run in the top five and that was probably a realistic expectation if we did a good job. Then with 90 per cent of the race done we were in contention to win, and it doesn't get much better than that. We had the strategy right, we had the late speed race, Greg was driving sensationally and we could so easily have won. Even in a 1000 km race, it is all about the fractions.

I've had some painful losses up there, but this was one of the worst. To be honest, with 15 laps to go I turned to Toni – which I should never do and I promise I will never do again – and said, 'We're going to win this.' We had the fastest car on the track, Greg was driving it really well and we would have come back onto the track with a 10-second lead after the final pitstop. I knew it was the fastest car because I was catching Tander early in the race and Greg was the fastest car on the track at that stage. Clearly, the car was fast enough to hold out any challenge.

But it is a cruel sport. When someone goes off the road on a 6.2 km racetrack and you get the luck of the safety car being called just when it's too late to get your own car over into pit lane, that's just ridiculous. It takes a lot to win that race and not much to lose it – it is one of the reasons why it is such a special race to win, there is so much out of your own control.

It is our grand final, the one race you want to win. The ultimate challenge is winning the whole year, but the reality of our culture and our tradition is that this is a 'stop the nation day' in Australian sport. Every team puts its biggest effort into this one day; if you can't afford new bits every week you hang onto them for this weekend – everyone is at their absolute best for this weekend, and that was why I was so wrapped. For our car, from a relatively small team (which now no longer exists) on a relatively low budget, to be the fastest car was just amazing. If we'd won the race, it would have been an incredible result for all concerned.

It would have been a great way to round off one of the arrows in the Skaife Next logo. A sixth Bathurst win would have been amazing.

The arrows in the logo represent the four parts of my work life. The first arrow in the logo was racing, and the next one was the automotive industry because clearly I've always been around cars and love the industry. The third was based around media, and the final one was 'other', which was basically other things I've been interested in, like circuit design and other business ventures.

John had done a lot of work on assessing me around those four criteria. He also assessed me in comparison with 15 of the superstars of motorsport, from Bob Jane through to Jim Richards. He then packaged it all up with a recommendation of six or eight opportunities that he felt I should pursue.

I found that paper really motivating, and that made the final step of selling my stake in HRT to Tom so much easier. I didn't need the ownership of HRT to drive my future, I had plenty of other opportunities and in some respects they would be easier without HRT. I had the chance to buy him out – and I had investors ready to do that – but I ended up making a decision with my head, not my heart. It was one of the biggest decisions I've made in my life and it was a good one, with the Global Financial Crisis hitting the motor industry particularly hard in 2009, especially given the troubles at GM in the States. I felt relieved not to be facing the commercial turmoil of team ownership.

It made absolute sense to me to sell out at that stage, to step back from it all and have a good think and even a holiday. From a media standpoint, I was fortunate that I had opportunities to do some things there and other opportunities that have come up since, like heading up the Car of the Future program, Directorship of V8 Supercars Australia (TEGA and AVESCO combined) and the design of the Townsville and Homebush tracks. It's those things that have given me back my spark. I had obviously been on the board of V8 Supercars before and I helped with the Canberra track, so it wasn't unfamiliar territory, but it was now more enjoyable because I could stand back and have a proper look without my team owner's hat on.

Life after racing has been as demanding time-wise as it was when I was racing, which is good. It's probably hard in some ways because there's not the same infrastructure around me that I was used to, but it's been a really good change. I probably worked harder in 2009 than I've worked for a long time because it's been about establishing the next steps and where we will head. It's been really flattering because there's been a lot of automotive industry discussion about me doing things in retail or in various businesses and I'm really interested in some of those opportunities moving forward.

The Skaife Next document was pretty extensive and we had a lot of meetings and a lot of discussions to finalise it. It all started with a briefing and three or four meetings, then

John went away and did some research and returned with a draft. We had a final recommendation meeting where he collated the last parts of the research, and he delivered that to me around August 2008 – all 75 pages.

The document contemplated me retiring at the end of 2008 or 2009 and we discussed that quite a lot after John finished his work. As the 2008 season became more of a chore I thought – why prolong it, the time was right.

For a lot of reasons, Bathurst in 2008 was one of my least satisfying race weekends, but I don't think it weighed too heavily on my decision. There were a lot of background business choices to be made, and I felt that through the year there was lots of plotting going on from different people, including some of our major sponsors, to change the driver line-up around. I knew Garth had pretty much become the lead driver in the team, which again was a sign for me because I didn't really care. If I was as motivated about it as I had been throughout my whole career, I would have put more energy into changing that. To sit back and say 'I don't really care' was a pretty good barometer for me not wanting to be there and not valuing the level of competition and my status in the sport as much.

The decision to retire slowly crept along – there was no defining moment, no light switch where everything became clear. My continued disillusionment and the fact that I was getting less enjoyment from it was becoming too much to ignore.

Quitting racing was one thing, selling the team was another, and they aren't directly related. I'm so much more relaxed and comfortable not having the team that it was clearly the right thing for me to do. Up to then I had a number of people whose lives I had a direct responsibility for and I had to generate the multi-millions of dollars required to keep operating at the highest level. Over Christmas in 2008 after selling the team, I wasn't getting the phone calls. It was fantastic, probably the best time in my life for off-season relaxation.

There is no money in owning a race team if you want to win. Absolute fact. If there was money in it, you wouldn't be competitive because people would go and grab money off the top of it and put it in the bank. The only guys who ever win are blokes who spend every dollar, and when you spend every dollar clearly the return on your investment isn't that great. I didn't feel as if buying HRT was an unbelievable opportunity to earn a massive amount of money; that was certainly not the thing. I did it with my total interest as a racing person.

With GM's dramas in 2009, coupled with the knowledge that HRT's agreement with Holden was up for renewal at the end of the year and the rumours that Holden through its head of motorsport, Simon McNamara, was shopping around for a new race team, I was just so relieved when it wasn't my worry any longer. When Holden announced that Roland Dane's Triple Eight team was coming on board it was water off a duck's back because I was absolutely far enough away from all of that to not be concerned.

I'll always be worried about how Holden Racing Team sustains itself – I'll always be concerned to see that it continues as a top level team and that it remains prosperous, especially when I see the guys at the race meetings. There are blokes there who are close personal friends and that all means something to me. When they won at Bathurst in 2009, I was one of the first on the phone to ring Richard Hollway and say, 'Well done, mate.' Those guys had all been such an important part of my life, so while I have concerns for them I can never remember feeling so relieved in all my life. I was totally relaxed, and that was a good thing.

10

THE THINGS THAT MATTER

For me, it was never about getting a bigger boat or the latest toys, it was about the purity of the concept: of racing cars against other people, about seeing how deep you could go under brakes, how far you could push on a given day on a given track. It was about being the best race driver possible and that meant both on and off the track. In every facet of a very complex sport, I wanted to build my knowledge and I was hungry.

To me it was like a normal business – you run a gap analysis looking for weaknesses and places for improvement and then find the puzzle pieces that are missing or aren't good enough and work on making them better. If you did the same analysis on any driver running in Australia today, you'd find they all have gaps, whether it's Jamie Whincup or Garth Tander. Or even a Michael Schumacher, for that matter.

It was important to try and be complete in every aspect of the sport. I wanted to be the best and I wanted to win races. In my mind, if I did the very best I could, the rest would sort itself out, and that included money and some of the other perks. I've had boats and jet skis and there were plenty of bonuses off the track in addition to the financial rewards, but I've never been good with idle time which means I've never had a lot of time or desire for some of the trappings of the sport. Getting my pilot's licence has been on the radar probably half a dozen times and I should go and do it, but clearly from a safety standpoint it's something I'd want to do really well and I've never had the time to be as proficient as I'd like. In reality, I guess it just hasn't been that important or I would have found the time and that may be because it wasn't going to help me win races or to relax. When I finished a race meeting, there was no way I wanted to head off to the airport and organise my flight schedule and then fly a plane back to Melbourne.

After a race, I needed to unwind, to have a beer with the boys and then go to the airport and jump on a plane . . . to me that always seemed the relaxing way of getting the simple things in life in order. Even now, just being part of the media, at the end of the day I'm worn out because I've had to think about a lot about a race – all the race strategies – and had to make sure we've covered the race properly. And now it's not thinking about one or two cars, it's about 30 cars. It's exhausting in a different way to how it was in the past. Sometimes it's nice to go and jump in a helicopter and get to the airport quickly, which I do sometimes and I don't mind paying the price in terms of getting my wallet out – but in terms of owning one and having to fly home, it's not for me.

I think what happens in professional sport, and perhaps even any profession, is that if it's really what you want to be doing, it can be all encompassing, you are drawn more and more into it. I always felt that I had to eat, sleep and breathe motorsport to get the best from myself. When other blokes were at the pub having a beer, I was hanging around thinking about the next set-up sheet for my Formula Holden. Some people look at it and think I missed out on a few things because of that approach, but I think in the end I would have missed out on a lot more if I hadn't done what I felt was needed. Probably the only other guy I know who's worse than me is Nathan Buckley – he's just full-on, which is one of the reasons we're good mates. There's a lot of attention-to-detail work we both love and we often laugh at each other about how stupid some of our habits are.

When Mitch was born, a lot of people thought it would slow me down, but it gave me a different perspective. I remember standing in front of the shock-absorber machine one day re-rating shockers and I knew that Mitch would have a sleep in the afternoon between 2.30 and 4 and I was going hell for leather because I actually wanted to go and see him when he woke up. Some of my focus had changed and what I learned was not to sweat the small stuff. I still wanted things to be perfect, but I learned to relax on some of the things that ultimately didn't matter so much. I became more efficient and simplified things. I didn't want to change my desire for doing the best job I could and I think I maintained that focus while getting better with my diary. It was a strange time for me. Family and mates had always been important to me, but this was different.

Mates had always been good to provide an escape at times and I've been lucky to have some pretty good ones outside of motorsport. If I was under the pump and working my bum off, it would only take one night out with them, have a couple of beers and to talk about anything other than motor racing and everything was fixed.

I still keep in touch with some of the guys I grew up with on the Central Coast – whenever I'm up there I go and have a beer and we get all our families together. I don't feel like that's any different to how it's ever been, and I really value that. Mum and Dad are still up there, so we do still go there a bit and it is such a great part of the world.

Dad and I have always been fantastic friends too. There's only 19 years between us, so we're more like mates than we are father and son, but I've got a very healthy level of respect for him. He's a very bright guy and really capable; he could do anything he set his mind to and he's always been a perfectionist. No doubt this is why his business was so successful.

Nothing that Skaifey ever did was by halves. We made stainless steel exhaust systems for heaps of performance cars in the Central Coast area before anyone else. We were the first to have a pipe bender and we'd stay back in the workshop late at night and make three or four at a time. If it was even half wrong, it would just get thrown out.

Dad has a pretty fiery temper; he's Jekyll and Hyde in that respect. A very passionate and gentle bloke when he wanted to be, but then a real hard nut and serious taskmaster at other times. His father was the same but a bit more extreme. Pop was at a level that not many people could work for him. The level of demand and expectation were similar between the two, which was just the highest level of rip-tear-and-bust and get stuff done to absolute perfection, but the intensity did drop off a bit from Pop to Dad to be a bit more sensible and more humanly realistic, but it was still very hard to work for the old man. Nothing was ever right and that part of him rolled into our sport stuff too. If it was my sister Lisa's dressage horses, they needed to be pristinely prepared and they were. A lot of that was very similar with Mum too and those values in me came from both of them. Mum's attention to detail was, and is, superb.

If you were going to wash the car, it needed to be perfect and that's a great thing – if you teach kids to be mediocre, then they'll be mediocre. Clearly you have to be sensible in all of that expectation, though. When they're five and they can't reach the roof of the car they're going to miss that section. I remember when I was that age, I missed a piece in the middle of the roof on a car once and the old man ripped into me and said, 'Why didn't you stand on something?' So next time I did stand on something. He was hard, but he is just a fantastic bloke and he did so much for me. Clearly, I've learnt more from him than any other person on the planet.

We are softening as a family, though. I've tried to modify the bits that have got him into trouble at times, but I am very similar to him in a good way. Mum and Dad funded all the first few years of my racing and to demand of me to put in my pound of flesh was perfectly healthy. If we went interstate for a race meeting, we had to be back at work to open the shop the next day. It would have been easy to arrive back at Wyong at eight o'clock in the morning and go have a sleep for four or five hours and come to work after lunch or something, but that just wasn't the go. Even the edict of not being able to work on the cars in business hours was smart, although it might mean we were working back on the race car until nine or 10 at night. They were very powerful messages for me to learn; it was the business that funded the racing and you had to look after the business. If we'd been slack in preparing the car we wouldn't have won as many races as we did and perhaps I wouldn't have been where I am today.

If you want to do it, you've got to put in and do it properly – give 100 per cent – it is quite simple.

The real backbone of the family was Mum. She is a loving, beautiful, soft and gentle lady who cared for us enormously and, as busy as she was, always prioritised the family above all else. Mum also had an innate feel for the business and for customer expectation, what people wanted from us and what we had to do to deliver quality service. From a family standpoint, she was very much like that for us, and things never got out of control. You would never walk out of our house without your shirt ironed, which meant when we got home from the workshop after spending a day serving customers and then a few hours on the race car, Mum would still be ironing clothes and completing all the household requirements. It was just a normal part of our family life and those levels of effort are very much the foundation for how I operate today. It's not necessarily the same for everybody and we've all got different ways of going about our lives, but for us those stricter guidelines were very important and she certainly was at the heart of all that.

My sister Lisa didn't really want to be in the tyre service business, she just didn't like it and couldn't find the motivation to be involved with it. She's certainly a different cat – a very interesting and beautiful girl. So when she was leaving school, the business was going pretty well in Melbourne and we brought her in to do the merchandising for Gibson Motorsport. We were really the first to approach that side of the business in such a professional manner selling Nissan Motorsport merchandise.

She is an ideas girl and she has the intelligence and discipline to turn those ideas into action. She can be a bit left-field sometimes, but where she gets to as a result is actually very good most of the time. After doing a bit of work for us, she worked in the UK for five years or so, but she stayed working in motorsport with outfits like Prodrive and then ran an HR company specialising in the placement of motorsport personnel. When she returned to Australia near the start of 2000 she worked with me for a while again. She was good at looking after my sponsors, making sure they got value for money from their involvement.

Then she started the Australian Motorsport Show and has recently sold it and these days she's a fantastic mum tied up with her kids. Cooper and Riley are ripper little blokes who get a buzz from anything automotive, but with those names and the family they came into that was always going to be the case. Their dad is 'Krusty', Richard Hollway, who was my engineer in the HRT days and that in itself presented challenges.

It was a bit weird when they first got together; normally

you'd be warning your mate about your crazy sister, but it wasn't like that this time. I said to her, 'Don't you burn this one because you'll bugger it all up for me with him.' It only reeked of drama for me – I had a very strict warning for Lisa not to upset Richard because he was so important to my racing. But it's worked out well for both of them, and me, which is perfect – they're a beautiful couple.

I suppose at that stage I was going through a bit of drama myself with Belinda. I met her in May 1991 and we were married in November '93 and she was obviously around for those couple of great Nissan years before we tied the knot. She was very supportive and we did a lot of European racing and had a really great time. It was a very vibrant, busy and successful part of my career.

She wasn't really a motor-racing person, which was good in most respects. She did enjoy it and she got her brain around it, but she gave me an escape a lot of the time, the ability to drop out of the motor racing zone and into a 'normal' world, and that was probably the thing that we grew apart on as time went by. She was probably sick of me being engrossed in motorsport, my expectations and the racing industry, and also the level of time and energy that I was applying to it. When we separated in 1999, Mitch was four and I guess Belinda and I just didn't get on as well anymore, we'd drifted apart and our priorities were different.

It was a very difficult and strange time for me. Getting my gear and leaving the house and having Mitch understand that I was leaving . . . was way up on the Richter scale of the hardest things, bar none, that I've ever had to do. The most difficult thing in my life was to tell him I wouldn't be at home!

I rented a little place only a couple of kilometres away to make sure I was really close to him. That part of my life was very difficult, stressful and emotional, but the following year I met Toni. She was the production manager at Network Ten for motorsport, golf and lots of other things and we started to see each other in 2000. Life is about peaks and troughs and when you're in those troughs, like I was in '99, sometimes it's very difficult to see the light at the end of the tunnel. On the racing front, I won most of the races but I didn't win the series; on track it was all getting better after an extremely tough couple of years.

But it was an extra tough year for me and not just because of what was happening with Belinda. One of my best mates, my trainer, Andrew Crouch, had died and between Belinda and I splitting up and Andrew, I was not really having the best time. I remember in that off season having to get my brain around what I had to do – I had to get my life in order.

Life lessons can be good in some ways, no matter how tough they seem. All that shit led into the best phase of my career, the three championships in a row. Personally, though, it was a lot about just trying to get my act together and Toni was sensational with it all. I'm glad she was there to help me and share the success with me. She is the nicest person I've ever met. She's just gorgeous and she was fantastic to be around. Again, she didn't know a great deal about motor racing and she didn't really know about me. She didn't know how competitive I was, so that was a bit of a surprise to her as time went by.

It was all lovely and then she started to see some racing

from the inside which maybe opened her eyes – she didn't really know about the mongrel part of the M Skaife package until she started to become involved in my life at the track.

Toni is an incredibly clever, capable and driven person. She has this way about her that I was drawn to – she's stylish and savvy with great people skills. She is a far better communicator than me and has been outstanding mixing her work and business life with the demands of motherhood. The girls, and Mitch, adore her.

When Toni said to me after a couple of years that she wanted to have children, I was unsure about how and when. I knew how difficult those early days could be and I wasn't sure how kids would fit in to our already busy lives. But of course that is a short-sighted view. I'm so glad we decided to have our girls; the sense of family that we have now is complete and watching the three kids grow is a daily reward.

She is just fantastic with Mitch too, she puts so much effort in. When things come to an end like they did with Belinda, there is going to be grief. Sorting out my arrangements with Belinda was hard and at the end of the day, all I endeavoured to do was make sure that she and Mitch were looked after. After that, Mitch's relationship with Toni was very important, just as it was for Belinda to get on with her life. Belinda has married again and she's got another little boy so she's moved on with her life now and that makes a big difference to both of us. I talk to Belinda every day because we're always talking about what Mitch is doing and who's picking him up, where we're going and what's going on, so it's great now that we've got a good relationship in place.

For both our families it was important to get access and custody absolutely right, and the energy that Toni put into ensuring that she and Mitch have a good relationship was extreme. They're really close and that is great – we'll be at home and Mitch will just walk up and give her a cuddle, but it could so easily have been different if they hadn't both put in the effort.

Any time you have big life decisions there's going to be a question mark over whether you've done everything you could. I think both Belinda and I did our best to stay together, but the reality is that it doesn't always work no matter how much you try. I would never recommend to anyone that they separate, but if it can't work, if you're on different pages and you're not operating in a way that's going to be conducive to a nice relationship and a nice family environment, you need to deal with it. Life's too short to not be happy.

You're always going to have feelings for the mother of your child and you'll want for her to be happy and looked after and for her to have a nice life and that is what I have tried to do, but that time was definitely the hardest part of my life. I no longer had open and free access to my son, which was very weird and crushing. On Christmas Day, you feel it more, that's for sure, but you feel it every day. Some of the things that I really looked forward to, like waking up in the morning with a cuddle from him, were gone and it was extremely hard to deal with. We could do a whole separate book on the Family Court, but I couldn't understand why my access to my son was restricted simply because I was the father, not the mother. Anything that's predicated basically on women being better parents than men is wrong – I know it is marginally better now, but it didn't help me at the time in understanding the unfairness of the system.

Jeffrey Browne was my lawyer for all things motorsport and business and through all that and I sat in his boardroom when the solicitor from the other side came in and said – and I'll remember these exact words forever because I couldn't believe what I was hearing: 'How much are you prepared to pay to have him for a Wednesday night?' Honestly, my restraint was amazing, because I could have absolutely choked him on the spot. What we were arguing about was whether I could have dinner with Mitch or have him overnight – which still to this day gets me. That whole issue of how much you're prepared to pay for a Wednesday night; that will live with me forever.

Dads only getting access to their kids every second weekend is just wrong as a base level concept. I know some dads don't or can't put enough effort in, but I wasn't like that and it wasn't easy to be treated that way. If I wanted to go and pick Mitch up from school or to take him to footy training or go and see him at the swimming carnival, I should have been able to do that any day of the week. But the system had other ideas. Thankfully it has changed and access for fathers is better now.

Mitch can now decide for himself and it's quite a sensible relationship. Belinda has him for a week and I have him for a week, and he loves it because there's really great continuity. When he's at Belinda's I still talk to him every night, and the same in reverse. It's made it like a proper family relationship and in the circumstances it's as good as it can get; not that it felt like it was going to get to this stage when we were going through the legal drama of the Family Court.

A lot of the early access, like being able to see Mitch on Wednesday nights, was around me paying spousal and child maintenance, and I did all that and more. As I said before, I did everything I could to make sure both Belinda and Mitch were as well looked after as they could be, and I sleep easy about that side of it. I basically paid for what I wanted to be flexible arrangements because of the nature of my work life, but it's only in the past three or four years that it has become genuinely sensible. So for many years it was just torture, and in many ways it was no different to other blokes in the same situation, which to me was just wrong. Toni's support was the key to having good quality of life.

Again that's where my life committee as I call them, Whitey (David White) and Ned, really came into play and they were just a fantastic sounding board at the time, as they are today. Amazingly, this period was also the most successful part of my career, and to me this goes back to the root of all the conjecture of whether I'm naturally a good driver or have to work at it. To be able to keep going at the highest level, to deal with some of the things I had to put up with – a lot of which no-one knew about because I didn't want it to make the papers and which will remain a secret now for exactly the same reasons – answers the question over natural ability. Yes, I worked hard at what I did, but to use racing as an escape, to come from last at Clipsal in the wet to win after what led into that race meeting says a lot to me about natural ability.

Most people didn't know how tough I was doing it, that I was able to shut away portions of my life when I was at the track and use motor racing as an escape. It's really easy to sit in a race car while the boys are changing shocks and springs and detour into another land, so I had to be at the top of my game. It would have been very easy to head back onto the track without my focus and that could have had two consequences – I could have mucked up the set-up or crashed.

Race weekends were absolute escapism, and it was great to have the ability to really enjoy the fun when other parts of my life weren't much fun at all. I've never wanted to share any of my personal feelings – I'm not very good at it, anyway – and I never wanted a sympathy vote or whatever. There were times I would have liked a bit more understanding, but if I wasn't telling people what was going on, that wasn't going to happen, and I accepted that as the cost of privacy for both myself and Belinda.

Some people thought I was arrogant when I just bolted from the track, jumped on a plane and headed home, but I wanted to get some time with Mitch and I didn't have much choice over when I could or couldn't do that. On those Wednesday nights or on my weekends with him, my feeling was: just don't even pick the phone up. Do not even contemplate going and doing a sponsor deal or a dealer launch on a Saturday or a function – it could have been for the Prime Minister on that Sunday, but it was just no way! At the start of that year, we'd put those things in place and guys like Paul Weissel, HRT's PR man, and Craig Kelly and even some of the people at Holden knew that if they wanted me to do something it had to be done by 3:30pm on a Wednesday afternoon. That's what the situation was.

Mitch changed my life in so many ways and my daughters Mia and Tilly have done the same, even though they came at a time when I was busier than I've ever been in my life. They gave me focus and understanding – just the knowledge that there is a little person relying on you changes the way you do things, and I reckon a lot of that is pretty healthy. I hear people say, 'We're going to have a baby and this will bring us closer together.' It's one of the most difficult things you ever do in your life so if things aren't rock solid it could do the exact opposite. No-one gives you a handbook and you don't get a little guide on having a family, or on how to be a great parent. I mean, there are books but they don't really tell you about the level of commitment and a level of thought that is much greater than I would have ever considered it to be. I find it really interesting that my mum and dad had me at 19 or 20. I wasn't grown up at 19 or 20; I wasn't ready in my head or mature enough to be a good parent.

On the other side of it, though, I can remember Dad saying that one of the great things about having kids early was that the gap between us was small enough for him to come water skiing with us or playing footy or whatever. He said he was young enough to enjoy it all, but in terms of how much you know and what your life skills are, I'm really not sure.

I reckon a lot of my growing up was being around Dad in the business because you're just there and you're a part of it. When I was 10, he was 30 and was in full flight and you were either with him or you were not. It was great that he could have his family around him in the workplace; not many people can find that balance in their life . . . and I really value that experience now. We simply had to fit in.

Obviously parts of my work life have been easy to share with the kids, especially with Mitch who's a bit older than Mia and Tilly. Mitch being around so much has probably helped him to deal with some of the stuff that goes on – it can't always have been easy having a father like me with so many critics out there in the world. He probably doesn't even tell me half the things that have gone on. There would always have been kids who are Holden fans and been really supportive and think his dad's OK, but the world doesn't just revolve around red and there have always been plenty of fans from the other side who would have been less than complimentary and also those who were critical of my weekend's performance – 'Monday's experts'.

I'm sure he's copped some flack, and if I crash out of a race or whatever, he'll always say, 'Oh, this bloke gave me a bad time about that today,' or whatever. That part of it was quite tough, especially when he was still young and impressionable.

If Mitch does decide to race cars at least he's had exposure to both sides of the ledger, he's seen both good times and bad times, and he's seen both positive and negative responses from the fans. He's had some drives in go-karts but I've never pushed him. I'd like to think I've been the same as Dad with that and I'm really just there to help Mitch with whatever he chooses. Dad always said, 'Boof, if you want to go and play football or car racing or whatever, if you're going to do it, have a fair crack at it.' The same applies to Mitch.

He's a funny young bloke because he's got really good skills. It's a lot like great cricketers or great footballers, he's got a lot of time. When I watch him he looks like he's in cruise mode but when you click the stopwatch he's going quite fast. He's done a time at the Oakleigh go-kart track which would have put him in the top 10 at a big go-kart meeting earlier in the year, so he's obviously going alright in terms of speed.

He's got really soft hands, he's got a really nice feel for it. But I don't know whether he's got enough mongrel about him. He's way too nice at the moment, which is a beautiful thing to say because it's not a negative in life for him, but I'm not sure it will make him want to be a race driver.

He's much more of a free-wheeler than me – he's much nicer and has a beautiful disposition. But as he gets older I see some of the intensity that I have about things; like his fitness, for instance – he looks after himself and he's doing a good job. He'll often be up at six o'clock so he can train before he has to go to school. If I had to have a bet, I would say if he wanted to race cars, he probably could.

Mia and Tilly are just so totally different to each other, and to Mitch for that matter too. It's one of the great things in life because you could never foresee two such different people from the same parents, which is a lesson in nurture and nature, I suppose, and it's like living with two Tonis and two Marks. Mia calls herself 'Mi-Mi' and is a drop-dead gorgeous princess – she's a clone of her mother. The other little one I call 'Johnsy', as in Andrew Johns the rugby league player, because she should have been a boy except for the way she looks. She is the tiniest little girl with a mop of blonde curls – she is just so spirited, though. She is stunning looking but is absolutely full-on with a pain threshold right up there; she just terrorises Mia. She'll purposely take something from Mia and run away and thinks that's a great game. She'll hit her head and she never cries; she has a level of intensity and aggression that's totally different to her sister.

Very early on with Mitch, I learned that you have to get onto their wavelength if you want to really communicate with them. I had to know what pressed his buttons and I found that part of being a parent really interesting. It's like the two girls, what motivates one doesn't work on the other, and if you want to get anywhere with them, you've got to understand what makes them tick. It's always controversial about whether you smack a kid, but sometimes they respond to that and sometimes they don't. It's almost ingrained from day one as to what style of disciplinary action will work and what won't.

Tilly, for instance, has had this thing going where she just hits everyone. But what do you do? You smack her back and sometimes if you've startled her it's worth doing, other times it's meaningless. It hurts her feelings more to put her in the naughty corner and stand her there alone, so she can't be part of the family. That hurts her way more than slapping her on the back of the hand. Naughty corner – what modern day bullshit! But it works for her.

To me, as a leader and business owner, I try to work out what motivates each person: how do I get the best out of that person and what do I need to do differently? What I learned about myself in the process is that what really matters to me is people. My family and its well being is right up there as the greatest of motivators, but I didn't buy HRT because it was a great business model. Yes, I thought I could make it work, but it was more about doing something for the people in the team. They were my other family, and even though the costs were high, I have no regrets because I tried to do the right thing.

11

SPHERES OF INFLUENCE

I'M REALLY ENJOYING this next phase of my life and I've been fortunate to be doing work that's different and provides me with other areas of enjoyment. Obviously I love the industry so I like being involved, and now I love telling the story rather than being the story. For the best part of 20 years, much of what I did on 10 to 20 weekends a year was of interest to people; now it's my interpretation of what others are doing that is important.

I'll continue to run in the endurance races as long as the opportunities are there to run in a race-winning car with the right co-driver and, importantly, as long as I feel I'm competitive. I always said at HRT as team owner I'd decide when the time was right to step away, and while I think if circumstances were different I may have been able to run a few more competitive years, the clarity I have now after stepping away from the day-to-day grind is that I made the right decision. I won't be retracing my steps on that front, and I'm looking to the future rather than trying to relive the past.

My media work has been interesting. My gig with Seven is quite different to what I do on Triple M, which also quite different to doing this book. Skaife Next came with a rush and that meant 2009 was as busy as any other year for me after having my first real summer holiday in two decades. Much of what we did was well planned and executed by Ned and Boxy at ESP and that was all good, but the smokey for me was the invite from Tony Cochrane to join the V8 Supercar Board as an independent director and then also to look after the planning work for the Car of the Future program.

What I really enjoyed there was getting to exercise my brain in ways that I hadn't since the original problems with TWR. I spoke earlier in the book about how I enjoyed product planning and development and to me the Car of the Future was just that. We sat down and analysed the market as the core of the business plan, we spoke with the stakeholders of the sport, set some targets and then went out and developed a plan which we released first to the board and then to the team owners in November 2009. I think by getting active again in the sport and cherry picking the things I wanted to do, I started to get back my love for the sport.

I've enjoyed seeing my work on the Car of the Future evolve, to see my ideas coming back into play, and I loved the unanimous support of the board to implement the project despite what some of the detractors were saying during its evolution. We had goals for things such as build cost and opening up the door to other manufacturers, and clearly some people didn't like some of those ideas, but we – as in the board and generally the industry – saw both of those things as critical elements. I think in the end, we understood the DNA of a V8 Supercar and we had no intention of diluting what is a world class motorsport product.

Getting back in the car for Phillip Island and Bathurst was great – my little break from the driver's seat helped me rediscover my love of racing. Some people commented on how relaxed I looked during those two weekends, and I was. Those closest to me said my attitude was reminiscent of 2000. There were predictions of all sorts of dramas between Greg and myself, perhaps because we are both pretty headstrong characters, but they never materialised. We both had one goal – to win Bathurst – and we nearly did it, but as I've said along with a million others, motorsport is a cruel game. We had that race, we had the speed, the track position and the strategy to win the race, it was looking good until they called the safety car for a crash on top of the mountain and just caught Greg as he was passing pit lane entry. In that instant we lost our track position because we had to run a lap behind the safety car before our late race stop for fuel. If the race was green, we could have done that stop and still be leading by eight to 10 seconds; instead of that we were 11th after the safety car period. Greg did a tremendous job to fight up to almost a podium position.

I came back from my January shutdown with Toni and the kids and I was able to look at the sport from a different angle because I wasn't involved in the pit-lane politics and the drama. I was now able to take a global look at it. It isn't that my understanding changed in any way, it just didn't matter in the same way it used to. To come along with my helmet for a couple of test days and then to do the same at the two race meetings was perfect for me – I really enjoyed it.

Brock used to say, 'Things happen for a reason sometimes,' and maybe that's a little pie in the sky but that is how it felt. I have absolutely no regrets about selling my half of the race team, and with all the GFC dramas and GM going into bankruptcy the timing of that didn't concern me – I didn't have to live those issues in the same way. I certainly haven't put away the idea of owning another race team, but it was good not to have one in 2009.

Skaife Next was all about setting up the rest of my work life. At some point, I'll increase my automotive industry involvement so I'm doing more than just things like Car of the Future or media work, but right now I'm taking it all in and trying to work out what form that involvement will take. I have enough time and financial stability to cherry pick what I do and it's only 18 months since full time retirement.

If I stay fit and can drive in the practice days that are allocated at race meetings as well as the test days, I know I won't be any worse off than I was in 2009 in terms of how much driving I did and how I went. I still think I have a lot to offer, and now if I keep racing there with Lowndes he can never catch me for Bathurst wins!

Once I have finished my racing, then maybe I'll look at owning or running another team. I've had numerous approaches but the timing isn't right at the moment. I'd love to have another red-hot crack at that without all the encumbrances of being captain and coach and all the external forces who were working against us for their own goals. I think the business of a racing team has evolved into such a big entity and the level of complexity means you can't drive and run the team.

In hindsight, there are lots of things I should have done differently when I bought HRT. For instance, I should have immediately put on a great general manager or CEO; I couldn't do anything about the business structure because that was done as part of our original agreement with Holden, but I should have brought that to a head too. We were really a customer team for Holden Motor Sport and then Walkinshaw Performance, which just drove me insane, especially given some of the people I had to work with at that operation.

If, for instance, I had John Crennan running the business side of the team it would be a totally different story today. Number one, I think I'd still be in there racing full-time. Number two, we would have won more races. Number three, I would have enjoyed the phase. Number four, he would have protected me from a lot of the drama. I really needed a bloke like John Crennan to make it work. I think we saw that when I had Craig Kelly as acting CEO for a year, we won Bathurst and things started to get back on track. I needed to be able to take a step back at times and his involvement allowed me to do that.

I reckon the way the business model looks now for a V8 Supercar team is pretty positive, especially when all the benefits of the Car of the Future come into play in 2012. If you can run a two-car team for around five to six million dollars and you're getting a large chunk of that from V8 Supercars, running a team is absolutely a viable business. With the cost savings from the Car of the Future, you'll able to run two cars for the kind of money you needed in 2005 to run one, and that makes the business model financially achievable.

I'm working on trying to get back to something like a Thursday block-out day, but since my retirement announcement it's been really hectic just getting everything in place. But we're getting there. Motorsport has been a part of my life since I was six, and I'm pretty sure it will always be there in my life.

I was going to the racetracks with Dad at that age and I can certainly remember lots of race meetings on Dad's shoulders at Oran Park or under the Ron Hodgson bridge at Amaroo Park. Mum would get there first thing in the morning and she'd take the table and land it in a spot in the shade and we'd hang there for the day to watch every race. My passion for watching great drivers happened very early and I remember watching Pete Geoghegan in the Craven Mild sports sedan coming onto the straight at Amaroo and watching his hands. A little bit of a snapshot into my world is that if Dad told me something, it was gospel. He said if you ever had two hands on one side of the steering wheel you were in trouble, and then he explained to me why and it made sense. So even as a little bloke I used to watch drivers come onto the straight at that corner and the average blokes would have two hands on one side of the wheel, and when it got sideways it took them too long to catch the car from sliding.

I was always very interested in those drivers in the corners, the way they turned the wheel, how they applied correction, and what their throttle control was like. And I can always remember the absolute finesse and skill of a guy like Pete Geoghegan, who'd slide the car with one beautiful correction and he had amazing throttle control. There's a little technique I use sometimes, to flick the throttle on and off very quickly to bounce the car on the front wheel to regain front grip in slow corners, and it actually comes from that. With Geoghegan you'd see the beautiful slide and hear the smooth throttle application, which compared harshly to the guys at the back of the field with no throttle finesse and hands on one side of the wheel. I called it the sports sedan method, and in this era it is really easy to spot it on a data trace of throttle usage.

Those beautiful skills were what I wanted to emulate when I started racing. They really live with me in terms of who I watched and who I thought drove well. There were some great XU-1 battles between Brock, Colin Bond and Bob Morris at Amaroo and I just wanted to be in there. Colin Bond was a real favourite of mine too; his car control was fantastic, which probably stemmed from his days as a rally driver; over the dog leg at Oran Park what he did with a car was fantastic to watch. Jim Richards and Brock were sensational just because of their flair and the way they drove and I always thought that Allan Moffat was just the best; his whole act was the most professional. Allan Grice was the most aggressive and he was a great passer, great at overtaking moves – he bluffed most blokes into letting him through. Bob Morris was a really good race driver and really hard at it. There were so many drivers in that era to admire, and I watched and learned and embraced what I wanted from each of them.

I always used to think the way that Brock turned at the

corner was the best; that Jim Richards' overall car control was the best; that Allan Grice's braking and overtaking was the best; that Peter Brock's first lap was the best; that Allan Moffat's application was the best; that Colin Bond's flair was the best. I remember very clearly saying to Dad that if we put all those blokes together we'd have a pretty amazing race driver.

If you'd written down all the things you had to be very good at based on what you'd seen, you'd have had to start a new column for the parts of a race driver's make-up that were changing with technology and innovation. You could be more valuable to a team if you were able to give a little bit more in terms of feedback. Allan Grice became very good at reading the tyre and he did a lot of tyre testing and was very good at that part of it, and that made him a critical part of any team. I wanted to be able to tick all the boxes in my first column, all the driving and racing skills, and then add to the next column with the parts I was evolving as a test or development driver.

When I started to line up against those blokes on the grid it was quite a weird time. In my first Touring Car Championship start, I qualified alongside Brock at Oran Park and I looked across and my leg was shaking. There's an element of sympathy – do I really want to beat this bloke because I've spent so long admiring him. But then there's this other element that says, 'I'm going to fix him up, I want to beat him and do whatever I have to do to beat him.' I remember in 1989 having an absolutely fantastic battle with Grice in the wet at Winton for the podium and Grice was always the one who was bumping blokes and all that stuff. I gave him a few bumps in the slow corners to give him the message that I was serious. Those days are very important in the development of your skills and reputation – especially at 22 years of age.

As a lover of the sport, getting on the grid was quite a large transition and the front of the field was absolutely first class in those days, with those guys still at their peak and then a bunch of us young guys working hard to beat them. Grice, Morris, Bond, Brock, Moffat, Richards, Larry Perkins and Dick Johnson are easily as good as the best of today in terms of the pointy end, and then you had me, Glenn Seton, Tony Longhurst, Neil Crompton and Tomas Mezera all pushing them. It was a great time for the sport, a real changing of the guard that I don't think I've seen since.

On the track I've had some great rivalries and guys I've just loved racing, but there are probably four who really stand out – for a variety of reasons. I've spoken a fair bit about Jim Richards, and he was clearly the best touring car driver in the world when I started racing with him. Craig Lowndes was again a teammate and we had a series of great battles that continued well after he left HRT. On the other side of the fence it was Glenn Seton and Marcos Ambrose. Glenn and I are still close mates, but rivalry in this sport didn't get much bigger than him being the 'Blue' factory Ford driver with Peter Jackson when we were sort of at the height of our powers in a 'Red' Holden with Winfield on the car. That phase of the new Holden-Ford category was a great time, and we both had great teammates too. He had Alan Jones, and when Alan turned it on he was as good as he'd ever been, and I had the same with Jim Richards. Channel Seven's Mike Raymond used to call Glenn the 'baby-faced assassin' and he was a lot like that. He had a laconic, cruisy nature off the track – a little bit like Lowndes in some ways – but he was a very committed race driver with a hungry attitude and fantastic car control.

He was maybe a bit low on the mongrel stakes compared with me, but he was very gifted. I've done plenty of bumping when necessary, although I've never purposely just smashed someone out of the way to beat them, except for that race at Amaroo Park with Tomas Mezera, but Glenn intimidated in a different way. Glenn was as good as you'd ever see in terms of natural ability and when he was at his best, he was very hard to beat.

Lowndes is different to me too. I have a couple of bumps just to apply pressure to those I am following, but Lowndes is like morse code, he just keeps on running into the back of the car in front – he is relentless. I wouldn't say he's actually a great overtaker, but he ends up making passes that look great because he worries the bloke in front into a mistake. That treatment upsets some more than others; personally, it didn't disturb me at all because I loved the challenge of keeping him behind me, but I know for instance that it really annoys Garth Tander and Rick Kelly – and that just makes Lowndes do it more. You need to be able to say, 'I don't care how many times you run into me,' and then control the situation. You need to limit the angle at which he hits you – you can even position it purposely so that when he does hit you, it's to your advantage. Dealing with Lowndes means you can prop it in the middle of the corner so long as you haven't been hit getting into the corner; if you've got your car balanced, you have control. There's a lot of science and a lot of gamesmanship in the ability to not yield to him, but it was always a real challenge and he was great to race against. It was also great to turn it around on him when you were chasing and deliver some return punishment.

Lowndes shows the car a lot when he's following too – you will always see him pulling out of a slipstream just so the driver in front can see him in the side mirrors, and that's one of the biggest differences in our technique. I might do that a couple of times to demonstrate that I'm going to have a crack somewhere. I definitely won't show it at the spot I'm going pass the bloke, though, but like his tapping, Lowndes is relentless although sometimes it doesn't work for his speed. In the braking zone for Siberia at Phillip Island, he just continues to show the nose of the car there and it slows him down in a spot where he'll never pass. The good guys just take that as a rest – you can drive off line there all day and you won't ever get past someone who hasn't made a mistake, but it has worked on plenty of people over the years.

Craig definitely knows those who crumble and he likes to try and take the upper hand with everyone. That's one of the reasons he and James Courtney have crashed so many times – James just won't yield, sometimes to his detriment. Craig tries to force a bit of supremacy on him and James says, 'Get fucked, I don't care who you are.' So they crash. Others who are bit weaker, Craig will put a bit of pressure on and he's through in no time. He does get away with some things he shouldn't, but good luck to him if he does. He definitely takes liberties and half the guys find that intimidating.

It is important to know your rivals, to know who can push in what way, who is likely to do something strange, or if they have a track personality that you need to be alert to. Guys like

John Bowe, for instance, you just knew as soon as you drove up behind him it was going to be hard work – to a ridiculous point sometimes, even in his heyday. I'm not saying it is bad as such, just that you need to understand totally what you are in for, and that includes the guys you're unlikely to be racing because you'll have to lap them at some point, or pit strategy might lump you in with them.

Marcos Ambrose was very impressive from the minute he landed in V8 Supercars and there was a lot of gamesmanship, probably more than most, and we reciprocated. I knew straight away he was quick; I mean, he was on pole for his first race in Melbourne and I made sure I told him that he must have cheated, that he must have driven around the inside of turn four up the inside of the tyres. There was a tyre that had been moved a bit near the end of the session when he was faster than me, so I walked up, shook his hand and asked if he'd gone up the inside of that tyre. I made sure I put a question mark up about how he did it. I think he out-qualified me at Phillip Island a couple of weeks later, which was the first round of the series, and it was pretty impressive for a kid to come from nowhere and do that.

It was on everywhere with him. One really good one was when I speared him in the braking area for turn four at Phillip Island and I purposely just smashed into the back of him – not to spin him off, because it was so early in the braking area that he would've saved it, especially because he had such good car control and is pretty gifted; it was to wind him up. If you cop a tap early in the braking area there it's wild, and I thought this is a little entrée into how hard this is going to be for him.

But the best one of all was at Oran Park where we both went out of the gate full-on and I sped up the inside of him and turned him around at BP Corner. So on the first lap out for practice we came off the dog leg while everyone else was wobbling around, and we were into it, he turned in to the inside and *thump*, I spun him around and put him in the paddock – which for a non-event, just the first lap of practice, was very funny. Whenever we're having a beer, all the boys still laugh at that – it was excellent.

The race we had at Oran Park in 2004 was great too. We both won a race each and scored the same points but he ended up winning the round. The only reason he actually won in the end was that I was going to smash into him coming into the pits, I was all locked up and sideways and I was probably doing 20k faster, but if I'd hit him we would have blocked the pit entrance, so I basically pitched left and drove on, staying on track instead of pitting. It cost me time. But there was no let-up that day – there may have been a hundred metres between us but you couldn't have done a harder race in your life. When we both got out, we were buggered, and he walked up to me and he said, 'Man! We were fucking tapped out!' They were his exact words, and we *were* absolutely tapped out. It was just fantastic and there were a fair few battles like that with him over the years.

Consistently in their era, they were the four guys I rate as the best. I've had good races with Tander and others, but it was never the same. I've spoken about my part in generational change in the 1980s, and to me that started with me as the elder statesman in the first year of the VE in 2007 with Tander and Jamie Whincup. The opening laps of the race at

Queensland Raceway were as fierce as I can remember, with Whincup, Tander and myself. That was as wild as it ever gets, we were purposely running into each other at more than 200 kilometres an hour and bumping each other down the main straight. It was really good, really intense. But it was a great message of generational change – I was now the older guy and I was in the lead with guys 10 years younger or more, probably the best of the current crop, trying to pass me. I wasn't going to cut them any slack.

But it wasn't just about touring car people for me – I drew influence from other race drivers and other sports. Emerson Fittipaldi was a childhood hero and then Alan Jones – this was during the time we started to get better coverage of Formula One here.

Ayrton Senna for me was just unbelievable. When he died in 1994 we were leading the championship and the world's best driver being killed in a car had a significant effect on me. That was a very difficult period and took a lot to get my head around. Obviously I was always very impressed by Schumacher but he just didn't have the same appeal, and none of them today inspire me the way Senna did.

We were really into any form of sporting stuff as a family and we had a wide range of tastes and influences. Rugby league was big for me and a lot of very gifted rugby league players had a big impact – Bob Fulton was the biggest one. But I also used to pay a lot of attention to guys like Laurie Daley, Andrew Johns and Wally Lewis, just in terms of how they went about what they did and the time they had – how they were able to process the information and get a result and how they made it look easy.

Boxing was the same too. Dad was a massive Ali fan and I was too, and I've got a heap of his videos. I watched how he operated when he was at his very best and how good he was with his hand speed and his ability to move his head – it's just outstanding to watch him in full flight. The blokes who've captured my attention are the ones with enough natural talent to be able to show something extra, some form of flamboyance or flair.

As a young bloke, I thought I was going half all right in rugby league until I played against Greg Alexander in a schoolboys' competition. He just had the ball on a string and he made us look like gooses and we got flogged on the back of that performance. He just made us look ordinary. This was a kid who could read the game, he had great speed and obviously plenty of ability. I knew at that time that I couldn't ever play like that. It was actually quite a big moment for me because I thought that if I couldn't play the game at that level, then I should be into something else.

Greg Norman was right up there for me too, one of my real heroes. I've been lucky enough to meet him a few times and he's a good bloke too. Again though, he's got incredible skill but he's also got flair and a bit of larrikin earthiness about him. You could go through almost every sport and have a look and you'd see where the real heroes are, the ones with enough natural ability to put in that little bit extra. In a team-based context, they are probably the ones you love to hate if they aren't on your team, like Nathan Buckley. From a Collingwood standpoint everybody loved him. But from a total AFL perspective, a lot of people didn't – but only because he was just so gifted and so committed.

I'm a world champion copier and if I think there's a really good way of going about something, I'll take it. There's little bits of all these guys in me. I've taken a note of the bits I like and I've put them into my game in one way, shape or form.

12

IT CAN BE A CRUEL SPORT

I COULDN'T BELIEVE it when the Holden Racing Team was only allowed to race under some form of special dispensation back at the start of 2007. It felt like a personal attack on me, but more than anything it was far from being in the best interests of the sport. That there was a question mark over the validity of HRT and of me and that there was a chance we weren't going to be able to race was staggering. I don't have a lot of fond memories of that time.

There was aggro everywhere sorting out the issues between HRT and TEGA as the administration body of the sport. A lot of it was based on Tom Walkinshaw's commercial involvement in the team and my arrangements with Walkinshaw in terms of what services he was providing and how that then correlated with the terms and conditions of the Teams' Licence Agreement. There was just so much drama about how the investigation was unfolding and from a team perspective there was a lot of media hype about whether the team was going to get through this investigation. In the background a lot of the other teams were voting for us not to be there, which was just extraordinary. For people to be challenging my integrity probably upset me more than anything else; that some of my peers could say I'd do anything that wasn't within the regulations was a pretty hard pill to swallow.

It was an absolute nightmare. I reckon I learnt more in that timeframe about the real character of people than I'd ever learned before. I knew which way people were voting and then they'd pick up the phone at night and ask if there was anything they could do to help after voting to wipe me out. It was just the ultimate hypocrisy.

It took a lot of effort to keep it all together – to tell Todd Kelly, for instance, that it was all going to be OK and that we'd be out there racing when I really didn't know that was the case. I did believe everything from our end was on the up and up, but the process – including the ability for other team owners to vote on our fate – had left me with doubts. There was a lot of used car salesman in me at that time – I had to keep people motivated, to keep the cars rolling out the door and be ready not just to race but set the pace when I really didn't know what was going to happen.

There were so many things that were awkward in addition to the staff issues. When you've got to send an invoice to a sponsor they don't necessarily pay immediately when they think they mightn't have a race team going. So there were cash flow dramas. We were spending a huge amount of money on legals and I had to obviously keep the boys away from that. In the background there were obviously issues with Tom and me sorting out the business structure and what we were going to do moving forward. Holden had a big stake in it and we had to keep them abreast of all the developments – they were fantastic in terms of their level of support and how loyal they were. You don't get guys at the level of Denny Mooney and Alan Batey as the top bloke at Holden and effectively his 2-I-C involved and jetting off to meetings unless they are 100 per cent behind you.

I don't remember a time that had as much emphasis on me trying to sort out dramas rather than getting ready to go racing. I could have done a better job at the UN than what we were trying to do. It was very different to just buying the team and working through all of that; this time I was much more involved and had a lot more at stake. This was my money and my livelihood that was under threat, and you don't just sit back and let that go easily. This wasn't just about going racing anymore, this was about my life and my family.

I remember a meeting in John Hewson's office in Sydney when he was on the AVESCO board. He was there with Quentin Procter from the top-tier law firm Minter Ellison and Kelvin O'Reilly who was running TEGA, and on our side of the table was myself, Tom Walkinshaw, Alan Batey and Fiona Harden, who was Holden's general counsel. The aggro got to such a level that they were all talking about heading for the Supreme Court, and Alan and Tom started to pack their gear up. I don't remember jumping to my feet any faster in my life to keep it all controlled and for us to negotiate an appropriate settlement for us to keep racing, which we did. In three weeks we had a complete Deed of Settlement done and we were able to move on. Obviously I can't share the details of that, but they were pretty wild times in terms of what it all meant, and there'd been a very real threat to the team and my investment.

I remember jumping on a plane at one stage with every agreement the team had, things like sponsorship agreements, service contracts and the employee contracts that TEGA wanted me to substantiate so that we could prove that I was actually controlling the team and not Tom. I met Kelvin at the airport in Brisbane at 7.30 pm and we spoke for two hours and I flew back that night again. With that sort of effort I wasn't thinking about understeer and oversteer or shocks and springs. It was about trying to ensure that we were absolutely compliant with the TLA, and by the time we got it all fixed I felt it was like an endorsement of my ethics. What surprised me, given the level of emotion, was that we were able to sort it all out in a way that didn't create monstrous problems from a personal standpoint. Kelvin O'Reilly was good to deal with, as was Quentin Procter. John Hewson was also fine. They were approaching it from a regulatory point of view, and people and personalities (a lot of people didn't like Tom because of what went on a few years prior with the collapse of TWR) really didn't figure the way they did in the media – the only agenda was one of TLA compliance, not of keeping Tom Walkinshaw away from the sport. Holden was totally supportive and fine too, so at the end of the day we got through the whole thing with not too much damage; certainly nothing long lasting, other than a few years off my life expectancy!

The sensible approach was that HRT should never have been at risk of losing its Teams Licences, or as they are known now, Racing Entitlements Contract (REC), but if you took the industry view – as in people in pit lane voting – it was gone. It still winds my clock to think those people could conceivably think it would be OK not to have a Holden Racing Team in pit lane. I've always said motorsport is a mongrel business, and that shows it quite clearly. There were people holding their hand up to get rid of us so they could move two spots up the grid and maybe even have a crack at our sponsors. The level of competition is not necessarily as clean as I'd like at times, and that is just as true off the track as on. Sometimes people see a possible gain for themselves without being able to see the big picture.

First and foremost, I've always believed we should all work together to make the pie as big as possible – then I want the biggest slice I can get. What you do to beat each other on the track is absolutely open slather – do what you like within the rules. But to make the sport as good as it can be is almost objective number one and then when you've all got the same level playing field to work from, then how do you go off and beat the opposition?

Privately, I made sure that I communicated with the key guys very clearly during this time and that they spread that message around the place, so that if any of them heard something on Triple M or read something in the *Herald Sun*, they knew what was going on before the media. We were pretty good at cutting those things off before they became a raging fire. There were two trains of thought inside the team – some of the less experienced guys were literally wondering if we were going racing at all, while others had confidence in me being able to fix it and negotiate a way to a sensible resolution. The senior guys were pretty positive throughout this drama, and that made it easier to keep the workshop ticking over while I dealt with lawyers.

I honestly believed we had done and were doing nothing wrong, but that doesn't always mean the cards fall your way. Fred Gibson used to always say, 'We'll just bullshit our way through it,' and I was certainly doing a bit of that. I never wanted to lie to the guys in the team but I was very careful with how much I told them because if they actually knew the extremity of the issues and they knew the real ramifications then we would have lost some staff who were worried about job stability. In the end, we didn't lose any people through this period where it could have been a real blood letting.

When we won in Perth, I'd missed two flights to get there because I was still in Collins Street with lawyers. In fact, I ended up on the last possible flight that could get me there on time. Kelvin laughed about it too; he said, 'What we've got to do is hold you back.' He used to make jokes about the nearer the miss of the race meeting, the better I went, which was just a little aside from the aggro that we were having over the phone every day about how we could get the things fixed. That was the fifth round of the season and this had been going since before Christmas.

It was a time when there was so much going on and just to get to the race meeting was an achievement in itself. It was great for me because I could finally escape the shit and just concentrate on the car. It was almost like a reprieve to get in and drive.

Yeah, I was working really hard at it. I was doing laps of Collins Street and hadn't been to the gym in three months and yet I was still able to go out there and win races and a round. I wouldn't have known what the set-up was when we got to the track, I wasn't doing any preparation for the race meeting . . . it was just a very different time for me.

To tell you the truth, I was lucky I still had the driving. I remember thinking at the time that if Collingwood was under investigation about stuff that they had going in their agreements with the AFL, it would be Eddie McGuire blueing and he never got to kick the footy because he was simply a suit with a view representing the club. Nathan Buckley was the captain and he would get to kick the footy, but he wouldn't be involved in any of the drama. So in a funny way I remember thinking that it was good to be at the helm and driving the car because it gave me that escape from the constant attack. It was like a surprise present for all the aggro, and it wouldn't have been the same in any other sport I can think of. However, the mental energy that it all took did impact my driving. The desire to win became a commercial necessity for the team – not a personal one.

We had some great supporters through it all, though, many of whom could easily have jumped ship and made their own lives easier with their own boards. James Erskine and Tony Cochrane from SEL were 100 per cent behind HRT – they could see the big picture of the business. Greg Smith from Mobil was fantastic; he remained committed to the team and was sympathetic and understanding of what was going on. In motorsport we're actually really in a service business and you've got to be very careful about how you service those clients and you have to manage very well up and down the chain. At the big businesses there's often a motorsport manager you have daily activity with and you have to manage that in a different way to the MD when he is around.

It's not the sponsors' team but they feel like it is, so how much do you tell them? What is the relationship like? You need to be able to sell them on the concept of it being their team without letting them have control of how it runs. For factory teams, it's even harder. This whole period could have been massively destructive for our relationships with our sponsors. But Mobil was great, Holden was great, and our supporters were sensational. Many fans indicated that they would have been lost to the sport if we'd been rubbed out, and we got through it unscathed with everybody retaining their sense of ownership.

Even when we first bought it, I always said that Holden really owns Holden Racing Team. As I've mentioned, that's the reality because Holden retains the IP; I was really just licensed to run the factory outfit for them in a way, like anyone else at the helm. I was just a caretaker, even if it was my money on the line.

Most of those guys, like Greg Smith and Denny Mooney at Holden, are still mates of mine because we put in the effort to make it work. We communicated with them honestly and they never left a conversation at the time wondering if I was spinning a line. I knew I could tell them a lot too because I trusted them with the information I was giving them – I was very fortunate to have those sorts of people behind that whole cause.

Denny was ecstatic when we got it all sorted and he hosted a function for us and all our sponsors and whoever else we wanted to bring along. All of Holden's senior management were there, and Alan Batey, who fought with us in the ditches, hosted the evening. They had it in the foyer at Fishermans Bend and took the guests up into Holden Design and showed them cars they shouldn't see and it was a great Holden way of demonstrating their support for us.

Personally, when we managed to get it all sorted out it was the ultimate relief for me. When you're a factory team you're expected to win and I think all the dramas made us take our eye off the ball for a little while, so I felt a real sense of 'Righto, now let's get on with it – let's go and win the races and do what we have to do.'

I knew at the end of the whole drama that in many ways we had the structure of the sport wrong. That my rivals could vote as to whether or not the Holden Racing Team was allowed to race was just wrong. That people who knew they couldn't beat us on the track could resort to that was just mind blowing. I'm sure if it had been an independent board and someone had sat back and looked at it from a total business point of view it would never have got the legs that it did, but the board wasn't independent, and that was, and to a certain extent still is, an issue.

The biggest thing was that I always wanted to compete at the highest level and beat the best blokes, and that was changing.

Maybe all I needed was to go away with Toni and the kids and recharge, but that wasn't going to happen while I still owned HRT and while I was negotiating with Tom to buy half of our team. I didn't have a break at all from the start of 2007 to the end of 2008, and I was feeling it. Even when we'd come to terms on the partial sale, I still couldn't just take a month off to recharge. I was definitely behind the eight-ball compared with other drivers.

Once I made my mind up to retire, I felt much better about it because the demands of being a professional race driver and owning a team clearly were excessive. I was very comfortable with the retirement decision, it was logical and right, and there were some pretty significant world economic issues that were happening simultaneously that I was pleased I didn't have to ride through. When GM went into receivership and there were big sponsorship dramas in all sports, I remember thinking how cool it was not to be part of it, which is an attitude I wouldn't have had five years before that.

The second part of being comfortable with not driving full-time was my work as a commentator for Channel Seven, and being able to talk about the sport and continue to live it from outside the driver's seat. There were definitely times throughout 2009 that I did miss climbing into the car, but that feeling wasn't always there. I wouldn't have done the long-distance races if I didn't have that feeling at times, because I needed some competitive fix. To do those couple of races with Murphy and because it was a Melbourne team and there were a fair few guys who I knew quite well, I felt like I could really contribute to making the car better and putting something together that was going to go reasonably well. I really enjoyed myself too – it was seriously like I hadn't been away – and in the first part of Bathurst when I caught Winterbottom and rounded him up and then set off after Tander, it felt like I'd been in the car the whole year.

But clearly, for me, there will be other opportunities so

long as I feel like I'm still doing a good enough job. The new rules that each full-time driver has to stay with his own car mean that Lowndes and Whincup for instance can't pair up; for me, there are effectively more options open where I can actually win the race, which is the same for the fans. I had some really fantastic offers before Christmas 2009 and I didn't rush my decision-making on who I was going to race with at Phillip Island and Bathurst. I made a little checklist for myself of all the things that were important. Number one was what was the chance of a result because it wasn't really about money; there were bigger offers than the one I accepted. Joining up with Craig at Triple Eight was, I felt, my best opportunity to win. We'd driven together before and we've been great rivals and I have a massive amount of respect for him, and we are good mates. Teaming up again 10 years on is very cool.

It was also about the team and the car. With three wins in the past four years they certainly know how to build a car to win that race, they are clearly the benchmark team at the moment and that was appealing. I know how much testing I'm going to do to make sure that I can do the best job possible. I think I've got a few more in me yet, but I don't know if it's possible to catch Brock – I'd have to be pretty lucky to do that – but I do know that as long as I am with Craig, he can't catch me!

If it gets to the point where I can't go to Bathurst thinking I can win, I'll step away – I have no desire to just make up the numbers. It isn't about earning more money, as a lot of people have said and written, it is about winning again and enjoying the experience.

2009 was an excellent year in terms of me just getting the next phase of my life organised and getting things in order a bit more. Moving into new offices, having new people around me and working through the plan that we did with John Crennan was all a big thing. Then when I went back on the V8 Supercar Board, started work on the Car of the Future and working on the racetracks for Sydney and Townsville, we were as busy as we'd ever been, but I'd had a holiday and was fully recharged and ready to get into my new life.

It was a different sort of busy, though, with a whole new set of challenges. So much more diversity but less intense and certainly less politics. I was able to choose the bits that I liked and the bits that I could do a good job on. I really enjoyed the commentary stuff with Crompo, Larko, Matty White and Beretts – they're a very professional group of guys and it was a great mix of experienced people in the TV compound with some really young guys as well. Working again with Ross Holder as the tactician was good too, it was like a really well-rounded race team. Given that this had become the biggest part of my working life, it was refreshing to really enjoy it and I'm sure Toni would say I was a much better person to be around. In fact, she did comment on that. I overheard her talking to one of her girlfriends, saying that it was just like old times.

One question mark for me was how much I'd miss the driving, and then next was around whether I could talk about the sport in a way that is genuinely positive and good for the viewer, given how jaded I felt. You might think you can do it, but until you actually have a go you don't really know. Would I then enjoy the weekends away at a sport which has been my life? Would I enjoy the weekends away with not competing? So there was a lot of stuff that I didn't really know about what it was going to look like.

I've been pleasantly surprised by the number of work opportunities and the number of things that have come to me since the start of 2009, like the V8 Supercar work and Car of the Future, which are easy projects for me because they're my interest. But there have been other things too, like the Stick Shift on Triple M, which are not in my natural zone.

I had to work harder in 2009 than a lot of people might have thought, but there was a lot of pride on the line and I couldn't just subcontract it to someone else. For instance, I certainly didn't want to do the Car of the Future project and not to do it well. It was incredibly important for the whole of the industry and I wanted to do the best job possible. The same with the track design and event at Homebush after it took so many years to get off the ground; the workload attached to that was just enormous and the way the event came off and the look and feel of it was great. The Sydney market is very important to everyone at V8 Supercars, and the Olympic Park precinct was packed with more than 180,000 people to watch our inaugural street race at Homebush.

The circuit design work came a bit from left field but I've really enjoyed it; however, there are lots of other bits and pieces outside the normal motorsport and motoring world that people have spoken to me about. I haven't really made up my mind as to what projects I want to get into or where I'm headed with those at this stage.

Now that Homebush and Townsville have been bedded down, I'd like to see some more permanent racetracks.

There's a lot of chat about Barbagallo being redeveloped and I've spoken to the government about that and would like to be involved. There's another project, up in the area that I come from, the NSW Central Coast, that is a great opportunity for motorsport – it's just next to the Hunter Valley and it's a real petrol-head heaven. It would be pretty special for me personally to work on something in that region, but I do believe it'd also be great for Australian motorsport. There are pockets all around the place that are begging for motorsport facilities, and if we can get them up and running more than just a racetrack – with a conference centre, a museum or a hotel and all set up for corporate work with car companies, with driver training and an automotive precinct – it could be really successful.

I am not good at idle time, although I must admit I've enjoyed having two good summer breaks with Toni and the kids, but after each of those it's been pretty full-on. Firing into all the work has been great and the results have been good too. I think Car of the Future will be really good for the sport – it has already been really well received and it has been given the unanimous thumbs-up by all the stakeholders and, most importantly, the team owners.

We're effectively going to 'Open up the shop front' and allow other manufacturers into the sport, and I think we'll see at least one other manufacturer grab the opportunity. Anytime that you can increase the size of the pie and make the business bigger, everybody wins – it helps sponsors, it helps television and it helps all the stakeholders. There is a really bright future for V8 Supercars; in the worst economic times since the Second World War, we've grown through the phase amazingly. No other sport in the country has even looked like improving as an overall business case, so that is a very positive outcome. From that base, if you can add other manufacturers to some of the teams that are not now being supported by Ford or Holden – without detracting from Ford or Holden's involvement – then I think it's a really exciting time.

Tony Cochrane is one of the directors of Sports and Entertainment Limited (SEL) and he effectively took over the management and promotion of the sport back at the end of 1996. He has to be credited with a lot of the success we now enjoy – he's been fantastic for motorsport in this country. I drove him down to Phillip Island in 1996 after SEL was appointed to help with the marketing, before it became a stakeholder itself (SEL owns 25 per cent of V8 Supercars Australia and the teams own the other 75 per cent), and I took him through all the problems with the sport from my own point of view. We've been mates since that trip, not that we haven't had our arguments, but the good thing is that we never hold a grudge – we're able to move on when you have finished the debate. He's a very passionate person about all things and there's no one in the V8 Supercar community who could argue that he doesn't do great things for it. He is visionary and he's much more committed to this sport than people think. He's strategically got a very good brain for what the business needs, and under his guidance V8 Supercars has been a sporting success story. He is a great mate and I value his friendship immensely.

In 2009 I was also involved in an initiative known as the Captains' Forum, which was a project put together by John Bertrand and John Eales to see what can be done to make sport in general bigger in Australia and collectively how sport can help the community even more. I spent a really enjoyable couple of days with Kate Ellis, the Federal Sports Minister, and the other 'captains', working through a lot of ideas and initiatives based on what sort of impact we can have on health and participation in sport and activity. Sport has been good to me, so to be able to put a bit back is a good thing.

I've led a very fortunate life to date and I think there are great things ahead. I think I've learned enough to really capitalise on what lies in front of me. Every time I do something, I learn a little more too. I really enjoyed the Captains' Forum because I was working with a bunch of people who felt the same way; they were all very high achievers in their sport and all they wanted to do was to make a difference.

I'm 43 now and my life has changed a lot in the past two years, but there is so much left to do. I always said I want to be over and out and lying on a beach somewhere when I hit my early 60s. I'm pretty sure even then I'll still be doing something with my time, but I certainly want to get to a point where I can start to walk away and enjoy it all a little bit more.

I'm lucky that for the next few years I can go back and drive at Bathurst; that sort of thing only happens in motorsport. It would be like Nathan Buckley lining up just for the AFL Grand Final – he just can't do it, even if Collingwood makes it. The ability to do what I'm doing is unique to motorsport, and it is just that our sport is different – not that it requires anything less physically, it is just different.

Sitting back today as a non-regular driver, I suppose

I've had some time to think about how I'd like to be seen by people. My record is one thing, but I'd like to think that people would say I was someone who always gave it 100 per cent and was competitive, but fair. The way you go about your sport sometimes is a really important thing and, yes, there have been plenty of heated aspects of gamesmanship over the years and I was always trying to win. But at the end of the day I can honestly say I've never shoved anyone off the road by mistake, and I always reckon that's a way of separating the goods from the bads.

Perhaps people may even think I did a pretty good job. Who knows . . . ?

13

OTHER PERSPECTIVES

Fred Gibson
'Mark first came down to Melbourne because we were looking for young guys to join the team, but he had to work as a gopher in the workshop on the chance he may get a drive at some stage on the condition that his father stayed out of the way. It was nothing against his father, but I'd seen it before and it never works – to both their credits they accepted that and Mark joined us. When you hear about his Wyong escapades, like crashing cars and doing the sort of things that all young guys do, this was not just a big step for him but a good step too.

'He wanted to be a race driver and he was the kind of guy who would do whatever it took, even if he didn't like the rules and even if it was taking longer than he wanted. He fitted into the team fairly well because he was a go-getter. He's pretty focused on what he does. I compare him very much with Whincup today. Whincup's driving very well, he's focused and a serious racer – and the other drivers aren't as serious as he is and that's why he's winning races. It was the same with Mark when he had learned enough to put it all into action.

'Comparing drivers is never easy, but they talk about Lowndes and Skaife and always refer to Lowndes' natural ability. Skaife didn't have that natural flair that Lowndes has got, but that doesn't mean he wasn't as good. It's a bit like Moffat and Brock – same situation, totally different people! I drove with Moffat and he was such a serious and committed guy, his throttle control was outstanding and he was a better "natural" driver than people gave him credit. People didn't understand Allan that well either – the general public thought he was an ass because he was so devoted to his motorsport he didn't always come across that well. He lived and breathed motorsport and so did Mark. But he did also have some fun doing it, even if people on the outside never saw it.

'When Mark came down here and teamed up with Seto and Tratty [Glenn Seton and Anthony Tratt] they had a good time. But when Mark went motor racing it was serious stuff.

'Thanks to his father, he was already good with business when he came down to us and he virtually ran the Special Vehicles Department when we started doing the Skylines for Nissan Motor Company. He made money for the race team by the way he organised himself and a couple other guys – not many drivers could have done that as well as he did.

'But primarily we brought him down to race cars. I was

one for youth back in those days, but you had to get a good young guy with a good head and bring him up through a sport. If you do that right he becomes better at it, and Mark excelled to a point more so than Glenn. Mark wanted to be involved in everything we were doing, whether it was the business or the development of the car or putting the engine together – he wanted to have his nose in everything that was going on and he learned from that.

'So that was all experience which he's taken forward and I suppose sometimes it can be an enemy also because it was easy for him to think he knew everything. Sometimes the guys would say, "Mark has a point," and sometimes you might say you didn't agree with that point and then you'd go and butt heads with him. And believe me, there was plenty of head butting at work with the engineers and the senior guys. But that was his learning curve.

'One of his great strengths was testing. Even before data the feedback he had about a car and what it was doing was first class. He did most of our testing even from early on, because he had much better feedback than Glenn. But he didn't just have good feedback, he had the ability to sit with the engineers and over a period of time work out what the engineer was thinking as well. When data came along he just learnt how to read that. But he blew Glenn away on how he wanted to feel the car and how he wanted it to be better.

'A lot of people don't know the real Mark Skaife. That's the problem. He's a "people person" but he doesn't suffer fools lightly and that has been an issue at times. I forget the guy's name, but when the Formula Holden ran out of petrol at Winton one day because this guy hadn't put enough fuel in, he got the flick the next day. We call Mark Mr 110 per cent and my wife Chris used to say to him, "Mark, you've got mechanics who are giving you what they think is their 110 per cent, but to you, it's 60 per cent, but they can't give any better than that," and that's something he had to learn. He expected his 110 per cent out of everybody because that's what he said he's giving!

'But the whole thing is, some people haven't got the ability to give more than they're giving. He expected everyone to be the same as he was. He'd come from being an apprentice tyre technician in Wyong to being one of Australia's best race drivers and he did that because he worked hard at doing it. It doesn't matter what he does – if he was sitting down doing paperwork, he'd be 110 per cent at that too.

'Even today, he punishes himself over his commentary; he is always trying to be better. That is why he needs good people to talk to him when he's in the car; his view is that he is going to go as fast as he can and will put all his effort into that. We had to pull him back a few times in the car; at Bathurst one year all we wanted him to do was maintain a 10 second lead over second place, which was one and a half seconds off the pace he could do, and we had to keep talking to him to get him to drive to the pit board.

'In the car he's got the red mist down at some stages and he needs people to help him. He used to hold his breath on qualifying laps – he'd do a whole lap, suck his breath in and do a qualifying lap and absolutely wring its neck. That's when we used to say over the radio, "Breathe, Mark, breathe."

'When we first started racing, Jim used to blow him away in the same car – the cars were exactly the same but Jim was always quicker in qualifying, quicker in the race and would always finish ahead of him. Mark could never have beaten Jim in those situations and we understood that. I got Jim at the time because I wanted one of the most experienced drivers in the car to bring these young guys along.

'Over the time of all that, Mark became a better qualifier than Jim but in the race Jim would still beat him because Jim was consistent. Mark would be a second quicker, two seconds slower, a few tenths here, a few tenths there, and not consistent. As time went on Mark became more consistent than Jim, so he was then out-qualifying Jim and then beating him in the races. But Jim understood that also and the two of them get on so well, and Mark owes Jim a lot because he helped him like you wouldn't believe. Mark had me nurturing him from the pits and Jim nurturing him from a driver's point of view and not a lot of other drivers would have done that.

'I'd rate Mark as high as any race driver I've seen in Australia and I've been around for a while, and he got there because he has a certain level of talent and 100 per cent commitment. He watches everything and analyses everything and goes out the next day and does better.'

Craig Lowndes

'Mark is a very competitive person. He's very focused on what he wants to do and how he wants to achieve things, which meant when he joined the team I just had to focus on my own thing and worry about getting the car faster and making it a better race car. He and I worked really well together because he was so technical about the cars and methodical about what he wanted to do and how he wanted to achieve things, where I was more "Give me some more turn or some more drive and let's go out and race". I was a bit more on the "seats of my pants" sort of thing where he analysed and always wanted to make the car better. He was fantastic!

'We had plenty of great races, but I really remember some of our battles at the Clipsal 500. When we were teammates we were obviously trying to win for ourselves, but also for the team, and that made it a little hard at times. My first year in a Ford was different, though, and we actually had a coming together in the Sunday race, which we had a laugh about afterwards.

'I think when that happened we had the better car at that point of the race and I wanted to get past and I decided to do the switchback on him. But we knew each other too well; in essence, he knew what I was going to do and I worked out pretty quickly what he was going to do to try and stop me. So we played our little game together and we ended up hitting and I put a hole in the radiator of my new Ford and he had a problem with the front of his car. We laughed later, but not at the time.

'There is always good and bad in any relationship in any sport. He came into the team after Peter retired and obviously took his position. But he also came with a lot of confidence and a lot of things that he wanted out of the car and himself and everything else. As a team, he really pushed us along and he certainly pushed me into doing my best at every round.

'When I was leaving the team we didn't really talk about what I was doing and why, but now I think he's faced some of it himself I'm sure there will be a time that we sit down, have a beer and have a chat about what happened, who did what to who and who got screwed more. Maybe after we win Bathurst together, that would be a good time.'

*

'When it came to driving together at Bathurst in 2000, it was well documented that I was leaving the team, so I rang him up and told him that regardless of what I was doing in the future, we were going to Bathurst as teammates and that I was going to give him 110 per cent to win the race and to help him win the championship. At that stage I never thought I'd race a Holden again, let alone have the chance to race Bathurst with him again, but here we are 10 years later trying again.

'When Roland asked us to put a wish list together for possible Bathurst partners, Skaife was at the top of my list because we've got such a great rapport and such a great respect for each other and he clearly still has the ability to do the job. We didn't get the result we wanted in 2000, and who knows maybe we would have if he had've pulled his finger out a bit more, but now we have the chance to rectify that.

'It would be something pretty special to be able to win a Bathurst again and especially with Mark. I have so much respect for him as a driver and person. We had a lot of funny times together; it wasn't all just about the cars. The driver training days after a race meeting were always a good time to let our hair down, and despite his race weekend intensity he was always good for it after the meeting, when neither of us really wanted to do anything but recover. It made those days a lot easier.'

*

'I read and hear all the time people saying Mark wasn't a natural, but that was crap. He was very methodical about how he approached things, how he wanted to get the best out of himself, the car and everything else around him. But he had natural ability – we've all got the ability or we wouldn't be here, it's just a matter of how much you apply that focus. He was very good at extracting everything out of a car and himself, and his record stands on its own.

'We were opposites in the way we approached the sport and we had great times together. If an engineer of the time asked me what I needed and I'd say, "I need a bit more turn or rah-rah-rah," and they'd tell me I've got it and I'd just go out and drive it. Whereas he would go right through the data and every minute or second of his time to try and find that tenth of a second that he needed to find.

'We're two different characters and that's why as a team it was probably the best balance.'

Todd Kelly

'I think I was Mark's second longest serving teammate after Jim Richards. I was with him for five years and to manage a relationship as teammates for that long is quite difficult. There's not many drivers who come out of a five-year stint together and shake hands and still get along.

'A lot of people from the outside probably think that Mark's not one of those guys, but the whole time I was there he was fantastic. I'm not saying he's old but there's a pretty big age gap between us and he taught me a huge amount of stuff about driving and pretty much with everything. We used to spend a lot of time together and to see how he approached everything and how he went about being a race car driver was a huge part of developing me. I was very lucky to be able to spend that time with him.

'There were some good times and there were times when we hit each other. There was one at Eastern Creek but that wasn't too bad, although it was at the start of the race and we were on the front row of the grid together. I think there was another in the same year in Darwin where we went into the first corner together and folded our mirrors in and had a bit of a bump here and there.

'But there were only two or three times that we came together on the track in a major way and he's so intense and competitive it was always a bit of a drama, as you would expect. The good thing about him is that by the end of the day or the next day when he's had his say, you're all cool again and you can go out and do the same thing again, if that's how it is. We're both racers and he understood what that meant.

'Even when he was responsible for the team, I always saw him more as a competitor and a teammate than as my boss. Out in the workshop he was off doing all his stuff which I'm fairly familiar with now, but that never really impacted our relationship.

'I was witness to the whole thing with Mark and what was happening with TEGA and TWR, and every time we got to a track I could see all the shit that he was dealing with and I used to get in the car and think, "You poor bastard, having to go through all that and having to drive." I really felt bad for him a lot of the time.

'That was the end of his full-time career and he was still capable of being on the front row or winning races and that stuff had to affect his performance. In my opinion, when he retired he was still good enough to win a race and there's not that many guys that get to the point where they want to retire and they're still at that level.

'So it was sad to see the last five years – they should have been his most enjoyable.'

*

'He was the benchmark driver when I joined HRT, no doubt about that. You'd go to some of the simple tracks and there'd be hundredths of a second between you. But then you'd go to a joint like Phillip Island or Eastern Creek and he would just go *bang* and be three-tenths clear and you had no idea how he managed that. When I was able to run with him at the faster tracks I knew I was doing a pretty good job, especially at Eastern Creek – I think he's an absolute master of that joint.'

*

'Winning Bathurst in 2005 is probably my biggest achievement with HRT and with Mark. For him to have won the race and driven it over the line is massive for a driver. But as soon as he crossed the line, he said "Happy birthday, mate." That just goes to show what sort of a guy he is. I could name about 25 other blokes who'd be cheering and carrying on and the last thing they'd think about is the teammate that drove the car with them. But that's why the relationship was fantastic and it was an enjoyable five years being his teammate.'

Marcos Ambrose

'When I came into the sport there was no one to beat but Skaife. He was top of the pile, the king of the kids, and had pretty much got himself into a position where he was dominating. If you were going to win races, you had to beat Skaife first.

'Eras change and move, and I came in at the height of Skaife's reign of the sport. He was a worthy competitor and he taught me a lot and, to be perfectly honest, he made me the racer I am today. You need a challenge to harden you up and I had that with Skaife and Lowndes in particular. You've got to remember, this was my first paid drive and I had to beat not just a bloke who was dominating, but the most successful driver in the history of the series.'

*

'I remember my first race in V8 Supercars, it was at the Grand Prix in Melbourne. It was my first attempt at qualifying and it was actually my first time on new tyres. I'd done a test drive on Bridgestones but I had no chance to put new tyres on, so I basically went out and we had two sets we could use, maybe even three at the time. I had completely botched up on the first sets and missed every corner; we had an oil leak and could only do two laps at a time before I had to come into the pits and top up with oil.

'I was basically thrown in the deep end there and there was about six minutes to go in the session, enough for one final lap and I knew I had to make it stick. The track was getting faster every lap and I'd been in those situations before in Europe where you only get one lap to qualify, so I knuckled down and got the lap.

'There's a high speed chicane out the back which if you mess it up you can straight line it, but if you mess it up on purpose you can actually gain a lot of time. So when I busted off the lap, quite naturally the first thing that had gone through Mark's head would have been: "he must have cut that back chicane."

'I didn't, of course, and got the pole. A brand new guy coming into the sport, nobody knowing who I was or what I was capable of, it would have looked outrageous, and Mark was the first guy to come to my window. He didn't accuse me flat-out but he intimated quite strongly and had that wink that said "I know that you know that I know" kind of thing. We can look back at it now and he was wrong, but I can understand why he would have taken that position and he was keen to let me know what he thought.'

*

'We've never had any words that I can remember, which is more than I can say for people like Murphy, but we had some great battles. Our rivalry was really subliminal – it was the actions we took on the track and against each other rather than on-track dramas that really set up the duel. It was showmanship and one-upmanship on the racetrack and it just wasn't very verbal. Like anyone who's a champion, they're a champion because they are ruthless and they're aggressive and they'll do whatever it takes to win, within reason.

'He had this mindset and that's why he is and has been the champion and will continue to be in life. He's had some ups and downs like anybody, but if anybody's gonna rise up from the ashes and come back it's going to be a character like Skaife because it's what makes him.

'It took me a couple of years to beat him. I came into V8 Supercars in 2001 and didn't win my first championship until 2003, so I had to build the team around me and get confidence and grow into the sport – all those things you have to do. I had time to watch what he was doing to make him so good, and I copied him a lot in the way that he approached his racing and the level of professionalism that he had.

'I used him as the yardstick – if I could beat Skaife, I knew I was going to be somewhere near the front. It worked sweet because I took down the guy who appeared to be invincible. When I came into the sport in 2001, who was going to stop Mark Skaife? There was no one in the field that could. It was a big challenge and it ran deep.

'I always wanted to be on the racetrack first because it gives you options, and even that became a battle. We ended up going down to the end of pit lane about half an hour before the session was going to start and getting all hot in the seat for nothing. It came to a head at Oran Park. We were both gunning to go out first and my car wasn't coming in quickly enough and he was all over me – we got into each other like we were racing and it was only the start of practice.

'There's plenty of great races we had too, and they are not always that obvious either. We were so close in our speeds that it was really challenging to hold him off. You couldn't let him see a weakness either because he'd take advantage of it. I stalked him at Phillip Island a few times, and that place was really his house, a high speed/high danger track. You've got to have a lot of confidence and a lot of commitment through the corners, and I stalked him for a few races there and I didn't win a race there for quite a while. When I beat him there, it gave me the confidence that I could beat him anywhere.'

Brock on Skaife when he equalled his ATCC win record (as told to Andrew Clarke)

'Give him the kudos he deserves, he's doing a fantastic job. It hasn't been that easy for him in many respects, there's always a challenge, and it wasn't as if Skaifey was born with a silver spoon in his mouth. He's done the hard yards, he's been in good teams and he's worked hard at making sure that he's had the results in those teams too. He is intelligent, he is committed and all of that's good practice.

'When Skaifey came along [to the HRT] he fitted in very well right from the start, and he was able to win over the team, which is one of the traits of a successful driver. We're focusing on Mark Skaife here rather than the team or teams, and rightly so because the responsibility is on a driver's shoulders once the flag drops.

'He was on the numbers over in Perth and I mean obviously it's a matter of time [before he registers another win] and look I've never been one for keeping count. There's certain numbers of races I've won and I thought "Oh gee that's good," and just to think that I was ahead of someone's probably a big surprise, not to think that they've caught up. It's inevitable and given the number of races and the way that it's sort of worked out these days it's going to happen. I mean he's probably only going to be around for another couple of years or so but that's probably his choice on how he wants to see his career unfold, I guess.

'My focus was on endurance, on Bathurst I suppose, but having said that of course every time you go out there you want to give it your best shot. It'd be fair to say that I became a bit more pragmatic as time went on and said our team needs to win Bathurst ... but having said that I can absolutely understand the need to win every race you go into, and that's just the way it is when you're a competitive human being and you're never going to go out there and give it less than your best, that's for sure.

'He's shown his interest in the sport in general and, who knows, in the future he might have a go at some of the other different categories that sort of pop up here and there, but it's quite obvious if you're going to win at Supercars you've got to be dedicated to Supercars – that's all there is to it, there's no other ifs, buts or maybes. So at the moment I think he is the most dedicated, committed bloke that's out there and he's getting the just rewards.'

Toni Skaife

'I am a believer of fate when it comes to love, and so I know that there are reasons beyond my control that I met the man I now call my husband, Mark Skaife.

'For some, Mark is a Holden hero, one of the most successful touring car drivers in our country. For others, he is an arch rival, a record to beat or maybe just an all round pain in the bum. For me he is all of those things and then some! Well perhaps not the record bit, but certainly the latter!

'He is my partner in my life, the father of my children and he is my biggest fan, just as I am his. He makes me feel like I am the luckiest woman alive. His passion and dedication for me as his wife and then for our family is a true testament to the person he is. He is unfailing in his love and commitment. Our relationship is the pinnacle of my life and the thing that grounds me. Mark is as solid as a rock. In my opinion, I could not find a more decent human being to share my life with.

'He makes me laugh at least five times a day, and most days this is before I've even left the house for the office. He puts so much effort and energy into keeping our home a vibrant, safe and an emotionally stable place for our children. He's always done this, even when things were not going well for him.

'We started our relationship early in 2000. There was a lot going on for him personally at the time. He was fighting for basic access to Mitch and that was tough for him. But I will never forget this whirlwind of a force in my life – this man who was full of energy, inspiration and motivation. He was the most upbeat person I had ever met, he was also the most charming. There was no doubt about it, we were just mad about each other.

'We've always had an extremely close bond, so to watch him race was at times very hard, especially when he was deserving of a result but didn't get one. Most of the time it was an honour share this part of his life with him, albeit sometimes tough. To watch him artfully take to the track week in week out and extract every last of energy from himself to win was truly amazing. I will never forget that feeling of pride and absolute joy for him. Truly, his dominance in 2000, 2001 and 2002 was as one would expect – just euphoric for us both.

'I think I know him better than anyone, and I can tell you

that he is one of the most intense people you will ever meet. Everything in his life has meaning and order. But like all of those who are close to him, it's easy to feel like you are the winner in the friendship. He is a dedicated mate, whose passionate nature comes through at every level of his life. You only get 100 per cent with him.

'There have been times in recent years where I knew every minute of every day was a challenge for him – those final racing years. I could see him trying to be all things to all people – a businessman and team owner, the general manager of the team, a racing driver, a dedicated father to a teenage son, a supportive husband helping out with his two year old and a six month old as his wife returned to her career. His nights were already sleepless, but he still shared the load with the night waking. During this time, he lost his beautiful grandmother who he was really close to. These were extremely difficult times for him – and us all, but he never faltered from his family commitments.

'It was hard to watch all this go on and looking back now, I can see that getting through it was a demonstration of our love. I guess for me I took his retirement hard. I cried often. I could understand the reasons he had come to his resolve, but I have always felt that there were other forces at play and some not so ethical things that contributed to the way he felt about his driving. Mark and I are extremely compatible, one of the reasons is our values, and our appreciation of what is right and wrong. I remember through these times, just hugging him and reminding him what a good person he was – and he was and still is. I watched as he fell out of love with his lifelong love of motorsport – it was excruciating. If I can make another analogy along the lines of love, to me his retirement was like leaving your wife or husband because you suspected them of cheating on you, only to find months later that you were wrong and that someone had mischievously misled you into believing the thing that you feared the most. On that issue, I'll leave it at that.

'I am so proud of Mark for so many reasons, his racing credentials are just a small part of that. He has left and will continue to make his indelible stamp on the sport that makes him tick. At times I envy his drive and I know others do too. I am extremely proud that in his new life, he has embraced his pursuits with the same Mark Skaife vigour and passion as one would expect. He is exciting to be around and I'm just enjoying this time with him immensely.'

Andrew Clarke, unpublished article, November 1992
Mark Skaife is perhaps one of the most maligned Australian Touring Car Champions in history. Such has been the speed at which he has climbed to the top of the local motorsport tree, that virtually every one of his rivals carries some sort of grudge against him and the aging motorsport media hasn't been able to cope with a champion who's younger than they are.

He's often appeared impetuous on the track, arrogant in private and immature in many respects. But that's now in the past – the Mark Skaife of today is a well balanced 25-year-old racing driver, one with enough natural ability to mix it with the best in any field. If he bit the bullet, there is a chance of fighting his way to Formula One. He is good enough, but it is a big step.

It is that sort of ability and, in many respects, the open door of opportunity that has stood him against the world in so many respects. Even today you can still read how Jim Richards was told to let his younger team-mate win the 1992 title.

But Skaife fired into the series the hungrier of the two, smack bang on form thanks to a good pre-season and desperate to sew up his first ATCC title. He won the first round fair and square, and then led his team-mate for the rest of the year, officially claiming the crown in the season finale at Oran Park.

'There's always going to be knockers,' Skaife explained a couple of weeks after claiming the title, 'that's how it is ,you know, and there's always going to be people that believe you're not really worthy of doing those things.

'I try not to listen to them and all that shit, but obviously it does get to you at times. So to have close friends and family that are supportive can only be a benefit, and I suppose I'm lucky there.'

On that score he's got a family that is as keen as mustard. His mother and father are regulars at his races and in many respects are his staunchest defenders. I remember a letter sent to me by his mother when I was editor of *Racing Car News*, after one of my columnists had written a scathing attack on Skaife. A few other letters flowed in from that column as well, mostly supporting the author's assessment.

Skaife's sister, Lisa, works for Gibson Motorsport and his fiancee Belinda works only part-time and is nearly always there to help. 'Belinda and I have been living together now for about a year and she's been unbelievably good support. Prior to Oran Park I wouldn't have been the best bloke in the world to live with for two weeks, and she copped that really well.'

The other strength he now possesses is maturity. He can cope with the shit fights that are such an endemic feature of motorsport, and now he has the right mental approach to race consistently throughout the duration of a race.

'What's very difficult about driving touring cars in Australia is that not only do you drive against the top dozen drivers in Australia every time you run, you drive against very experienced top drivers.

'Speed-wise, probably for a few years now, we've been as fast as we need to be, but the balance of being fast yet finishing races is something that doesn't come easy. I think that Australian touring car drivers make it very hard on you in that respect too, because the Brocks, Richards and Johnsons, and all those guys that have been around for so long, are so consistent and so good that you can sometimes look as fast, but to do a whole race as fast as them is very hard.

'So in 1989 when there were times where I went almost as fast as Richo, he beat me every time in the races. The cars that we are driving now are very hard cars to drive – they have big horsepower and little tyres. So it's probably harder for young blokes in that respect to make the progression, it can only come from spending time in the cars. But once you've got it, you still have to retain your speed and that's one of those things that's hard to evolve.'

His famous incident at the Australian Grand Prix meeting a couple of years back – when he rolled and destroyed one of the new half-million dollar Godzilla racing cars – brought the knockers out of the woodwork. But team manager Fred

Gibson retained his confidence in the young charger, and Skaife put the incident behind him with nary a thought.

'I don't think of Adelaide at all, to be honest. That particular day, I didn't do anything that I would not normally do. The car would not necessarily do that again tomorrow if I did the same thing.

'We're professional racing car drivers, we're there to drive the car 10/10ths every time you get in it. The more times you get in, the more times you're likely to have a biff. You look at all the top drivers, they've all had big biffs.

'It's one of those things that you're not going to get away from because that's what you're there to do. I didn't dwell on Adelaide at all – I just got back onto the job and I copped a bit of criticism for it, but it could happen again tomorrow.'

Skaife is one of the few fully professional racing drivers in Australia, he works at Gibson Motorsport, runs his own Formula Brabham racing team and spends his life around motorsport. The life of a professional racing driver in Australia is not quite the same as it is in Europe; there are no multi-million dollar salaries and few genuine playboys that lounge around the swimming pool when not strapped into a racing car.

'I suppose in Australia you can't really earn enough money just out of being a professional race driver, so if you talk to any of the other professional racing drivers, whether it be John Bowe, Jim Richards or whoever, they've always had other business interests. If you just talk about being a professional racing driver, our obligation is to be fit and to be at our best to drive a car and do whatever promotion activities that we've got to do for our sponsors.

'So as a professional racing driver, we do the racing, the testing, the fitness and the background work to make sure that we're good enough to do the job properly.

'Outside of that, I assist Fred in the workshop. I also do a bit of stuff with driving schools and things outside the team, plus I do a bit with my father's automotive businesses in New South Wales. So I keep pretty busy between all that.'

Considerable work is done in the gym, mostly on aerobic fitness as well as body strength, although Skaife is a firm believer that there is no better training for race driving than doing lots of testing. And he's had plenty of that over the past few months, and he says this is part of the reason for his growing consistency.

'I think with the amount of testing that I do, and the amount of driving that I do between the Formula Brabham and touring car that I'm in pretty good shape, nothing is any better than match fitness. It's just like footballers, the same thing goes for car drivers – you spend more time in the car, the fitter you are, and you can't simulate the sort of forces that are on you in the car. Probably two hours in a race car is as hard on you as an hour of squash, easily!'

Skaife says his first Australian Touring Car Championship is the result of 10 years' work, not just one. And behind those 10 years were various people who helped train him into the driver he is today. Obviously Fred Gibson and Jim Richards rank highly in any conversation, but there are others too. people like his own father and Barry Seton (Glenn Seton's father) regularly crop up as his major influences and guiding hands.

But it is Jim Richards who has probably helped Skaife the most since he joined the Nissan team back in 1989.

'Richo's such a straight shooter that I can ask him something and he tells me the right answer – we get on great as mates but we really are competitive against each other. Like every time we're in the car we try to beat each other. And that's good for his driving and has been especially good for mine.

'I don't think that I'd be as good as I am now without him. I'd probably like to think that I could be as good without the help of guys like Jim and Fred, but it definitely would have taken me longer. I believe as a young guy coming into touring car racing, you are just not going to be competitive for two or three years. Then you've got to be competitive against the best drivers in the country, and the best driver in the country is Richo.

'I didn't really think of topping 1991,' Skaife says of his improved fortunes in 1992. 'You've just got to take each year as it comes. Winning the touring car championship is something that I've always dreamed of doing, but it's difficult to say whether I thought we could go better than last year or not because I didn't really think of it like that. All you do is you start the year thinking, "Let's try and have the best year we can have without dwelling on the past or thinking of the future too much."'

Just where Mark Skaife will spend 1993 is open to debate. He is openly searching for a budget to run the International Formula 3000 Championship, and that budget is a cool $3 million. F3000 is the logical extension of his three years in Formula Brabham, a racing formula that is based on the chassis used in F3000 with locally derived Holden engines, and it is also now the accepted final stepping stone to Formula One.

Skaife believes it will be possible to mix F3000 with touring cars in Australia, although a full ATCC would be unlikely if he was able to chase the Formula One dream. The Nissan team, of which Skaife has been a member since leaving the Ford Laser series back in the mid-1980s, is important to him. But while playing as part of a team is important, so too is Mark Skaife.

'I suppose this is a really close knit team, we're real good mates. We have a beer together and things and it's a good place to not only work, it's a good place to be involved. And I'm sure that sort of loyalty and commitment is very hard to find and very hard to build – we've sort of built it over a fair few years and the team's a very good team.

'But I do still think of Mark Skaife because when you're 45 you've got to be happy with what you've achieved – I don't want to be 45 and say I should have had a go at this, or I should have driven something else, because I had too much allegiance to just doing touring cars. I'd like to drive for Gibson Motorsport touring cars for ever, but I still want to do some of my own things.'

The benefits of open-wheelers have long been documented in motorsport journals. An open-wheeler such as Skaife's SPA Formula Brabham is a purpose-built racing car, one with no compromises to performance. The smallest of changes to the suspension in the SPA make large changes to the way the car performs, there are more variables with multi-adjustable suspension and wing settings, and more ways of testing and developing towards the ideal set-up.

'Probably more than anything the SPA makes you very critical of the touring car, and that is probably the biggest advantage. You try to make the touring car do things like the open-wheeler does, so you're very critical of the performance, the handling, the braking.

'The more time you can spend in any car the better you'll be. The Formula Brabham has been a good car because its got a lot of different things to tune and to change that you wouldn't have with a touring car, and I suppose testing-wise that's been an advantage. It's also something that I like getting in and having a drive.'

The Formula Brabham presented other obstacles, like driving two completely different cars in consecutive races on the same day. Like racing for the touring car championship in a champagne-soaked race suit after claiming the ADC. But that's all in a day at the office when you are mixing the ADC with the ATCC.

'We had the two touring car races and the one Formula Brabham race, after the Formula Brabham race we'd won two of the three and would have been very easy to say, "Oh shit, I'll run fourth or fifth now and I'll win the touring car championship." But really, that's not being very professional, that's not the right sort of attitude.

'We sat in the car prior to the race and I remember saying to myself, "Let's get this thing off the line as good as we can do and let's give them buggery." Because to be honest, I thought the BMWs would give us a bad time in the second race and I wanted to get as big a gap as I could early on.'

Which is exactly what he did, blitzing the field all the way from the green flag to the chequered flag just as he had in the first touring car heat and Formula Brabham race before.

The results of the season have made it look easier than it was, the handicapping of the Nissan GT-R keeping the team on the run and working hard towards its goal of three touring car titles in a row.

While handicapping may have made life tough for Skaife and the Nissan team, it is now that handicapping system which looks set to rob him of his chance to defend Nissan's Bathurst crown. 'I suppose the intention of making the racing closer this year has been a good thing, and you couldn't complain about the quality of the racing for the year.

'I don't really believe in handicapping, but the result has been good so far. The reason we really won the championship was because we were so competitive at the start of the year. Our cars were good cars at the first round, and they've been consistent and reliable since. If you look at John Bowe, he's won nearly as many races as we did, but we got more points.

'I can't remember us ever having to drive the cars as hard as we have this year. If you ask the boys how many brakes we've destroyed through the year, they'll tell you how hard we've been pushing. I would like to think that if it was a Sierra or BMW or whatever, we would have had a reasonable chance of winning the championship, but the Nissan has made it easier because the car is still a very good car despite the handicapping.

'The four-wheel-drive makes it a very consistent car, so lots of times you don't qualify all that well because that is not it's strength. For one lap, 4WD around Lakeside is of bugger all difference or advantage, but for 50 laps it's definitely an advantage. If you look at the car, with a heap less horsepower and more weight, we went as fast this year at most tracks as we did last year. So if you think about that, the car and the team have made a good job of making it that good.'

As Winfield Racing's test driver, Skaife has probably spent more high speed laps behind the wheel of a Nissan GT-R than anybody else in the world. He debuted the car in Australia two years ago, and after two years of solid work Godzilla is now a much tamer beast. The car now handles much better than it did last year, and it uses its brakes to full effect as well – often braking as late as the 500kg less BMW M3s.

'The car is a little more settled, but it's probably just as hard to drive because its got more momentum from being that bit heavier. If one of the things [a Godzilla] steps out of line it's a hard car to gather up – its 1500 kg and it's a big and fast car, when you have half lost control of it, it feels like it takes forever to gather it back up.'

Whether or not Skaife appears at Bathurst with the car is open to debate, and in reality it will have little impact on the significance of his achievements. At 25 he is an Australian Touring Car Champion. At 25 he is a dual Australian Drivers' Champion and a Tooheys 1000 Champion at Bathurst.

He is also perhaps our brightest international racing prospect for many years. So who knows what trophies Mark Skaife will have added to his mantelpiece by the time he turns 26.

Jon Evans, *V8 Supercars: The First Decade*

Aboard the right machinery and within the best team, no one can thoroughly dominate a weekend from practice through qualifying and on to a sweep of all races in the same way as Mark Skaife. In his prime at Holden Racing Team, Skaife proved to be a belligerent, competitive, determined and tenacious character intent on riding rough shod over any rival; even teammates.

For example, at the height of Skaife's rivalry with Ambrose, the two teams even fought to be first out of pit lane on a Friday such was their endeavour to win the mind games that make this as much a cerebral as a physical battle.

Skaife's aggressive driving technique has him hunched forward over the wheel literally controlling and correcting by almost anticipating the necessary movements. While not a 'classic' driving style by any means, the effectiveness can be judged by his imposing record. Skaife's ability to concentrate on everything around him to his advantage, virtually 'Schumacher/Ferrari' style, can be exemplified by just how difficult it was for erstwhile HRT teammates Lowndes and Bright to go their separate ways on development and resources.

Andrew Clarke, *2006 V8 Supercar Yearbook*

V8 Supercar racing's most celebrated duck was broken in New Zealand. Mark Skaife had not won a solo round since the Clipsal 500 in 2003, and for the man who dominated from 1999 to 2002 (with 22 wins and three championships) that was a pretty lean spell.

Speed had not been Skaife's issue during the drought. Time and again he sat on the edge of a win, but it fell from his grasp for one reason or another. Yes, he had recent wins at Sandown and Bathurst to his name, but they were shared, and he desperately wanted sprint round honours again.

Luck played its hand during that time, but many believe you make your own luck. Pretty much every gamble he took backfired, bits of his car broke while others stood up to the pounding. Maybe only half a dozen times in those 33 rounds did the car let him down, the other 27 or so were due to scenarios in which he placed himself, and if you know Skaife, you know full well he doesn't deal well with such things.

Not that you could knock his modus operandi, though, as he has driven that way for pretty much his entire career. Blindingly fast in qualifying (he is still perhaps the best Shootout lap driver in the field), he has numerous times turned a pointy-ended qualifying performance into a round win – 37 times in fact. So aside from getting back on the winners' list, he was now also equal to Peter Brock for Australian Touring Car Championship round wins.

His strike rate (one win every 4.7 rounds) is higher than Brock's (5.7), and although it is not the historical best (Allan Moffat with 3.2 and Marcos Ambrose at 4.2 lead the stats since the championship moved away from being a single event), it is pretty useful, especially given that he started his career in a class car. The only real issue was that the last three of those wins were such a long time coming, especially after his seven wins in season 2002.

So what was different this weekend in New Zealand? In short, nothing really, the cards simply fell his way for the first time in a long while, but then, he did keep his nose clean.

He was consistently quick throughout the weekend without being dominant. Tander and Lowndes were quicker at every outing, but infinitely more troubled in the races, both wearing the wrath of race stewards for alleged indiscretions.

Even Ingall was line-ball with Skaife speed-wise, but he struggled where Skaife was dominant, which was in and around the compulsory pitstop (CPS) in each race, but particularly the first on Saturday.

With local hero Murphy already out, Skaife turned on the heat once the safety car left the track at the end of Lap 4. Tander was given a Pit Lane Penalty for jumping the start and Skaife started the work needed to get his first CPS in shape. Starting his 10th lap, the call came over the radio to pit next time around, and that acted like a switch and Skaife was now on the edge for 2.82 km.

He nailed the in-lap, setting a good time on the opening two sectors and then jumping on the brakes for the pit lane entry at the absolute perfect moment. He said later he was almost out of control in the braking zone for pit lane so late did he throw out the anchors, and in the end he wouldn't have been at 40 km/h for very long before the line that marked the pit entry. He banged into Rob Starr's stop board and then gently moved the car away, with its tall diff and speed limiter making the exit from his pitbox as critical as any other part of the stop, even if it wasn't spectacular.

Skaife chugged back into the fastlane, flicked the steering wheel button that turns off the pit lane speed limiter and climbed onto the track to set a blinding time on cold tyres. His two laps surrounding the CPS were 1.9 seconds quicker than Steve Richards in the Jack Daniel's Racing Commodore, who was the next best in and around his CPS. Significantly for Skaife, though, he was nearly 3.5 up on Ingall who pitted one lap later and resumed the race a few seconds adrift but still in a nominal second place.

According to *RaceFax*, HRT changed Skaife's rear tyres in Race 1 quicker than any other team, but it was only 0.3s quicker than the stop for Richards. This means Skaife made up 1.6 seconds on the track over the two laps, and with a lap time less than a minute. To put it in perspective, a margin that size was more than the difference between the fastest car (Lowndes) in qualifying and the car in 30th (Porter).

The reverse grid race saw more of the same from Skaife, albeit in less dominant fashion, and in Race 3 with a small cough from his Commodore he was beaten over the two keys laps by Lowndes. But in terms of immediate challengers, he blitzed them when it counted.

Andrew Clarke, *V8X*, issue 16, 2003 – 'Control Freak'

Mark Skaife said at the announcement of his HRT purchase that he is still a control freak, and that he now liked the fact that he had control of his own future. But he knows he now has a bigger challenge in front of him if he wants to keep winning.

'One of Holden's first comments was that we were going to have to put a business manager in place, hoping to keep my eye on the ball and focused on the racing. And that to me is valuable, because Holden values the first element of my driving and the second element of team ownership in the right order.

'At Winton the overall car speed was OK in the open, but it wasn't very usable in traffic, and I probably didn't drive it as well as I could have. It wasn't one of my best performances, but I can't qualify how much of this has impacted on it.

'I've probably worked harder in the last month than at any

point in my whole life; however, you can't put that down to a per-tenth each lap, or a percentage thing, I don't know what that quantifies as.

'I'll be the first one to know if it affects my driving, and probably the Richard Hollways and Rob Starrs of the world will be the next to know; they might even know before me. So we'll just have to put things in place if it happens.'

Skaife said that if his performances were starting to suffer, he would have to sit down with the team and see what was needed to get his speed back. If that failed, he'd just have to accept fate and sack himself.

'If I'm not doing a good enough job, that's how it is,' he said.

Extract from *V8X*, issue 38, 2007 – Andrew Clarke with Mark Skaife

AC   When Tom Walkinshaw came back it was supposed to make Mark Skaife's life easier. Do you think it's achieved that goal for you so far?

MS   It has, because Tom and I have not had a bad word. This is again where things have been misreported; we have not had a bad word on anything to do with racing. We are on the same page with how we want to go racing and what the team needs to do and what Walkinshaw Performance as the new Holden Motorsport needs to provide. Where people have said, and this is classic media speculation, that we've been at odds is just miles off the page, and the other part is that we'd had this thing going where people saying it's Tom versus Mark, but it's been Tom and Mark.

AC Did you have an argument with Walkinshaw after Phillip Island as people were saying?

MS No.

AC In the last *V8X* we reported the rumours of a vote post-Bathurst about Mark Skaife's future, do you know if it happened and do you care? I know you were pretty angry when you rang me to 'discuss' the story.

MS Well look that's the first time I'd heard it, and you know how lively I was when I spoke to you about that because I was absolutely off the bike about it. That's the first I'd ever heard about that. To me that's just absolute crap and I will be the one who determines when Mark Skaife retires. I'll be the one because no-one knows it other than me because I'm the one that pulls the helmet on and gets in the chair – no-one knows whether I'm performing at the level that I need to perform. I mean, our closest engineers and closest staff probably know me better than anyone else in terms of how I approach my racing, and if Richard Hollway or Dave Swenson or Robbie Starr said to me, 'Skaifey, you look like you're struggling,' I'd be the first one to put my hand up. But I'm also aware and absolutely totally conscious of the fact that my lap times – qualifying, for instance – will be the thing that will show up and determine whether I'm driving the car OK or not. I don't want to be part of Holden Racing Team's future as a driver if I'm not performing at the highest level. I've said on many occasions that as soon as that happens I will be a big enough boy to step aside and put a young guy in the car.

AC It's a hard thing, though, isn't it, as a sportsman, knowing when to pull the plug?

MS One of the things that incenses me is that every second question I get these days is how long are you going to do it for? I know that Jim Richards was probably the world's best touring car driver in his early-40s and he was enjoying it and he was fit and he was relishing the opportunity to get in the car. If I make my life and my scenario work in a similar way, I believe that there is another four or five years, if I want them. It may be only one or two if I decide that I'm not enjoying it enough . . .

AC You'd want to go out on a winning note, though, wouldn't you? You wouldn't want another rough season like this to be your last one?

MS I wouldn't. I think 2006 could've been one of my best seasons ever and it just didn't work out like that. So you know that's the harsh reality of motorsport, isn't it – it's a very complex business and we've already discussed some of the things that went on in '06 but you know it could've been an absolute ripper year for us but . . . I could've had one of the best years ever. If we'd won seven rounds we wouldn't be talking about 'Wasn't it a drama' – we'd be saying what a great year. It's such a fickle game.

MARK SKAIFE CHRONOLOGY

1967
- Born 3 April 1967 in Gosford, New South Wales

1981
- Started racing go-karts

1984
- First car race at Amaroo Park – Holden Torana XU-1 Sports Sedan

1985
- New South Wales Laser Series –2nd for Tyretown Racing

1986
- New South Wales Laser Series –2nd for Tyretown Racing
- Victorian Laser Series – 1st for Tyretown Racing
- Bathurst – Mark Skaife/Peter Williamson – DNS – Toyota Celica Supra

1987
- Australian Touring Car Championship (ATCC) – 17th (12 points) – 0 Wins / 0 Podiums / 0 Poles – 1 of 9 Rounds – Nissan Gazelle for Peter Jackson Nissan Racing (Gibson Motor Sport)
- Australian 2.0 Litre Touring Car Championship – 1st – Nissan Gazelle for Peter Jackson Nissan Racing (Gibson Motor Sport)
- Bathurst – Mark Skaife/Grant Jarrett – 19th – Nissan Gazelle for Peter Jackson Nissan Racing (Gibson Motor Sport)

1988
- ATCC – Equal 28th (0 points) – 0 Wins / 0 Podiums / 0 Poles – 1 of 8 Rounds – Nissan Skyline HR31 GTS-R for Peter Jackson Nissan Racing (Gibson Motor Sport)
- Bathurst – Mark Skaife/George Fury – DNF – Nissan Skyline HR31 GTS-R for Peter Jackson Nissan Racing (Gibson Motor Sport)

1989
- ATCC – 9th (22 points) – 0 Wins / 1 Podiums / 0 Poles – 8 of 8 Rounds – Nissan Skyline HR31 GTS-R for Nissan Motorsport Australia (Gibson Motor Sport)

- Bathurst – Mark Skaife/Jim Richards – 3rd – Nissan Skyline HR31 GTS-R for Nissan Motorsport Australia (Gibson Motor Sport)

1990

- ATCC – 14th (9 points) – 0 Wins / 0 Podiums / 0 Poles – 8 of 8 Rounds, Rounds 1-5, 8 – Nissan Skyline HR31 GTS-R, Rounds 6-7 in Nissan Skyline BNR32 GT-R for Nissan Motorsport Australia (Gibson Motor Sport)
- Bathurst – Mark Skaife/Jim Richards – 18th – Nissan GT-R for Nissan Motorsport Australia (Gibson Motor Sport)
- Australian Drivers' Championship (ADC) – 3rd (23 Points) – 0 Wins / 2 Podiums – 5 of 8 Rounds – Spa FB001 for Skaife Racing (Gibson Motor Sport)

1991

- ATCC – 2nd (132 points) – 3 Wins / 8 Podiums / 3 Poles – 9 of 9 Rounds – Nissan Skyline BNR32 GT-R for Nissan Motorsport Australia (Gibson Motor Sport)
- Bathurst – Mark Skaife/Jim Richards – 1st – Nissan BNR-32 GT-R for Nissan Motorsport Australia (Gibson Motor Sport)
- ADC – 1st (135 Points) – 6 Wins/ 7 Podiums – 7 of 7 Rounds in Spa FB003 for Skaife Racing (Gibson Motor Sport)

1992

- ATCC – 1st (234 points) – 4 Wins / 7 Podiums / 2 Poles – 9 of 9 Rounds – Nissan Skyline BNR32 GT-R for Winfield Team Nissan (Gibson Motor Sport)
- Bathurst – Mark Skaife/Jim Richards – 1st – Nissan Skyline

BNR32 GT-R for Winfield Team Nissan (Gibson Motor Sport)
- ADC – 1st (90 Points) – 3 Wins / 5 Podiums – 5 of 5 Rounds – SPA FB003 for Winfield Racing (Gibson Motor Sport)
- FIA Formula 3000 International Championship – 2 9th – Reynard 92D Mugen Honda for 3001 International

1993
- ATCC – 6th (87 points) – 0 Wins / 2 Podiums / 2 Poles – 9 of 9 Rounds – Holden VP Commodore for Winfield Racing (Gibson Motor Sport)
- Bathurst – Mark Skaife/Jim Richards – 2nd – Holden VP Commodore for Winfield Racing (Gibson Motor Sport)
- ADC – 1st (110 Points) – 4 Wins / 5 Podiums – 6 of 6 Rounds – Lola T91/50 Holden for Winfield Racing (Gibson Motor Sport)
- Married Belinda, 13 November

1994
- ATCC – 1st (285 points) – 4 Wins / 8 Podiums / 3 Poles – 10 of 10 Rounds – Holden VP Commodore for Gibson Motor Sport
- Bathurst – Mark Skaife/Jim Richards – DNF – Holden VP Commodore for Gibson Motor Sport

1995
- ATCC – 6th (145 points) – 1 Wins / 2 Podiums / 0 Poles – 9 of 10 Rounds – Holden VR Commodore for Gibson Motor Sport

- Bathurst – Mark Skaife/Jim Richards – DNF – Holden VR Commodore for Gibson Motor Sport
- ADC – 7th (32 Points) – 0 Wins / 2 Podiums – 2 of 6 Rounds – Lola T93/50 for Gibson Motor Sport
- Mitch born, 13 June

1996
- ATCC – 9th (177 points) – 0 Wins / 1 Podiums / 0 Poles –
- 10 of 10 Rounds – Holden VR Commodore for Gibson Motor Sport
- Bathurst – Mark Skaife/John Cleland – 7th – Holden VR Commodore for Gibson Team Sega

1997
- ATCC – 13th (166 points) – 0 Wins / 1 Podiums / 0 Poles – 5 of 10 Rounds – Holden VS Commodore for Gibson Motor Sport
- Bathurst – Mark Skaife/Peter Brock – DNF – Holden VS Commodore for Holden Racing Team

1998 – (Not including Sandown 500 & Bathurst 1000)
- ATCC – 3rd (768 points) – 0 Wins / 4 Podiums / 5 Poles – 10 of 10 Rounds – Holden VS Commodore for Holden Racing Team
- Bathurst – Mark Skaife/Craig Lowndes – 5th – Holden VT Commodore for Holden Racing Team

1999
- V8 Supercar Championship Series/ATCC (V8SCS) – 3rd (1656 points) – 6 Wins / 7 Podiums / 2 Poles – 13 of 13 Rounds – Holden VT Commodore for Holden Racing Team
- Bathurst – Mark Skaife/Paul Morris – 3rd – Holden VT Commodore for Holden Racing Team

2000
- V8SCS – 1st (1570 points) – 4 Wins / 8 Podiums / 3 Poles – 13 of 13 Rounds – Holden VT Commodore for Holden Racing Team
- Bathurst – Mark Skaife/Craig Lowndes – 6th – Holden VT Commodore for Holden Racing Team

2001
- V8SCS – 1st (3478 points) – 4 Wins / 9 Podiums / 4 Poles – 13 of 13 Rounds – Holden VX Commodore for Holden Racing Team
- Bathurst – Mark Skaife/Tony Longhurst – 1st – Holden VX Commodore for Holden Racing Team

2002
- V8SCS – Mark Skaife – 1st (2227 points) – 7 Wins / 8 Podiums / 5 Poles – 13 of 13 Rounds – Holden VX Commodore for Holden Racing Team
- Bathurst – Mark Skaife/Jim Richards – 1st – Holden VX Commodore for Holden Racing Team

2003

- V8SCS – 3rd (1853 points) – 2 Wins / 6 Podiums / 3 Poles – 13 of 13 Rounds – Holden VY Commodore for Holden Racing Team
- Bathurst – Mark Skaife/Todd Kelly – 8th – Holden VY Commodore for Holden Racing Team

2004

- V8SCS – 12th (1294 points) – 0 Wins / 1 Podiums / 3 Poles – 13 of 13 Rounds – Holden VY Commodore for Holden Racing Team
- Bathurst – Mark Skaife/Todd Kelly – 14th – Holden VY Commodore for Holden Racing Team
- Married Toni, 21 August

2005

- V8SCS – 5th (1754 points) – 1 Wins / 4 Podiums / 2 Poles – 13 of 13 Rounds – Holden VZ Commodore for Holden Racing Team
- Bathurst – Mark Skaife/Todd Kelly – 1st – Holden VZ Commodore for Holden Racing Team

2006

- V8SCS – 16th (2036 points) – 1 Wins / 3 Podiums / 4 Poles – 13 of 13 Rounds – Holden VZ Commodore for Holden Racing Team
- Bathurst – Mark Skaife/Garth Tander – DNF – Holden VZ Commodore for Holden Racing Team
- Mia born, 10 March

2007
- V8SCS – 8th (379 points) – 1 Wins / 3 Podiums / 0 Poles – 13 of 14 Rounds Holden VE Commodore for Holden Racing Team
- Bathurst – Mark Skaife/Todd Kelly – DNF – Holden VE Commodore for Holden Racing Team

2008
- V8SCS – 14th (1644 points) – 1 Wins / 1 Podiums / 0 Poles – 14 of 14 Rounds – Holden VE Commodore for Holden Racing Team
- Bathurst – Mark Skaife/Garth Tander – 12th – Holden VE Commodore for Holden Racing Team
- Tilly born, 24 October

2009
- V8SCS – 31st (372 points) – 0 Wins / 0 Podiums / 0 Poles – 2 of 14 Rounds – Holden VE Commodore for Sprint Gas Racing (Tasman Motorsport)
- Bathurst – Mark Skaife/Greg Murphy – 4th – Holden VE Commodore for Sprint Gas Racing (Tasman Motorsport)

Summary 1987 – 2009
- ATCC / V8SCS – 216 Rounds – 5 Championships (92, 94, 00, 01, 02) – 39 Wins / 84 Podiums / 41 Poles
- Bathurst – 23 Starts – 5 Wins (91, 92, 01, 02 & 05) / 8 Podiums / 5 Poles
- ADC – 25 Starts – 3 Championships (91, 92, 93) – 15 Wins / 21 Podiums

ABOUT THE AUTHOR

Andrew Clarke is a journalist who has been covering motorsport for more than two decades. He was there when Mark Skaife began his career and plans to be there when it finally ends. Today he blends his work in motorsport and sport in general with communications and brand advice to professional services firms. He has two children, Byron and Gabi, and a wife, Jacquie, who tolerate his endless hours behind a computer screen and days away at motor races.

You've finished the book but there's much more waiting for you at

www.randomhouse.com.au

- ▶ Author interviews
- ▶ Videos
- ▶ Competitions
- ▶ Free chapters
- ▶ Games

▶ Newsletters with exclusive previews, breaking news and inside author information.

▶ Reading group notes and tips.

▶ VIP event updates and much more.

ENHANCE YOUR READING EXPERIENCE

www.randomhouse.com.au